THE
UNMASKING

THE UNMASKING

MARRIED TO A RAPIST

Kevin Flynn

THE FREE PRESS

A Division of Macmillan, Inc.
New York

Maxwell Macmillan Canada
Toronto

Maxwell Macmillan International
New York   Oxford   Singapore   Sydney

The Free Press
A Division of Macmillan, Inc.
866 Third Avenue, New York, N.Y. 10022

Maxwell Macmillan Canada, Inc.
1200 Eglinton Avenue East
Suite 200
Don Mills, Ontario M3C 3N1

Macmillan, Inc. is part of the Maxwell Communication Group of Companies.

Printed in the United States of America

printing number
1   2   3   4   5   6   7   8   9   10

Library of Congress Cataloging-in-Publication Data

Flynn, Kevin (Kevin J.)
     The unmasking : married to a rapist / Kevin Flynn.
          p.   cm.
     ISBN 0-02-910315-0
     1. Rapists—Texas—Family relationships.   I. Title.
HV6565.T4F58   1993
364.1′532′092—dc20
[B]   92-37379
                                                                 CIP

Lyrics from *Whatever It Takes* copyright © 1975, Lanny Wolfe Music/ASCAP. All rights controlled by Pathway Music, P.O. Box 2250, Cleveland, Tennessee 37320. Used by permission.

For Mut and Père

CONTENTS

PREFACE

"Mrs. Wyatt? How does it feel to be married to a rapist?"

With the threatening, anonymous phone call that she received hours after her husband was arrested for rape, Ronda Wyatt began to confront that precise question.

Ten years later, she is still seeking answers as she changes and grows into a stronger and more self-confident woman—raised out of the ashes of her marriage and of the person she thought she was. It did not take long for the town's grapevine to spread the news that the rapist had been caught. But it took years for Ronda Wyatt to recover from the shock of betrayal after learning that her husband of seven years, the father of her two young children, also a Christian man, lived a shrouded life of evil. By eventually overcoming her disillusionment and sense of failure, and battling the rage she felt at being victimized as well, Ronda became a different kind of rape survivor.

It had seemed preposterous that Eddie Wyatt was a rapist. To friends, Eddie was a pillar of decency. He had overcome his juvenile delinquent past after turning to Jesus, and established himself as a personable and hard-working fellow. To Ronda, he was a strong and loving man with faith and determination to make a better life. And yet, toward the end, Eddie had become increasingly withdrawn, both emotionally and physically. He seemed almost entirely uninterested in sex.

Even in the days following his arrest, in the face of increasing evidence against him, Ronda stood by Eddie, convinced that it was all some cruel mistake, that he could not have forsaken her only to force himself on total strangers. It was not until she heard the devastating admission from her husband's own lips that Ronda realized the world as she knew it was at an end; in fact, that it had never even existed. Her home, her children, the storybook marriage she had imagined since her childhood, would never be the same.

How it changed would be up to her. The questions that bombarded her along the way would slow her down and sidetrack her; despair and self-pity often tempted her. She had to come to grips with an understanding of her husband's crime that went beyond popular misconceptions. If Eddie needed sex, she wondered, then why wouldn't he make love with her? If indeed his rapes were not crimes of sex but of rage, then what was he so angry about? She had to learn how her husband's hidden rage could have come out in that way.

And then she had to consider herself. Was she worth loving? Was she attractive, inside and out? Would she be able to find love again? And if she did, could she once again freely experience it the way she so desperately needed to? For the sake of her children, and with determination to rediscover the loving heart within, Ronda fought against all the questions and doubts. This is the story of the transformation of a naive woman whose capacity for love and trust could have been forever diminished had she not discovered the faith, inner strength, and crucial outside support that would lead toward happiness again.

At points in this book, some names have been changed and some locations have been obscured. This includes the names of all the rape victims and their relatives, as well as the two men who were arrested prior to Eddie but were not charged with rape.

PROLOGUE

H er throat tightened up to the point of gagging when she thought of what might happen next. She could sense that cold shank of honed steel, the knife he had used to quiet her dog, Killer, soon being drawn across her own neck, slicing sharply through her throat. She could feel the tape cutting into her wrists, bound together behind her. The seventeen-year-old was defenseless against the palpable sensation of that straight edge cutting deep into her throat. The roiling queasiness in her gut, which had subsided as the numbing attack wore on, suddenly began to bubble again.

The car yanked sharply right and came to an abrupt stop. Inside the dark trunk, she rolled onto her side and bumped into a sharp-edged metal object. It was that thing that had rattled like a tool box when she was dumped into the trunk and the lid was slammed shut. She wanted to remember details like this in case she came out of the next five minutes alive. Her sight was cut off by one of her own socks, which was taped securely around her head, but her other senses had taken in every smell and sound of the last six hours. Despite the terror, she catalogued every sensation with the proficiency of a librarian. Her faithful mutt's last shrill yelp. The scratchy feel against her naked back of that abrasive, stiff-fibered carpet. The oily odor of the cramped car trunk to which she had been returned for final transport.

Her initial flood of panic had given way to survival instincts during the lengthy ordeal. She had tried to make him see her as a real person, not as an object. And above all, not to rile him, to do whatever he said, to say whatever he wanted. Maybe then he would not kill her.

The engine shut off and she heard him exit the car, his shoes scraping across loose gravel. She followed the sound to the rear of the car. The trunk lid went up and a bit of light seeped through the blindfold. It reminded her of that instant back at the house when her attacker suddenly stopped and demanded to know if she had seen him. He suspected that she had been peering through two small triangular spaces created down both sides of her nose by the tautness of the tape with which he initially wrapped her blond head. She denied that she could see him, but still he re-wrapped her face with the socks. The truth was that she had plainly seen the angry and twisted expressions on the man's face for most of the six-hour ordeal. He had so hurriedly wrapped the inch-wide tape around her head that a thin sliver where it did not overlap remained right over her eyes.

"C'mon," he said, lifting her by the arms and raising her out of the trunk. The brisk late afternoon air wafted over her shoulders, causing them to contract underneath her T-shirt. The chill descended to her exposed legs, as if the cold were grounded when her bare feet touched the asphalt. Then she heard voices in the distance, and sounds like children playing.

"Shit. Get in the back, bitch!" he commanded her, pulling open the car's rear door and aiming her inside. She landed on the seat, and her soaked panties began staining the fabric while he started the car and drove off again. This time the trip lasted only a minute before he stopped again.

"Okay, bitch, here it is," he growled. He pulled her out and led her only about twenty feet into a dank enclosure. The smell immediately conjured in her mind the image of a public rest room. This was it, she realized, tensing at the sound of his knife slipping out of his belt. He went behind her and grabbed her wrists. The blade slipped between them and the tape, then he sawed his way quickly through the tape.

"You wait ten minutes before you leave here," he told her. "You can wear these." Then she heard something soft flop onto the concrete floor near her feet.

At that, she heard the man turn and walk out to the car, which he'd left running. There was the sound of a car door slamming, the transmission being put in gear, and the tires crunching the gravel as the car drove off. She waited until the sound of the engine faded into the background noise before she brought her hands up to the tape around her head. She tore at it until it loosened enough to pull the socks from her eyes. Her vision, sensitive even to the subdued light in the public rest room, soon focused on a pair of drab green slacks near her feet, left by the man. She quickly pulled them on to cover her soiled legs. Now free, she noticed everything ached, from her face to her arms to her hips and legs. But most of all, she felt a searing pain in her most private parts.

The girl peered slowly out the entrance to the rest room. She now knew exactly where she was. There were the ball fields, and the playground, and the big open field of Dick Kleberg Park south of town. She saw some people in the distance, but she couldn't be sure her torturer wasn't among them. So she took off running north toward Escondido Drive. The soles of her feet stung from slapping the rough asphalt, but she fixed her gaze on the closest house and pushed herself forward. The house was a light brick rancher surrounded by a small chain-link fence. As she dashed across the road and up the driveway, she saw an older gentleman out in the yard. She ran past the big bay window and called to the man.

"Help me, please!" Allison Shaw begged him. "I've been raped! Please help me!"

Even though it was clear on the other side of town, it didn't take Eddie Wyatt long to drive back to his small, white frame house on Mesquite Avenue. Kingsville, Texas, wasn't that big. Once home, he began to tidy up because his wife, Ronda, was due back soon from work with the couple's two small children. He had already disposed of the tissues he used to wipe himself. Those he flushed down the toilet. He wrapped some paper towels around his buck knife, then lifted the lid of a storage box in the laundry room and dropped the knife inside. He returned the duct tape to his dresser drawer. Wetting a hand towel, Eddie scrubbed over the carpet where he thought he felt a wet stain, then tossed the towel into a laundry pile. Standing straight up again, he slowly scanned the boxlike, wood-paneled living room and stopped when he spotted something near his kids' presents under the small Christmas tree. Quickly striding across the room, he reached down and gathered two joints from the floor, then took them back to the bedroom, where he kept his small stash of marijuana.

Satisfied that the house was back in shipshape order, Eddie dragged a wooden dinette chair into the hallway and stood on it to reach the attic crawl space. He retrieved the cassette tape and Polaroid snapshots he had placed up there less than an hour earlier. Eddie pulled the chair back to the kitchen table, sat down, and relaxed. Presently, he put the cassette into his portable recorder, then hit PLAY. Background hissing began to come through the speaker while he picked up one of the pictures and examined it closely.

The young, blond girl in the photograph was completely naked on his living room floor, except for the blue sock and green tape wrapped around her head. Her legs were spread, knees slightly bent. As Eddie examined the photograph, voices began coming from the tape player. They were low. One was angry, the other frightened. That was not how he remembered it. Not at all.

Eddie suddenly snapped the STOP button, then sat motionless for several seconds. The tiny house was quiet again. His eyes looked over the other Polaroids, a portfolio of how he had defiled the young girl. A mood change was slowly washing over him, a familiar sensation that Eddie recognized as the start of another period of depression. Once again he realized that the act he thought would bring release from his anger and frustration had in fact made him feel dirty, ashamed, and confused.

With sudden determination, he gathered up the Polaroids, rewound the tape and ejected it from the player, then dragged the chair back to the hallway, underneath the attic opening. He moved the panel back and stored the pictures and tape up with the sundry items he'd been stealing during the burglaries he had committed around Kingsville. He had to hide everything before his wife and children got home. He had to act normal, like nothing had happened.

Ronda soon arrived home with Paul and Diana, who had spent the afternoon in day care. Eddie dreaded the encounter with Ronda for fear she would see guilt on his face. In the past, it had been late at night, and he could slip into the house without waking Ronda. Now that his shift at the Naval Air Station had changed, would she detect anything in the light of day, Eddie wondered?

Ronda walked in through the door off the carport and greeted Eddie with a smile, asking how his day had gone. He answered that he'd been out buying Christmas presents earlier, then had taken a nap so as to be rested before going in to work. Ronda suspected nothing unusual, he realized, and he felt sudden relief.

Paul, age five, and Diana, age three, were excited about Christmas, coming in four days. They jabbered at Eddie, but he did not appear to be focused on what they were saying. Paul wanted to go over to the park and crawl through the colored pipes in the playground, and Ronda asked Eddie to come along.

The park was two doors east of the Wyatt's house, just across Second Street. Eddie and Ronda brought up the rear as the kids made beelines toward the wide-open park. Off to the west, the sun was going down beyond the south Texas desert, and the air was getting chillier. Ronda wanted to hold Eddie's hand, like they used to do when they were newlyweds. But he held it stiffly at his side. While they made small talk, Eddie was distracted by other thoughts.

That's the end of it, he vowed. It had never brought him the satisfaction he expected; it had only made things worse. But this wasn't the first time Eddie told himself it would stop. While he watched his pretty wife playing with their two kids, Eddie's inner voice dragged him back to his troubled world. Yes, you will, it said. You're going to risk losing everything over and over until you finally do lose it. And Eddie knew the voice had to be right. It always was.

Ronda Wyatt could only guess at what was bothering her husband. Any time she tried to draw him out about his depression, he told her she would not understand. She pushed him to undergo counseling so they could both understand what was happening to their marriage. His refusal puzzled Ronda, who wanted and needed to be held, to be touched tenderly, and to feel affection from her husband. Now, she was becoming anesthetized to his rejection of any form of shared intimacy.

She had vowed her undying love to him seven years earlier,

but this love was threatened by the wall that Eddie had built around his troubles. It had already prevented their making love as they used to do, when they were still feeling the newness of their passion. There had been only two attempts at lovemaking in the last year. Sexual desire seemed to be drained from him.

Ronda suspected that she was the problem. Perhaps she wasn't pretty enough, lively enough, or interesting enough to spark those flames in Eddie anymore. Her failure to get him to feel better was dragging her down as well. She had hoped things would improve when they moved to the little Coastal Bend town of Kingsville. In Norfolk the navy had promised them that Eddie would not have to go to sea again if he extended his hitch for another two years. So off they went to Texas, Eddie's home state, with the feeling that they had bottomed out and could now look up.

But it did not happen. Eddie continued to shut her out. She knew none of his secrets. And it was tearing her up inside that she couldn't find the right things to say or do that would help him. A devout Christian, Ronda prayed that God would soon reveal everything to her, no matter how much it would hurt.

CHAPTER 1

A COLLECTION OF MISFITS AND LONERS

Occasionally, Eddie has talked about his experiences, especially in reform school. There are some things which he says he has never talked to anyone about. Once he told me that he watched as another boy was beaten to death. He had to learn to keep his feelings inside, and not to trust anyone.

—from Ronda's diary

M ost of his early childhood was nothing more than a haze now, but Eddie Wyatt could clearly remember this one particular morning. He was five years old, and the smell of eggs frying on the stove wafted back to the bedroom, invaded his sleep, and woke him with a hunger pang. That was his favorite way to wake up, and if he wasn't quick about it, his two older brothers would beat him to breakfast. Man, did he love fried eggs, slightly over easy, the way his mom always made them for him. He quickly slipped out of bed and padded his way into the kitchen, where he found his dad seated at the table, a plate of eggs waiting, and his mom standing at the nearby stove. They had been yelling at each other again, but stopped when the bleary-eyed youngster came in. Eddie grabbed his seat at the table in anticipation of a fatherly ritual. His dad always left something on his plate for Eddie to finish.

But before too many more things were said, Eddie's dad pushed his chair back from the table, stood up, and stalked out the door, leaving the house with both eggs still on the plate. Eddie looked over at his mom, then asked her if he could eat his dad's breakfast. His mother told him to go right ahead. As Eddie slid the plate over in front of himself and dug in, he thought, "I wish Daddy had stayed. I wanted to talk with him."

What Eddie had left of his childhood were only a few vague, unconnected memories almost pointless in their triviality, like that scene over the fried eggs. He did not know why the memory of that particular morning stuck with him through all the years. It was just one of those vignettes in which his father would enter and exit, like a character in the theater of the absurd. Another consisted only of a clear recollection of his father driving down the street loudly singing Doris Day's hit that was so popular at that moment, "Que Sera, Sera." There were only a handful that Eddie could recall. Most were played out in a small house on the west end of Avenue Q, near Offatt Bayou in Galveston, Texas, where he lived with his parents, two brothers, and three sisters. His parents tried not to fight in front of him, but they had little success. It made Eddie feel different from his friends.

Eddie's dad, George Walter Wyatt, had come back from World War II a far different man than when he had left, suffering a bad case of shell shock—what decades later was called post-traumatic stress disorder. In those days, war heroes were not supposed to feel stress. Those who did had to suppress it or risk losing their self-respect. George Wyatt found the answer to his emotional disturbance in a bottle of liquor. Still, Eva Angelina Wyatt tried her best to make their marriage work.

Eddie was the Wyatts' fourth-born, and when he came along on September 22, 1951, the family was living in Birmingham, Alabama. Three years later, George Wyatt took them to Detroit. That lasted only a year before they moved to Galveston, and the house just off Fifty-seventh Street between the cool bayou and the brown sand beach on the Gulf of Mexico. Eddie was the youngest boy. One sister was the oldest child, the other two sisters the youngest. George Wyatt supported his family as a painter, but money never came easily. He spent what he earned quickly enough on drinking and gambling. From Prohibition up through a state-led crackdown in 1957, Galveston was wide open for alcohol, gambling, and other vices. Bordellos jammed the humid and sweaty circus of Postoffice Street downtown. Casinos such as the Hollywood Dinner Club drew throngs of partiers. Slot machines, crap tables, and roulette wheels ran night and day.

As an adult, Eddie could remember a lot of tension around his parents' house over his dad's drinking and gambling. He told friends several times how his dad left the house and stayed away only to come back to the family for another attempt at reconciliation. Then the arguing would resume, and the hurt and confusion Eddie felt would rise up again. One day when Eddie was five, George Wyatt walked out the door and never returned. The family later discovered that he was living up in Houston, less than an hour's drive from Galveston, yet Eddie never laid eyes on his father again. He often wondered just what kind of man his father was, and why he never came back, even to see his kids.

Abandoned by her husband and with six children at home under the age of twelve to feed, Eva Wyatt found a job at a small grocery store, working long hours seven days a week to support her young family. Although the children's maternal grandfather lived with them, he was not a substitute father for Eddie. After he settled down as an adult, Eddie often told his friends that his mother had told him he had one problem after another, starting the day when, at four years old, the Galveston police had brought him home in the back of a cruiser. He had run off from the front yard, and police returned him with a sucker in his mouth.

When Eddie was seven years old, he took a toy from Weingarten's department store and started to head for the door. A female security guard stopped him, took him back to an office, and called the police. The officer, however, took one look at Eddie and told the woman to take him home and inform his parents.

The woman took Eddie to her car and followed his directions to Avenue Q. But when they arrived at his house, no one was there. The woman interrogated Eddie about his parents; getting no meaningful answers, she simply asked him to explain to his mother what had happened because she had to return to Weingarten's. Sure enough, when Eva Wyatt came home that evening, Eddie confessed everything, even though he could have been free and clear if he had just kept his mouth shut. Years later, Eddie remembered that rather than scolding or spanking him, his mom simply sat him down and talked with him. She told him that she loved him and she was sorry she was not able to be with him as much as he wanted. She told him she knew he wanted her around more often, but that it was up to him to do the right thing even when she couldn't be with him. Eddie recalled that he slept peacefully that night, feeling uncommonly soothed by his mother's attention.

Eddie started at Travis Elementary School but found no subject could hold his interest as much as the sound of the mild, Gulf water lapping along the rough beach below the seawall. Sometime around the fourth grade, he began to ditch school with a core group of youngsters who, like himself, had troubles. They spent their time fishing, hanging out at the Sea Horse bowling alley, or jumping off the pier at the Sea Breeze Cafe in double-dares to see who could reach the other bank of Offatt Bayou first. When the weather didn't permit, the youngsters soon enough found a vacant house near the school and broke their way inside.

They were not a gang in the sense of one-for-all and all-for-one. They were a collection of misfits and loners who could not develop caring relationships, even with each other. Later in life, Eddie told friends that he used to watch the so-called good kids going to school, getting into sports, and doing things with their parents, and he could remember wanting desperately to be one of those kids. With benefit of hindsight, Eddie said that he wished he had turned to Junior, Joey, or Gerald and told them that he was angry over his dad leaving, or that he felt restless and discontented. But he knew what would have happened. It would have been seen as a sign of weakness. They would have laughed at him, and told him to grow up in the real world.

Eddie occasionally caught disturbing glimpses of his friends' lives. One day in the sixth grade, Eddie went to Joey's house. Joey seemed a little nervous, and as Eddie followed him in the door he was thinking how strange that was. Joey, after all, had nerves of steel. Eddie had once watched him spear a cat in the alley and kill it for sport. Eddie sat down in Joey's living room, but no sooner had he begun to relax than Joey's grandmother came storming out of the back of the house, snapping a razor strap.

"You want it now or you want it later?" she screeched at Joey, who flinched when he saw her coming at him. She didn't wait for an answer, but started whipping the boy right in front of Eddie, whose eyes widened at the sight of it. In his whole life, Eddie had never gotten a licking from anybody. He made a quick dash to the door while Joey begged his grandma to stop. Eddie took off running back to Avenue Q.

The activities of Eddie and his youthful associates did not go unnoticed by Galveston's juvenile officer, Oscar Ekelund. He knew the boy wasn't going to school. Eddie and Officer Ekelund had many conversations over such things as shoplifting, ditching school, or breaking into vacant houses. The juvenile division was building a file on Eddie and his friends. Eddie signed a lot of papers admitting to different things such as ditching school. He also signed confessions to things he didn't do just to get out of Ekelund's office.

By the time Eddie was eleven, Ekelund had enough reports to haul him before a juvenile court judge.

Eddie first saw it in the fall of 1962, gazing through the smeared window of a security bus that brought him and several other boys from east Texas out to the hill and brush country. They had been riding the asphalt two-lane west out of Waco for a good forty-five minutes before they came up over a scrubby hill, passed through a collection of houses called South Mountain, and then started rolling down into a small river valley. At the bottom was a dinky little spot on the highway called Gatesville. The towns-people in this dusty seat of Coryell County were used to seeing these vehicles coming through town. The livelihoods of several hundred people—retired military from nearby Fort Hood, farmers, and ranch hands looking for supplemental income—depended on these human shipments, the children who were being housed north of town. "Guard" was not a word the state liked. The preferred euphemism was "youth supervisor."

In the center of town, the bus took a right turn onto the raod that headed up a treeless valley toward Jonesboro. Along the meandering Leon River, which looked like little more than a drainage ditch, Eddie soon spotted a collection of buildings about two miles north of town. Texas called it the Gatesville State School for Boys. Eddie called it home for the next six months, after a juvenile court judge in Galveston saw the truancy reports in his file, read about the stealing incidents from the Travis School, and saw that the boy was often at home without any supervision. Eddie fit the classic pattern of the 1,700 youths a year, on average, who were being sent to Gatesville.

There was hardly a kid in Texas from the late 1950s through the early 1970s who had not heard of Gatesville. Threatening a youngster with banishment to Gatesville was just about the most cruel and callous thing that could be done to a child. From El Paso to Port Arthur, Amarillo to Brownsville, schoolchildren were treated to the standard lecture from a juvenile officer, guidance counselor, or trusted teacher about the horrors that awaited those childen who could not stay in school or out of trouble. Often, a juvenile officer would pick out the biggest boy in the class, or the schoolyard bully, and have him stand in front of the classroom. Then the officer would tell the students that at Gatesville, this boy would be dog meat—and the counselors were right.

In the early 1970s, against the wishes of state juvenile officers but at the pleading of a team of poverty lawyers, the Texas Youth Council was ordered to shut down both Gatesville and nearby Mountain View, the maximum security unit. Eventually, the facilities were turned into women's prisons. In a federal court lawsuit against the entire Texas reform school system—sparked by lawyers on behalf of a girl who was confined as incorrigible because she refused to turn over the salary from her part-time job to her father—nationally recognized experts in juvenile justice inspected the complex at Gatesville and came away in a state of shock. The facilities that housed boys as young as eleven had conditions that were worse, they testified, than those at the legendary Angola Prison in Louisiana, then known as the nation's most primitive adult prison.

The unfenced state school was a complex of seven different units, each of which had dormitories, vocational training shops, and classrooms. It could hold up to 1,560 boys at a time. Typically, about one-third would be Anglo, more than a third black, and the rest Mexican-American. There was a surprising amount of racial enmity among the children. However, at Mountain View, just up the hill, there was officially sanctioned segregation, with blacks in one dormitory and Anglos and Hispanics in another. Frequently, the Hispanics and Anglos teamed up for defense against the blacks.

Newly burgeoning sexual capability was the weapon bullies and gangs used to terrorize their prey, and it was not uncommon for word to spread that some unfortunate boy had been raped the night before. As a result, real security for many of the children could only be achieved by joining a gang. There was a separate dormitory at Gatesville where youths with homosexual tendencies were placed together, a practice later condemned by a federal court along with the rest of the Gatesville–Mountain View complex. In the other dorms, members of the protective cliques would never even think of having sex among themselves. Homosexual contact with one another was taboo. But strangely, it was not considered a disgrace for a boy to mount a sexual assault on a boy from outside the clique. Indeed, that was an act of power, control, or revenge over a rival gang or individual, and was considered a heroic and manly thing to do. Some boys bragged about how they had "gotten" someone from another clique. In the code of the institution, the utter disgrace and humiliation lay in being the one penetrated by another boy's penis, and not in being the one doing the penetrating. To be the victim was the shameful thing.

Instead of generating sympathy, the victim would find himself the object of further hatred and scorn. Once word got around the compound that someone had been victimized, that boy could count on being the target of others seeking to further humiliate him for failing to defend his own rear end. He would be no better off than an injured deer in a mountain meadow trying to fend off a pack of hungry cougars. In so many terrible ways, the brutality and dehumanization at Gatesville and Mountain View were nothing less than reflections of the adult prison system.

A lot of boys ran away from Gatesville, but there was nowhere to hide in the wide open, rolling brush, especially after the "youth supervisors" gave chase on horseback with some of the forty-one bloodhounds kenneled nearby. The folk of the little town demanded such measures as part of the trade-off for hosting the reform school. Most of the children in the facility had come from the state's seven largest urban centers, and the local whites were edgy about the children of minorities and inner-city white trash.

Mountain View was where the harder children were housed. It could handle up to 480 boys. It consisted of nine dormitories, a school, and training facilities, and was surrounded by a double row of barbed-wire fencing. It had a security wing in which troublemakers could be kept in a juvenile version of solitary confinement. Mountain View was operated apart from Gatesville, and its specter was often used to keep the Gatesville boys in line. If they misbehaved, they got sent up the hill where, it was said, treatment would be much worse.

Eddie Wyatt never had to embellish any of the stories he shared about Gatesville and Mountain View. In fact, if anything, he held back. He never told anyone about the worst of his experiences at Gatesville. He did tell his friends later, however, that he managed to stave off sexual attacks mainly because he was smart enough to get into a clique that could provide him with protection from such things.

In some ways, reform school did show Eddie the value of reforming. In his classes there he discovered that he had the ability to learn and do well in his studies. But his resentment at having been sent away in the first place, and tremendous inner confusion as to why this was happening to him, canceled out any benefit he might have received. His emotional wounds healed with a scab he frequently picked at and reopened as he grew older, never letting it heal over completely.

The first time Eddie was beaten by a guard it was for going to church services. Shortly after arriving at Gatesville, Eddie learned that one of the ways to escape the boredom of his unit on Sunday was to go up to the Hilltop Unit at Gatesville where nondenominational church services were held each week. Eddie's family was Catholic by background, but even at age eleven, Eddie could not remember ever having been in a sanctuary. So one Sunday morning, when this guard came through the unit asking who was going to church that day, Eddie decided he would go along simply to get out and do something different, and he raised his hand with several others. The burly guard gathered the kids for the short bus ride. As he did, he informed them of one other thing.

"I'm gonna tell you right now, anyone who goes over to church is going to get whipped when you get back," the guard snarled to the bewildered children.

Eddie was puzzled. Perhaps he was joking. The guards were always edgy, it seemed, and it was impossible to know when they were joking with some of their pronouncements that seemed so ridiculous. More likely, he figured, it was just another game of ruthless intimidation the guards played to maintain control.

Over at Hilltop, Eddie relaxed and watched the service, in which a youth choir bused in from somewhere sang up a storm of Gospel numbers. The chaplain, who had handed out Bibles to the newcomers upon their arrival at Gatesville, read a verse from Matthew that, for some reason, stuck with Eddie over the years and had given him a strangely contented feeling. "Jesus said, 'Come unto me,' " the preacher boomed, " 'all ye that labor and are heavy laden, and I will give you rest. Take my yoke upon you, and learn of me; for I am meek and lowly in heart: and ye shall find rest unto your souls. For my yoke is easy, and my burden is light.' Boys, there is no burden so heavy that Jesus can't help you carry it."

After services, when Eddie's bus got back to the other unit and the kids filed off, sure enough the angry guard was waiting with a bent coat hanger. He used it relentlessly to beat each child as he got off the bus. Eddie remembered that guard's name for the rest of his life.

There was a special jargon in the reform school for the various torturous techniques the guards employed. The most popular was called "racking." This was where a guard would order a child to stand against a wall with his hands in his pockets. Thus defenseless, the child would be punched repeatedly in the chest and stomach. The intensity of such punishment would rarely be consistent with the severity of the offense. An inmate could be racked for four minutes or forty, all for offenses ranging from talking in line or raising his head during a haircut, to running off from a work detail.

Other forms of punishment included a "peel" and a "tight." When an inmate was peeled, he would be forced to bend over, and a guard would strike him hard on the back with a fist or open hand. In a tight, the inmate was forced to grab his ankles or toes, and a guard would whack him across the buttocks with a broom, either the handle or the straw end. A "brogue" was when a guard swung his booted foot and kicked a boy in the shins.

The offenses for which such punishment was handed out included wearing pants too low, leaving shoes out, or losing a baseball game. There were no written rules, not even a standard procedure used by management, for almost any aspect of reform school life. A child's monthly parental visit, for which his parents may have traveled several hundreds of miles, could be summarily denied by administrators solely on a whim. Most children received no visits anyway. Each school administrator had full discretion to make any decision based on any principle. Guards who tried to speak out against what they felt was brutal treatment of the children were ostracized, or advised to find work elsewhere.

Despite the frequent beatings Eddie received, he considered himself among the lucky survivors. He saw one teen beaten to death at Gatesville, and knew of others.

The Texas Youth Council provided some staff members trained in child psychology, but their caseload was so great that even the worst cases, the obvious psychopaths and emotionally disturbed, received only the pretense of a treatment program. Gatesville had a psychiatrist on duty only four days a week, for more than a thousand children. Only five or six boys were seen on a weekly basis. Other were seen only for a few minutes, and only to determine their reactions to psychotropic medicines they were being given. In just one of every twenty psychiatric cases did the doctor confer with the inmates' caseworkers. Thorazine was readily prescribed for the more aggressive children to keep them sedated.

After six months at Gatesville, Eddie Wyatt was sent back home to Galveston, where he was expected to put together the remnants of a normal childhood. The prospects of that were slim.

Things had changed on his end of town. While he was away, his friends had discovered drugs.

Scanning the crowd of teens at the Sea Horse bowling alley, Eddie looked over the girls, most of whom he knew, before he finally spotted her. What a beautiful face she had. Eddie wondered how he could have missed seeing her before. Patty Battaglia was a thirteen-year-old goddess. Her jet black hair was long and bouncy, framing a classic Italian face. She had a bright smile that made her eyes light up when she saw him. Patty lived over the alley from Eddie, on Avenue P ½. (Not only were city surveyors so unimaginative that they named the east-west streets after the alphabet and numbered the cross streets, they also named in-between streets "½" since the island's belly widened beyond the alphabet's capacity.)

Eddie hadn't taken notice of Patty Battaglia until, at the invitation of Patty's sister that afternoon on a city bus, he agreed to meet the girls that evening. He felt an instant attraction to her. After they spent the evening talking at the Sea Horse, he was unable to get her out of his mind. To his surprise, it was not merely a physical attraction. He had enjoyed the simple pleasure of just being with her. She seemed not only to understand his feelings but to have empathy for him. They were on the same wavelength, and Eddie went home excited about his feelings for Patty.

Eddie, fourteen at the time, was a student at Lovenberg Junior High. His academic habits, if anything, had gotten worse since his stint in Gatesville. Lovenberg was right off the beach at Thirty-ninth Street, and Eddie began to ditch school for the pleasures of swimming. He had no favorite subject at all, nothing at which he excelled to keep him interested in the classroom. But as his relationship with Patty blossomed, and he found it easy to open up to her, he began to feel motivated.

This brief flirtation with responsibility soon ran headlong into more alluring temptation.

Shortly after returning to his neighborhood from Gatesville

in 1963, a boy from across the street opened his hand to Eddie, and in his palm were several pills. Everyone was taking them, the boy said. They were hallucinogens. Eddie swallowed one without even thinking twice. He did not like the resulting feelings, but he decided to do it again. He felt he had to in order to stay in tight with the other kids. In short order, he came to enjoy smoking marijuana and popping amphetamines, although he never developed a liking for hallucinogens.

There was one facet of his adolescent development in which Eddie thought he was secure, and that was in the sexual arena. Eddie first had sex when he was thirteen. A friend of his had two sisters, the younger being twelve, who, according to the gossip mill, were laying all the boys. Soon after Eddie met the twelve-year-old sister, they went off privately and engaged in sex. Eddie was duly unimpressed with the entire episode, as his male friends treated sex in general. It was something automatic and physiological. In fact, his introduction to it was downright unpleasant. The little girl's breath stank. So the whole time he was on top of her, going through the motions, he was trying to avoid smelling her breath. In the end, Eddie felt that it was no big deal to have sex with this girl. It was simply another thing to do to belong to the crowd.

Eddie felt a change when he fell in love with Patty Battaglia. He did not merely lust for her. He craved being in her presence just so he could talk to her and do things with her. It quickly became a contest for Eddie to see whether he could get Patty to have sex with him. Time after time, he put pressure on his beautiful girlfriend to allow him to get inside her, and he came up empty. Patty was not a pushover. She had a strong Catholic background, and it did not waiver after her parents divorced and she was left home alone with her older sister. She was insistent that she and Eddie wait until they were properly married to have sex. She was very strong-willed. Eddie found himself doing whatever she wanted to do, going wherever she wanted to go. He daydreamed about the time when he and Patty would be married and she would finally consent to sex. He wanted that with all his heart, and his continuing failure to do with Patty what he and the neighborhood boys had done to many other girls was very frustrating. He had been able to display a cocky measure of control among his friends, but sometimes Patty led him around by the nose.

One day when Patty had a few cents in her pocket she grabbed Eddie.

"Let's go down to the store and get some candy," she told him. Eddie had some money, so he went along. Patty had less than ten cents, but she shopped around for that candy as carefully as though she were picking out a brand-new car. The clerk behind the counter was growing impatient. But a girl like Patty Battaglia would not be rushed into anything, as her frustrated boyfriend standing nearby knew well. Finally, she selected a few pieces of penny candy.

"You want to eat that now, or do you want me to put it in a bag?" the snooty clerk asked her. Patty was not about to be treated like an underclass slob.

"Put it in the bag!" she demanded, like some Main Line matron. That was classic Patty Battaglia. She and Eddie laughed a long time over the clerk's impudence. "Put it in the bag!" became their private catch phrase, which they employed to insult those who thought they were better than they or their west-end buddies.

Eddie and Patty spent a lot of time together, saving up their two-bit allowances to go to the corner store for candy and dreaming about their future together. Eddie confided many of his feelings to Patty, and she was the only person he felt could understand him. It was a corner of Eddie's adolescence that was unlike every other facet of his being. In school, in social settings, in his family, he had utterly no sense of direction, no goals. He didn't even want them. It was much more fun to party and use drugs, and much easier than trying to build himself up in school. In class at Lovenberg, he would stare out the windows at the light blue water of the Gulf. That was where he wanted to be.

Eddie was able to pick up a part-time job on the beach at the Hotel Galvez, at the foot of Twenty-first Street, but Officer Ekelund was on his tail again. To stay away from him, Eddie started to run away from home, sleeping at Patty's house or, if that wasn't possible, breaking into vacant houses and sleeping on the floors. He was going to make it as difficult as possible for the officer to get him this time. He did not want to return to Gatesville, although everything he was doing put him on that very path.

One day in August 1966, Eddie broke into a laundromat near Sixty-first Street and Broadway where he knew there was a soda pop machine. He forced open the coin box and made off with the money, intending to buy food because he had stayed away from home for some time and was hungry. But while hiking the Sixty-first Street Causeway across Offatt Bayou, Eddie was spotted by two police officers in a cruiser, who started toward him. Eddie wasn't ready to give up without a struggle. He jumped into the bayou and began to swim across. The officers commandeered a nearby boat and headed out after him, fishing him out of the drink and heading him straight back to reform school.

The second stint at Gatesville was psychologically harder than the first. Eddie was fifteen now, and in love with Patty. The juvenile court judge had given him an indeterminate sentence, so he had no idea how long he'd be there. He was angry and resentful that he was being cut off from the one person for whom he cared.

Shortly after his return to Gatesville, Patty came to visit him along with Eddie's mother. Patty almost didn't get past the guards, because visits were limited to family members. But it had been a long drive, more than 270 miles, and the guard had a soft heart for Patty's tears.

The visit tore Eddie up. The next time Patty wrote, Eddie found the pain of separation too much to bear. He wrote her one last time and angrily told her not to write to him anymore. For several months he waited to hear from her, hoping she would ignore his harsh words. He had not meant to push her away so angrily; it was just his way of lashing out. But no more letters came.

Unable to cope with the intense frustration his decision had brought him, Eddie and a friend made plans to escape from Gatesville. In December 1966, the two teens took off across the field surrounding the complex. Coming to a farm house, they broke in and stole money, food, and extra clothing. Then they hid out for the night in a nearby barn; a few hours later they were awakened by an eerie sound, the clanging of the metal bells around the necks of the bloodhounds. Apparently it wasn't the first time this farm had been used by kids running off the compound.

The dogs led searchers right to the hay loft where Eddie and his friend were hiding. Eddie was sent to the maximum security unit at Mountain View, where he was put to work smashing up chalky rock in a caliche pit as part of his discipline.

Beatings by the guards continued at Mountain View, and Eddie spent nearly three years in a state of fear. Slapping was popular, and on one occasion, when a guard accused Eddie of tearing a picture out of a newspaper, he began to slap Eddie relentlessly on both sides of his face. When Eddie awoke the next morning, both cheeks had been reduced to huge scabs.

If he was not fearing the guards, Eddie was fearing the wolfpacks of kids, and woe be to the boy who was a loner at Mountain View. Eddie quickly aligned himself with a gang of fellow Anglos, who found themselves teaming up with the Hispanics when it came to taking on the blacks. The cliques stayed tight and provided peer support as well as mutual defense, like little anarchic city-states of teenagers trying to inhabit the same corner of the world.

Sexual tension was a much bigger thing for Eddie and his friends during this stay in the reform school. The first time he was only eleven. Now he was fifteen and through puberty, and he had been sexually active on the outside. In the clique, Eddie found protection from sexual assaults by other boys, but he and his friends still felt a tribal kind of anger when a white boy from outside their group, a fourteen-year-old boy by the name of Tommy Harper, became the target of a gang of black teens. The blacks took Tommy's food and other possessions, and taunted him out on the grounds. But most importantly, Tommy Harper was going over to the black dormitory and giving sex to those black kids.

It angered Eddie and his friends a great deal because Tommy avoided all contact with the Anglo cliques. It seemed clear to them that Tommy wanted nothing to do with them, and they watched him with increasing rage. They knew what he was doing in there. He was disgracing all of the white boys at Mountain View. He was dropping his pants and bending over in front of

those horny black teens, and letting them use him to satisfy their
sexual urges. He was going down on his knees and giving them
oral sex. He was taking their penises in his hands and masturbating them. Eddie and his circle of friends seethed at such a
massive affront to their dignity. On several occasions, they collared Tommy and racked him in the fashion they had learned
from the guards. They warned Tommy not to return to the black
dorm.

But Tommy still went. The rage that the whites felt at this
was immeasureable. Something had to be done to punish Tommy
Harper.

That was not long in coming.

After several months of using Tommy as a sexual toy, the
black teens had enough. Tommy was tossed aside like a soiled
doll, and this seemed to increase the anger directed toward him
from the other youths.

One afternoon, a few weeks after he was freed from domination by the blacks, Tommy finished up a class and was walking
back across the grounds from the vocational area to his dormitory. One of Eddie's friends came up quickly from behind and
intercepted Tommy. With quick thrusts, he jabbed at Tommy's
throat with a homemade knife. As Tommy fell, blood pouring
from a gaping slash in his neck, the attacker stuck him several
more times in the back. Tommy bled to death on the walk. Eddie
heard about it soon after. Every member of the clique felt a
catharsis, a vicarious release of the venom that had been directed
at Tommy Harper. There was very little talk about it afterward.
In the years that followed, Eddie thought of Tommy often, but
for reasons he kept to himself, he would never talk about the
boy.

Those intense few years at Mountain View were interrupted in
January 1969, several months after Eddie turned seventeen, when
the juvenile authorities selected him as a candidate for a relatively
new halfway house program. Eddie found himself in a YMCA in
downtown Houston, which hosted the program. He was given a
job assisting a carpenter who was building homes in the area.

But Eddie did not like the regimen and reacted swiftly to the first promise of escape. One of the other youths in the halfway house persuaded Eddie to get up all the money he could scrounge and run off with him and a friend to California. On the West Coast, the three of them would drink and do drugs from dusk until dawn. That offer was a lot more attractive to Eddie than being a carpenter's helper, so he threw his last few dollars into the kitty with the other two guys to fill the tank with gas, and they drove back down to the YMCA, where Eddie hurriedly went upstairs to pack his few belongings.

When Eddie got back down to the street the boys were gone, along with all of Eddie's money. He stood on the sidewalk, all of his possessions in a bundle in one hand. Feeling rotten and duped, Eddie took off, wandering until he came to a church on the outskirts of downtown. He yanked on the large wooden door only to find it locked. Eddie parked himself on the stoop and cried.

"Man, this is the last straw," he cried. "Even God don't want me." Later, he called his brother to come and get him, and he went down the highway to Galveston and home for the first time in more than two years.

Two weeks later, after a drunken Valentine's Day party the previous night, Eddie borrowed his brother's car and headed out for a wild Saturday night on the west end. Eddie did not have much experience driving a car because of all the years he spent in reform school while his peers were earning their driver's licenses. Sure enough, he careened down narrow Avenue S, learning how to drive a stick shift on the fly. As he neared Forty-fourth Street, a car coming in the opposite direction forced Eddie to the right, and he plowed into the rear of a parked car. The owner came running out as Eddie tried to restart his brother's car, but the radiator had been pushed back into the engine fan and the car was dead.

Soon the police arrived, handcuffed Eddie, and put him in the backseat of the patrol car. He had no identification and gave the officer a phony name, but he saw them grinning. They probably knew who he was, Eddie figured. While the officer took a statement from the owner of the other car, Eddie slipped his legs through his arms so that his wrists were cuffed in front of him, yanked the door handle, and took off running through a nearby yard. The officer drew his gun and yelled for him to stop, but Eddie put on a burst of speed.

At that point, he heard several sharp cracks behind him as the policeman fired his gun. Eddie heard the whizzing sound of one slug rush past his right ear, but still he ran. He hopped a picket fence out into the alley behind the houses on Avenue S, and one of the pickets jammed between one handcuff and his wrist, slicing open a large cut that started to bleed heavily. He ran west toward Forty-fifth Street with the officer in pursuit and closing the gap.

Ahead of him, Eddie saw cross-traffic on Forty-fifth, one of the major arteries on the west end going from the railyards on the ship channel to the beach on the Gulf. If he stopped to check traffic, the cop would catch him. He decided it was do or die. He would dart across Forty-fifth without slowing down. If he made it, he could get away; if a car hit him, he could die. Without hesitation, Eddie ran from the alley out into the street, and ran smack into the side panel of a passing car. He went sprawling onto the asphalt, and flinched when a police car came skidding to a stop within a few feet of his face. The blood poured from his wrists so profusely that a newspaper article mistakenly said he had been struck by a police bullet.

Eddie was charged with several driving violations and with escape from reform school, since he had run off from the halfway program. The two weeks in Galveston County Jail was the hardest time he had ever spent behind bars, and his thoughts turned to suicide. It seemed as if nothing he did worked out for him, as if everyone was against him. He felt that once he had been tagged a troublemaker, he had been singled out to make trouble, and whatever he did fulfilled that prophecy. He felt incapable of breaking the cycle. The things he feared most, messing up and going back to reform school, were exactly what he wound up doing. He pounded in frustration on the jail door's wire and glass window until his right fist swelled up black and blue.

He was shipped back to Mountain View in short order, having blown his chance for a clean start. He had only been gone for a few weeks, a prime candidate for the halfway house who instead wasted an opportunity. Some of his friends there were not even aware that he had been away.

Eddie remained at Mountain View for almost another year. He began to apply himself to his studies and found that he did a fairly good job when he put his mind to it. He took some computer training, and his counselor told him that when he was released, he should visit the Texas Rehabilitation Commission, which would pay for further training. In fact, Eddie maintained such a clean record that final year at Mountain View that shortly after he turned eighteen, his counselor told him the authorities were going to release him so that he could finish his senior year in high school with his former Travis and Lovenberg classmates, who were seven months from graduation at Galveston's Ball High School.

Computers were interesting for only a short time, then the lure of drugs again proved to be more seductive. After Eddie graduated with his class from Ball High in June 1970, he went back to Houston and, through the Texas Rehabilitation Commission, began training at the Academy of Computer Technology. This was supposed to be the up-and-coming profession, and Eddie knew that if he could find his way around computers, he might finally hold the ticket that would cure his aimlessness. However, as much as he tried, he could not stick with it. He began to skip classes after he found a new girlfriend. Julie was about a year younger than Eddie, and she was heavily into drugs. He soon dropped out of the academy, and with Julie engaged in a summer of wild sex and drug abuse, ending with Eddie slipping a needle filled with heroin into his arm, right under the tattoo of a rose and the name "Julie" that he had had embedded below his right shoulder.

Eddie was well schooled in the drug world, and he had always thought of junkies as the bottom of the barrel. He had vowed that he would quit drugs before he ever got to heroin. But Eddie could not resist anything that his companions wanted him to do. Meager and superficial as it was, he needed the social approval too much. Eddie repeatedly set up barriers that he pledged not to cross, only to move them as the need arose, farther and farther toward the edge.

To finance his drug habit, Eddie resumed burglarizing houses. He targeted a west-end house near the golf course and Greens Bayou. Eddie's childhood friend Joey was also doing drugs, and Eddie easily talked Joey into going with him to burgarize this house.

On Tuesday afternoon, September 8, Eddie and Joey slipped into the front of the house. As they began to gather items to steal, they found there was not as much as Eddie had thought, other than a television set. As they prepared to leave, Joey glanced out the front window and noticed a car pull up out front. Two men in suits got out. Joey quickly sized them up as plainclothes detectives, and figured a neighbor must have spotted them and alerted the police.

"It's the cops!" Joey yelled to Eddie. They both panicked and ran into the kitchen. Eddie pulled frantically on the back door, but it was locked with a key and would not open. In desperation, Joey grabbed a chair from the kitchen table and hurled it through the kitchen window. Both teens jumped through the window and began to scale the rear fence as the detectives ran around from the front.

"Get down off that fence, you little bastards!" one of the cops yelled. Eddie and Joey made it to the other side and bolted across a field, splitting up when they reached Fifty-seventh Street. Joey decided to play possum and just walk along the street hoping he would blend in with other pedestrians. But the police quickly arrested him. He refused to cooperate, maintaining that he was alone in the house. Police knew he was lying because they had seen both teens on the fence. They brought in reinforcements and began a meticulous search of the west-side neighborhood, concentrating near a graveyard between Fifty-seventh and Fifty-ninth streets.

That was precisely where Eddie had gone. There was a swampy area in the graveyard, and Eddie dove into its murky water. He went underwater and held his breath for as long as he could, then came up for fresh air and quickly submerged again. Several times when he came up, he saw police nearby. This went on for about an hour, then, just as the police were preparing to move on, Eddie came up for another breath and found himself staring right into the smiling face of Sergeant Ray Rubio.

"Hi. You wanna come on out of there?" Rubio said. He yanked the drenched young man out of the pond, and put him in a downtown cell with Joey.

Less than three months later, on the Monday after Thanksgiving 1970, Eddie went before acting District Judge Hugh Gibson and pleaded guilty to a two-count burglary indictment. Gibson gave him two five-year terms, to run concurrently, and ordered him shipped off to Huntsville, the intake unit for the adult prison system—Eddie was now nineteen.

Eddie found the time he did in the adult prison easier both physically and psychologically than his years in reform school. He was sent to a unit for first-time offenders with juvenile records. There were no organized beatings, no racking, peeling, or brogueing by the guards, beyond isolated incidents. If he wanted drugs, they were exceptionally easy to come by. He had more drugs pushed on him behind prison walls than he ever had on the streets of Galveston.

Eddie was assigned to a road crew, and worked the excruciatingly difficult drag lines that cleared drainage ditches along the sides of rural Texas highways. He maintained a clean prison record, and less than two and a half years into his sentence, his name came up on a work-release list. He began training in welding with a company in Richmond, southwest of Houston, and for the first time in his life he was laboring at something he enjoyed.

Eddie had a small place in Richmond to bunk while he worked the job. He kept his first few appointments with his parole officer nearby in Houston. But Galveston was only an hour away, and he went down to his hometown on weekends for visits. There, he began to hang around once again with a rough crowd. It was not long before Eddie found himself wishing to be out from under his job training. He spent his weekends with his friends having parties on the beach, drinking excessively, and doing drugs, only to have to return to Richmond for work on Monday morning.

Eddie's restlessness built into discontent until finally he could no longer stand the thought of going back to work. Soon, he chose to quit his job, transfer his parole supervision to Galveston, and return home.

But Eddie never bothered to look for a job in Galveston, and met with his parole officer only once. In the meantime, he joined a group of guys who were pulling armed robberies. Eddie and some of his friends laughed about one of the members of the group, who seemed half crazy. This guy loved to rob just for the thrill of it. Eddie and the others would simply suggest a convenience store or some other place they could go to, and their friend would go in alone and pull the robbery. Then he would run back to the car and give them all the money.

They hit a number of places near Galveston and up the highway toward Houston. One night in June, on the southern outskirts of Houston, Eddie and his friends pulled up to a 7-Eleven store. Their half-crazy friend told them he was tired of going in and taking all the risks. Eddie and the others decided it was only fair that they all go in this time, which they did. On the way out, with Eddie holding the bag filled with money, they ran right into an off-duty police officer who had stopped to buy some things. They took off and led the officer on a high-speed jaunt during which the robbers fired their guns out the windows at their pursuer before he discontinued the chase.

Several days later, on June 24, Eddie was back in Galveston driving his yellow 1965 Buick Skylark down Broadway. He was cruising east on the main drag just after 8:00 P.M., and had just passed the big cemetery when he noticed two police cars gaining on him. At the Thirty-seventh Street intersection, the police cars sandwiched him to a stop, one of them sliding in with a screeching fishtail to block his path. Several officers jumped out and leveled shotguns at him, another triggered a bullhorn.

"Keep your hands on the steering wheel!" the cop yelled.

Eddie kept his hands in sight and froze. The officers came over to the car, looked inside, and spotted a handgun on the seat. One of the cops grabbed Eddie's arm and yanked him out of the car. He was quickly patted down and handcuffed, then thrown into the Galveston City Jail. Eddie soon learned that the driver of their getaway car from the 7-Eleven robbery had been arrested after his license plate was traced, and that he had confessed to police and named his accomplices.

The police laid every charge they could on Eddie, from robbery to carrying a concealed weapon to reckless driving. But by far the most serious was the charge of being a habitual criminal. With Eddie's prior record, the law allowed prosecutors to seek to have him locked away for the rest of his life. Cons call it "the big bitch." It filled Eddie with fear.

On Monday, following a brief court appearance, Eddie bolted through an unlocked glass door in the passageway from the courtroom to the cells. He could not handle going back to prison, not for life. Police quickly found him hiding in a nearby alley, and filed an additional charge of attempted escape. Back in his cell, Eddie was overwhelmed by the realization of failure at trying to make a life for himself outside prison. He probably would never see the streets again, he thought. Even his mother, who had always been in his corner no matter what he did, threw up her hands during a visit to the jail and told him there was nothing more she could do.

Eddie was so depressed that when the jail chaplain went through the cell block handing out the book *From Prison to Praise*, Eddie shoved it up under his bunk without even glancing at it. It was not until a few days later that he remembered it was there, and he took it out and read it through. The book spoke of the existence of a purpose in life, including his. Eddie had never thought of his life as possessing any purpose other than drinking, doing drugs, and committing the crimes that helped fund those activities. It told him that if he began to thank God for the purpose in his life, the oppressive clouds around his mind would begin to clear. That, Eddie thought, was the craziest thing he had ever heard. He shoved the book back under the mattress. Yet a week or so later, Eddie remembered the book, and said a short prayer. The only thing he could think of to thank God for was the fact that despite all the destructive things he had done, he was still alive.

When he was transferred to the state's intake unit at Huntsville, his cellmate shared some Christian tracts his wife was sending him. One of them depicted a man who had lived a life much like Eddie's, who then died and faced his eternal judgment. He was tossed into damnation, where there was great "weeping and gnashing of teeth." That image fixed itself in Eddie's mind throughout his stay in Huntsville. He could not even escape it in his sleep, as his dreams were filled with the sounds of terrible weeping and the gnashing of teeth. He woke up several mornings in a sweaty state of fright from the dreams. He began to remember things, like the time he felt strangely comforted at the church services in reform school and the despair he felt after trying to enter the Houston church only to find the doors locked.

Eddie began to read a number of the Christian books available at the prison, and he sometimes broke down in tears when he saw connections to the failures in his life. When his cellmate walked in on him one day and found Eddie sobbing, prison authorities transferred Eddie to another block to keep a closer watch on him. Eddie thought his new cellmate resembled the devil himself, a big man with haunting, pale blue eyes. Eddie was tormented by his guilt and fears of eternal damnation.

Then, while sitting alone in his cell one day, Eddie heard a voice inside his head, telling him to read the book on his shelf. Eddie had been hearing voices in his head since childhood, although invariably the voices had told him to do something wrong. This time, Eddie reached for the book, *The Way to God*, and found a multistep program for inviting Jesus into his life. He began to follow it, and between steps two and three he felt a strange sensation coming over him. It was an involuntary feeling, like a shuddering, and Eddie could swear that it was accompanied by some sort of presence entering his cell. He had felt the presence of evil before, but this was different. He felt a warmth rise through him and it made him feel so light that he thought he could float. It seemed that every worry, every thought of depression and loneliness, had been expelled, and he felt a joyful peace. Eddie broke down in uncontrollable crying. It was the first time in his life that he had felt an inner peace. He was certain that Jesus had come into his life at last, and he sensed that his life from that day forward would be different.

It was not long before that feeling bore worldly fruit and

changed Eddie's life in a very tangible way. One of his accomplices in the convenience store robbery came through his cell block, having been convicted and sentenced at trial. He saw Eddie and, with a puzzled look, approached him.

"Where have you been, man?" his friend asked.

"What do you mean? I've been in here," Eddie replied.

"I mean at the trial. They put on the witnesses, and they went through the whole robbery, and your name never even came up. The lady we robbed, she fingered all of us but you. How did you get out of it?"

Eddie was dumbfounded. But sure enough, he learned there was no police hold registered in the files on him for the Houston robbery charge. Somehow, in the process of revoking his parole and separating him from the others, his involvement slipped through the cracks of an overburdened judicial system. It was as though his entire role in the crime had never occurred. Suddenly there was nothing standing in the way of his full and complete release. There was no big bitch hovering over him. The next time the prison door swung open, he could walk out freely into the clean, fresh air, filled with the love of Jesus. At last he had found the strength and will to make a new life.

Eddie served out less than six months more before he was released from state prison, his 1970 burglary sentence fully satisfied. As he headed in the opposite direction from Galveston, in search of a Christian community that would help to nurture his newborn love for the Lord, Eddie swore he would never turn back. The new friends he soon made, including his future wife, Ronda, helped him hold on tightly to the belief that he was a completely changed man.

CHAPTER 2

LIES OF SILENCE

Used to be that my mind wondered a lot if there would ever be anyone to share with, laugh with, sing with, and cry with. And then he was there. Eddie. And we share, and laugh, and sing, and cry. He's so very gentle and kind, Lord.

—from Ronda's diary

"Vicksburg?" Eddie Wyatt shot out in surprise. He turned his head toward the side window to watch the road sign go by. "We're going the wrong way! We're almost to Mississippi!" Ronda Hunter, over in the passenger seat, had seen the road sign at the same time and quickly felt disoriented, having thought they were headed west the last two hours. It had been rainy and overcast all day.

"Oh, Eddie, you're right. They're never going to believe we got lost for *this* long," she said as her escort looked for an opportune place in which to turn around. They had been so preoccupied with getting acquainted that they never realized they were going through all those tiny Louisiana towns until they spotted the highway marker outside Tallulah that said "Vicksburg, 12 Miles," up ahead across the Mississippi River.

Eddie yanked the station wagon off the shoulder, did a half-circle in the wide spot of wet dirt, and stopped. He squinted through the rainy late afternoon mist to check the traffic, waiting until several cars went by in each direction before easing on the accelerator, now correctly aimed for Texas.

"Dang wipers," Eddie said, futilely turning the knob on the dash one more time. "Oh, Ronda, I'm sorry about this." Eddie had been fidgety, and Ronda sensed that he was nervous about making a good impression. Among all the male counselors she had known in her two years volunteering at the Teen Challenge center in Dallas, Ronda noticed that Eddie was the shy one, a quiet and serious young man. Her colleagues shared her assessment of this relatively recent arrival at the center, and they thought his quiet manner signified politeness, maturity, and sincerity. They told Ronda she could not have a better escort than Eddie Wyatt to take her to Monroe, Louisiana, overnight to attend the wedding of Angela Turnbow and Bob Thompson, two mutual friends from Teen Challenge.

Having lost two hours on an already long ride home to Dallas, Ronda settled back in her seat and took the situation in stride. Eddie seemed to be relieved that she took it so calmly. But nothing fazed Ronda Hunter. She was the practical, take-charge staffer at Teen Challenge. If she walked into a room where the preschool kids had dumped a mess all over the floor, she would smile, roll up her sleeves, and go for the broom closet. Then she would hug and praise each little boy and girl as she mopped her way through the chaos.

Ronda possessed the wholesome look that came with growing up in the rarified air of Denver, next to the Rocky Mountains. At twenty-one, she was slender and wore her light brown hair long, often with soft curls to it that swirled around her glasses and gently grazed her shoulders. She almost always wore a dress, or skirt and blouse, a habit born in her conservative religious upbringing. Her calm demeanor hid an intense desire to help other people. She was a soldier and her fondest wish was to be the wife of a minister.

Ronda knew that Eddie Wyatt was not the product of a divinity school, that he had been to a Texas reform school, the destination of many an aimless child in the early 1960s. As an adult of twenty-two, Eddie seemed to have found a purpose after showing up on the doorstep of the Teen Challenge center. The nationally renowned rehabilitation program had taken the wiry young man with the burglary record and drug problem and turned his life around. The Assemblies of God church operated ninety-eight Teen Challenge centers across the land, mostly in urban trouble spots. One study of the original Teen Challenge center in

Brooklyn found that 85 percent of those who stayed for the full program, which could take up to a year to complete, never went back to the drugs, the alcohol, the crime, and the depression— all symptoms of the low self-esteem that previously characterized their lives.

Everyone at the Dallas center figured Eddie Wyatt for someone who would advance that success rate. Eddie was Teen Challenge's model client, having gone through the program without a single instance of backsliding. He counseled youths about his experience in prison and in finding Jesus, and he was effective in reaching them. Preparing to enter welding school to pick up a trade, Eddie was determined to overcome all the disadvantages that he picked up as a kid on the streets of Galveston. The handsome, curly-haired young man seemed to have taken charge of his life, and his easygoing manner displayed a contented happiness with his new lot in life.

Ronda found Eddie to be quite attractive, at about five feet nine and on the light side at 145 pounds. She was aware from his tearful testimonies at church services that he came from a broken home. On his body he displayed the evidence of his wayward youth—a scar under his chin and tattoos of a snake and a rose with a woman's name. But now Eddie bore the marks of a new way of life. He had found self-respect in the program and seemed to truly care about other people.

Ronda Hunter had dedicated herself to salvaging city kids in danger of losing their lives to drugs, crime, or engulfing despair. She zeroed in on that aspect of each youth's personality that needed affirmation, and then set about in just the right manner to build up that person's self-esteem. Eddie needed that in his life as well, and he began to wonder what it would be like to have Ronda as his wife.

Off to the west, on the dark Texas horizon, Ronda could see the glare of city lights illuminating the misty sky. They were still more than an hour and a half out of Dallas. The glare ahead was probably Tyler, the small east Texas city near which the Reverend David Wilkerson had moved his operations in the early 1970s. Back in 1961, in an effort to turn around troubled kids, Reverend Wilkerson, a rural Pennsylvania preacher, had established his first

Teen Challenge in an old house on Clinton Avenue in Brooklyn's Bedford-Stuyvesant neighborhood in New York.

"I want to tell you, Ronda, that I appreciate all the work you do at the center," Eddie said as they continued on their extra-long drive. "You make it look so easy, and I can tell you from experience, it just ain't that easy for me."

Ronda was flattered by the praise, and tried to brush away her embarrassment. "I guess when you like something so much, it makes difficult things easier," she replied.

"I understand how you feel about losing Angela, too," Eddie went on, "because over in the boys' program we're gonna miss having Bob around. He's a good hard worker and I think the world of him."

"Well, Eddie, you know, Bob really cares about you," Ronda replied.

Above the din of the station wagon's engine and other traffic on the interstate, Eddie thought he heard Ronda say, "I really care about you." He appeared to be startled. Eddie turned to look at her, and waited just a second until she also faced him.

"Well, I really do care about you, Ronda," he said. Ronda looked puzzled as Eddie continued. "In fact, I think I even love you."

Ronda was stunned. She admired Eddie. Like the others at Teen Challenge, she was proud of the way he had progressed in the six months since he arrived, how genuine his commitment seemed, and how he was filled with the love of the Lord. Eddie Wyatt had even spoken in tongues, that emotional prayer language that some believe comes only to people truly filled with the Holy Spirit. But she wasn't quite ready for what Eddie had just said to her.

"Well, Eddie, I don't think I love you, but I might could get to," she said with a rural colloquialism. Their hesitancy finally breached, they rode on to Dallas having that heart-to-heart talk Eddie always wanted to have with Ronda.

Eddie and Ronda Wyatt marked the date in their memories. August 30, 1974. They often laughed when they thought back on the series of mistakes that kicked off their relationship that rainy day on the highway back from Louisiana. What would their lives be like now if not for that serendipity, those little bumbles that broke the ice and eventually brought them together as husband and wife? It was a romance made in heaven, they thought.

The dedicated young men and women at the Teen Challenge chapel on Beacon Street in rough east Dallas, tucked unobtrusively two blocks down from the Santa Fe tracks, were constantly being swept up in intense dramas. Their work with the lost souls of the delinquents, with the poor children from the nearby housing projects, and with each other as they struggled to make a difference in those people's lives, fostered intimate emotional bonds. They prayed together ardently and cried in each other's arms. These were youngsters from all over the map, fresh out of adolescence but not yet admitted to adulthood. They met and shared their deep pain and more fervent desires for a life that would take them away from often unhappy childhoods. In fact, within the span of about three years, the Dallas Teen Challenge center had fostered the marriages of seven couples.

Ronda and the others at Teen Challenge knew of Eddie Wyatt's particularly dramatic turnaround. In spring 1974, a director of the Dallas center, Jim Jessup, got a call from his counterpart at the center over in Fort Worth, where the program was geared to young women. He told Jessup that a man named Eddie Wyatt had sputtered to a stop in a clunker of a car out by the center's front lawn and wanted to learn more about Jesus. Jessup grabbed the keys to the Teen Challenge van and made the quick trip over to Fort Worth to get Eddie.

By virtue of his position with the Dallas center, Jessup shared one of the program's houses on Garland Avenue, at the corner of Saint Mary Street four blocks from the chapel, with the boys in the program. Jessup and his wife lived in a bungalow on the corner while the boys lived dormitory style in a building out back. The bungalow had a common area where the clients met for group sessions. Ronda and several other female counselors lived about a half mile away on Gaston Avenue, and occasionally harbored troubled girls.

Eddie had never met any Christian folks before, and he discovered that unlike the people with whom he associated while growing up in Galveston, those at Teen Challenge were caring. There were about a half dozen young men who went through the program in the spring of 1974 with him. But none of the others breezed through it like Eddie Wyatt did. Lyle Noah, the director of the east Dallas center, had been around long enough that he could spot a phony. Eddie struck him as authentic. There had been those who were faking it; some, referred as a condition of probation, just went through the motions; and others always came to a point where the problems that brought them to Teen Challenge roared back and tried to swallow them up again.

Eddie, however, seemed intent on learning all he could about himself and about Jesus. Noah watched the other boys go off in fits of rage or break down in crying jags when some unresolved inner conflict bubbled to the surface. With Eddie, that never happened. No tarnish at all marred his steady transformation from delinquent to responsible adult.

Shortly after arriving at Teen Challenge, Eddie was in deep prayer with the others when strange sounds spilled involuntarily from his mouth. To lay ears it sounded more like gibberish, but to believers in some Pentecostal churches, it appears as the language of the Lord, a gift to those who have been "born again" in the Spirit. For Eddie, surprised and confused, it was a rite of passage into a new life. Ronda and the other counselors were thrilled to see him undergo the experience.

Later, after the service, counselor Steve Griffith walked by a small room in front of the Beacon Street chapel and found Eddie alone inside, a look of consternation on his face. Steve, who had much more experience at praying in tongues that Eddie, sensed his friend's struggle over the strange new feeling.

"Is the devil trying to steal what you got from God, Eddie?" Steve asked him. Eddie stopped for a second and gave Steve a look, then quickly his tensed-up face eased with relief.

"Thanks, Steve, I guess that's exactly what he's trying to do," Eddie told him. "It *was* real and Satan's trying to take it away from me!" Immediately Eddie began praying again, and his words quickly lapsed back into glossolalia right on the spot. Those indecipherable utterances confirmed to Eddie and everyone else at the center that Steve's reassurance was right on the mark.

Eddie, who had always been a loner and a misfit, now belonged to a group of people. In the roar of approval from the crowd, it would be easy to overcome any remaining self-doubt. He could push off any nagging questions about his past and leave them unresolved, because they were not relevant to these people. Once in a while, if those old feelings of frustration, anger, and guilt began to surface, Eddie found that a quick litany of "Lord, help me" pushed them back in the closet.

Ronda Jean Hunter was a child of the rural American heartland. She was weaned on its values of hard work, honesty, and abiding faith in human nature. In the farm town of Fort Morgan, hugging the scrawny ribbon of the South Platte River on the eastern plains of Colorado, Ronda began her life within sight of Longs Peak. The summit, shimmering like a mirage a hundred miles distant, anchored the northern reach of the Front Range of the Rocky Mountains. Down east, in the sunset shadows of the mountains, the business of the broad plains Ronda knew as a child was flatland agriculture. Her hometown of 7,500 people was surrounded by heavily irrigated fields of grain, beets, corn, and soybeans. It was far from the Colorado of the tourist brochures. The plains of Colorado formed the western lip of the Dust Bowl, the highest and driest part of the Great American Desert that the pioneers a century and a half ago quickly bypassed to reach the fertile valleys of California and Oregon.

Ronda was born late one hot summer night in July 1953 at Fort Morgan Community Hopsital to Paul and Erna Hunter, who had been reared in this milieu out on the eastern plains of Colorado. After Paul and Erna married, they had stayed with farming only two years. The couple lived with a farmer for one year, before sharecropping with another fellow the next year. Those early days were lean, and Paul sometimes brought to table a young jackrabbit that got caught under the disks as he plowed the fields.

They lived in a trailer home so they could up and move with the work. Son Ron was born in 1952 over in Brush, a town of 3,300 ten miles downriver from Fort Morgan. Within a year, Paul had moved the family down U.S. 6 into Fort Morgan where he'd gotten a job driving trucks for the county. That's when Ronda was born. Her dad then got a job working on the oil and gas wells that dotted the landscape over the Denver-Julesburg Basin. But in time he was laid off. Perusing the want ads, he found a marine business in Denver that needed a mechanic to work on boat engines, so Paul Hunter moved his young family to the city, where his third child was born in 1957, a son named Randy.

It was as a boat mechanic that Paul Hunter raised his family for the next several decades. Moving into shady Denver from the treeless plains, they imported those clean-living religious values that were the family's wellspring. It was not at all unusual, when Ronda was growing up, for her parents to take in folks in need. Ronda was proud of her parents for that, and she tried to pattern her own actions after them. She could not stand the thought of any pain or upset being visited upon those she loved.

They attended an Assemblies of God church, a relatively young denomination that is the largest Pentecostal group in the world. The church grew out of the early twentieth-century fundamentalist revival that began in the American heartland, spread to California, and then worked its way around the Christian world. The revival began with spontaneous acts of worship outside the mainstream faiths, during which participants caught up in the fervor began speaking in unknown languages. Bible scholars came to believe that this speaking in tongues, or glossolalia, was evidence of the baptism in the Holy Spirit, which was first visited upon Jesus's apostles on the day of Pentecost. Those who undergo the baptism are said to be "born-again Christians," although not all speak in tongues. Theirs is a very personal faith built not around the institutional churches but on an individual relationship with Jesus.

When they first moved to Denver, the Hunters took up residence in a low-income collection of duplexes by the South Platte River off Santa Fe Drive, close to Paul's work. Once the family

got squared financially, they moved to a house on Center Street
in west Denver, a block away from the Central Assembly of God,
where the Hunters were members. It was in that church that
Ronda was hurt one summer Tuesday in 1961, at the age of eight,
when a swinging door banged her on the right side of her face.
Within days, Erna noticed her little girl was having trouble chewing. Her feet began to turn inward, and she was dragging her left
foot. Erna was worried because several months before the injury,
Ronda had been unable to close her left eye completely. Six days
after the accident at the church, her parents took her to Children's
Hospital in Denver, where a battery of tests eventually determined
she had a brain stem glioma. The inoperable tumor, present before
the accident but discovered because of it, was causing partial
paralysis of her left side. After three days in the hospital, doctors
sent her home and told Paul and Erna that Ronda was likely to
die within a year.

Prayer networks sprang up at Central Assembly and in other
churches in the area. During the prayer call, Paul brought Ronda
forward for the community to pray over her. Throughout the next
year, instead of coming closer to death, Ronda improved. Her
eyes, which had crossed following the accident, straightened. By
the following July medical tests turned up no sign at all of the
tumor. By her ninth birthday, Ronda knew she had a special and
personal relationship with God. He had kept her alive for a reason,
she believed.

The people in her family and her church also saw Ronda as
specially blessed. And as she grew older, it became important for
her to be the person her fellow church members perceived her
to be. She craved approval so much that she tended to deny
problems that might disturb the image. She would be whatever
other wished her to be. Her aim was to please, and at that she
became very good.

Ronda had liked school from the day she walked into kindergarten. All through her school career, she was drawn more to
the humanities than to the sciences. She grew to love reading,
and into adulthood favored novels about the triumphant struggles
of the common person, or the pioneers who battled against the

odds. Having acquired her parents' sense of protectiveness, Ronda would often hover over the classmate who was being shunned by the other children and take that child under her wing. She quickly made friends with one very obese little girl, and another time with a homely girl from a poor family who rarely bathed and smelled bad, so both of them would not be without a friend.

The Hunters later moved to suburban Lakewood west of Denver and attended the Assembly of God church there. The family's religious convictions helped separate Ronda from her classmates. Her parents forbade Ronda to learn square dancing in elementary school and modern dance in high school. The restriction meant there would be no senior prom for Ronda. But she excelled at home economics. She was reared to believe that a woman's place was mainly in the home, and she was preparing herself as best she could for that day.

She also had innate musical talent. With lessons, she soon became accomplished at the piano. Added to that, her soft voice lent itself to beautiful song. Ronda often sang while she did other tasks, such as crafts or cooking. Her family and friends grew fond of hearing her sweet voice, singing the familiar hymns.

Ronda began to date at age sixteen. These usually consisted of dinner, walking together, or reading together since going to the movies was also prohibited. At Alameda High School, she was part of a Bible club that met for prayer on Wednesdays before classes. She was very happy with who she was, as long as the people who mattered in her corner of the world approved. Her sheltered upbringing surfaced the summer before her senior year when she flew to Montego Bay, Jamaica, with a group of youth missionaries for the Assemblies of God. Outside a rural church, Ronda spotted a rooster doing to a hen what roosters naturally do to hens. She asked one of the Jamaican children what the rooster was up to. The embarrassed boy pawed at the dirt with his foot, while Ronda kept pressuring him. When the boy burst out laughing, Ronda finally realized what was happening in the barnyard. This naivete about sexual matters carried over into her adulthood.

When Ronda graduated from Alameda High in June 1971, her parents pooled enough money to send her to Southwestern Assemblies of God College in Waxahachie, Texas, a half hour's drive down the highway from Dallas. She planned to major in Christian education. These studies would help her to work at a pastor's side as his wife and helper. Since the Assemblies of God also ran the Teen Challenge program, the Dallas center put out regular calls to the student body at Southwestern to come into Dallas on weekends and witness to the street people on the fringes of downtown. Dallas Teen Challenge sent two vans down the highway to the college every Friday and Saturday to fetch the volunteers, and a group of Ronda's friends began to go regularly.

Ronda was reluctant to go along because she would be proselytizing to a very skeptical crowd. But pressure from those who were going helped her suppress her anxiety. The feeling around campus was that if one were truly a good Christian one would go to Dallas, and so she went each weekend. If it pleased others for her to make those weekend treks, she would be first in line for the Teen Challenge van. Driven by peer pressure and her craving for approval, Ronda sometimes felt like a disembodied spectator in her own life, watching it occur in front of her rather than particiapting in it.

Ronda finished her freshman year at Southwestern. She enjoyed her studies at college, but she quickly came to realize she could not afford to return in the fall of 1972. Money was tight at home, and because she spent so much time with Teen Challenge through the spring, she had not earned any money herself.

Lyle Noah had spotted Ronda as a very gifted volunteer, and asked her to stay at Dallas Teen Challenge that summer to help with the Kids Crusades, in which they went into the housing projects and taught Bible classes to children. Feeling so needed, Ronda was happy to stay. During that summer, Ronda was paid a minimal amount, about $20 a month, in addition to room and board. In the fall, Noah gave her a job as peer counselor in the girls' home, where she helped teenage girls work out their problems.

Ronda could walk blindly into harm's way, her faith in the basic goodness of human nature remaining unshaken even after discovering some of the dangers she had unwittingly passed. For example, she once counseled a depressed teenaged girl in the girl's home. It was not until after several sessions that the girl confessed that, during Ronda's first visit, the teenager had been sitting on a loaded pistol. She had initially planned to shoot Ronda. Now that there was no more danger, Ronda characteristically felt no nervousness at all.

When Eddie left prison in February 1974, he knew the worst thing he could do was return to his old haunts in Galveston. So he borrowed his brother's car and set out for Abilene in west Texas. He briefly joined a Pentecostal church there, but could not find a job because the kids from Abilene Christian College had taken them all. For no particular reason, he then decided to head toward Fort Worth. No sooner had he gotten the car onto Interstate 20 than it caught fire somewhere in the engine compartment. He pulled over to the shoulder, got out, and lifted the hood. The fire went out quickly, but he had no idea what was wrong with the car.

That's when he heard a voice inside himself. Eddie was used to hearing voices, not actual disembodied ones, but more like impromptu thoughts that regularly popped into his head telling him to do this or that. While this voice used to tell him to do bad things, the voice now was different. It said: "Trust me. Get in the car and start it up." Eddie had not touched a thing on the engine, but he thought why not? It seemed no crazier than trying to monkey with the engine. He cranked the ignition and the engine turned over. Amazed, Eddie pulled back out onto the interstate, confident that Jesus was leading him somewhere. When he got near Fort Worth, he started to recall some of the incredible stories of salvation he had read in *The Cross and the Switchblade*, Reverend Wilkerson's inspirational classic that was read by nearly everyone at Teen Challenge centers across America and which Eddie had read while in prison. He yanked the car off at an exit and stopped at a telephone booth, where he quickly thumbed through the directory. It turned out he was only two blocks from the Fort Worth center. He drove over to the building, parked out front, and shut off the car. When a fellow from the center came out to have a look at it, he discovered the water pump had given out and a fan blade had broken off and punctured the radiator. That car should not have been running, he told Eddie.

Eddie responded by tossing him the keys, saying "Keep it," and climbing into Jim Jessup's van.

When Jessup pulled up to the east Dallas center that day in March 1974 with Eddie, the young man had already made the necessary commitment to turn his life around. Soon Eddie began to give testimony in churches and in counseling sessions about how he had come to Jesus. He gave Ronda and the others a glimpse of a lonely youngster when he told his Galveston stories. They simply scratched the surface, but they constituted the only knowledge that folks like Ronda, Lyle Noah, and Jim Jessup had of Eddie Wyatt. The fact was that the past did not matter to them. Whatever Eddie wanted to reveal, however far he was willing to go, was far enough for them. The Eddie Wyatt who was their friend was an entirely different man from the youngster who thought the streets of Galveston belonged to him.

Eddie held his audiences at churches and in Teen Challenge sessions enrapt with his chilling testimonies. He told them stories of his experiences in Gatesville, how he had often been beaten and had seen other kids killed. He told how he had gotten hooked on drugs. In his quiet and even-toned voice, he talked about the time he heard the police bullet buzz by his ear. Then he told them about his fits of depression in the squalid Galveston jail cell, and how they had total control over him until he prayed his first prayer.

Eddie's Sunday testimonies quickly made him a star in the Teen Challenge program, and he was featured in the Dallas area's newsletter. Ronda admired the strength of the young man's character.

She saw him face up to his past, admit his guilt, and speak lovingly of his new relationship with the Lord. A warm smile would come over Ronda's face when she heard him talk. The rest of the staff at Teen Challenge, who worked more closely with him, felt even more pride in Eddie Wyatt.

Jim Jessup remained for several more months; later that summer he left to join a submarine crew in the navy. Jessup found Eddie to be very conscientious and very committed to making the program work for him. When Jessup made a point during Bible classes, he could see Eddie stop to think about it, assess it, then catch it and be ready for the next. It seemed to Jessup that Eddie Wyatt was his own man, that he did not rely on the opinions of others. Jim Jessup held Eddie Wyatt in very high regard.

Jessup was replaced by Jerry and Charlotte Holley, a young east Texas couple who came to Dallas to dedicate their lives to young people. The Holleys found Eddie to be quiet and cooperative, unusual and welcome behavior in a program for troubled kids. Eddie got up every morning for prayer, Bible study, and chores without the slightest complaint. He seemed to learn because he wanted to learn. While most people in the program required attention at odd hours of the night, simply needing to talk or to cry, Eddie did not.

When he did have something to say, Eddie did not waste words. So when he opened his mouth his friends usually listened. And his presentation could be riveting. One time, during a visit to one of Dallas's many Pentecostal churches, Eddie was scheduled to testify for five minutes. But he kept the congregation enthralled for a full three-quarters of an hour with his story.

After Eddie took notice of Ronda, he would sometimes say a quick hello to her in the office near the chapel and be on his way. Once Eddie got on the staff as a peer counselor, the two were around each other more often, usually at the communal dinner table. Eddie was attracted to Ronda from the beginning. She was someone who embodied the qualities he wanted in his own life. When he watched her work with the children, the teenage girls, and even the other counselors, he felt inspired and motivated by her. During the summer, Eddie began to express himself in verse, and penned a poem for Ronda even before they started to date. One part spoke personally of the effect Ronda was having on his newly reborn heart:

> *To one that's fallen along the way*
> *I'm sure it would change the darkness to day.*
> *But to me, that smile you often wear*
> *Brings a warmth to my heart*
> *That has settled there.*

When Eddie and Ronda returned to Teen Challenge from their Louisiana trip and announced they were dating, their friends were surprised. Their dates were nothing fancy, dictated by Teen Challenge's meager, token salaries. What Ronda earned above her room and board, she donated back to Teen Challenge and relied on her parents for spending money. Dates consisted mostly of walking hand in hand and talking about their hopes and dreams. Within a matter of weeks, their colleagues heard Eddie and Ronda talking about getting married.

Ronda believed, as did everyone at Teen Challenge, that such a profound change as the one that had overcome Eddie's aimlessness, anger, and frustration was too deep to be ephemeral. Ronda saw herself as perfect for Eddie. She would give him the stable home he lacked as a child. She would reward his commitment by being the best wife and mother of his children she could possibly be, surrounding him with love for the rest of his life.

Jerry and Charlotte Holley were somewhat skeptical. The deputy director and his wife thought Eddie could use a little more seasoning. Deep down, they did not want to lose Ronda. Those who had gone through the program had enough problems straightening out their lives without rushing into the lifetime commitment of marriage. But they felt that Eddie was a good man and that Ronda had a practical head on her shoulders. In fact, of the seven marriages that took place at Teen Challenge in this time frame, the proposed Eddie Wyatt–Ronda Hunter nuptials raised the least concern among the staff.

*   *   *

Sometime in September, less than a month after their first date, Eddie and Ronda decided to set the most romantic day they could for their wedding, Valentine's Day, less than five months away. Eddie made plans to leave Teen Challenge and secure a job. He enjoyed welding that brief time he did it on work-release in Richmond, so he found his way into a welding certification class in the Industrial Trade School in Dallas. He moved out of Teen Challenge and took a room in an attractive boardinghouse in a quiet neighborhood on Junius Street, across from tiny Munger Park and only several blocks from Ronda's apartment on Gaston Avenue.

Paul and Erna Hunter came down to Dallas on a vacation to meet their future son-in-law during the second week of November. They drove down in a powder blue 1964 Volkswagen that they intended to give their daughter as a gift. Eddie seemed gentlemanly enough when Ronda's parents met him, but they were apprehensive about their daughter's marriage to a man who had gone through the Teen Challenge program, success story or not. Paul liked to brag that Erna had a sixth sense about people and could size them up faster than a jackrabbit could scoot across a farm road. Erna just didn't have a good feeling about Eddie. And Paul thought Eddie a nervous sort who would not look him square in the eye when they talked.

But their daughter's happiness stifled their own feelings and concerns. Paul and Erna would not mar the obvious joy this relationship brought to Ronda by expressing their doubts. Their daughter had been reared well and was now on her own. They were not about to call her back for more lectures.

Eddie began a welding job at Litton Systems in Dallas for $3 an hour on November 6, just three days before Ronda's parents arrived for their visit. In two months, he would be up to $3.25. It was hard but honest work that he enjoyed. As a married man, he would have to start earning better money than Teen Challenge could pay. From the day that summer when Eddie was made a counselor until the time he left in late October, he had been paid a total of $350. At Litton, he would earn triple that amount just by the end of the year.

Ronda had faith in God, and she was certain that whatever tribulations came their way during their married life, her faith and Eddie's would pull them through. She kept in mind a biblical passage from Paul's letter to the Romans that reminded her of a simple truth. If God is for them, then who can possibly stand against them?

CHAPTER 3

HAPPILY NEVER AFTER

*It's a little after midnight, and Eddie's at work. I miss him
so when he is gone and when it's almost time for him to come
home, I get all excited inside to see him again. Today he smiled
at me when he saw me after work, and my heart leaped to
grab it and press it deep inside. I hid it in a corner there to
pull out and remember. Lots of my corners are filled with happy
memories.* —*from Ronda's diary*

Around Thanksgiving, Eddie and Ronda decided to jump into
the powder blue Beetle and make the eight-hundred-mile
drive to Denver to spend the holiday with her folks. They got a
late start out of Dallas, and by the time it was dark they were
not yet out of east Texas. Eddie wanted to drive straight through,
but both he and Ronda had put in long hours at the center that
day.

It was very late at night when Eddie pulled off to the side of
the highway to take a rest. While he and Ronda were talking,
Eddie moved closer to kiss her. The kissing got to be pretty heavy,
and Eddie's hands began to roam over Ronda in places where a
man had never touched her before. It stunned her when she
realized that Eddie intended to have sex with her, right there in
the Volkswagen, parked at the side of U.S. 287.

"Eddie, we shouldn't be doing this. I'm afraid I'll get pregnant,
Eddie," Ronda pleaded. "I don't want to be pregnant for my wedding. Please don't."

"I know what I'm doing, honeybun," Eddie said, trying to
soothe Ronda. "I've done this before."

After having heard all his testimonies, Ronda had no particular
reason to believe that Eddie was a virgin. But his statement con-

firmed that she was not the first woman with whom Eddie would
be intimate. That realization hurt her for a moment, but right now,
the present was much more threatening than the past. She had
always prided herself in maintaining control, and for the first time
she could remember, she was failing at that. Things were happening too fast for her.

Somehow, Eddie maneuvered her into a position where he
could remove enough clothing from both of them, and he was
able to penetrate her. It hurt, but not as much as Ronda had
feared. As she laid back and let Eddie have his way, her gaze fell
outside the car's windows and fixed on three huge tree trunks
that were blacker than the nighttime sky against which they were
silhouetted. The stark picture burned itself into her mind.

After Eddie was finished, he fixed his pants, and restarted the
Beetle. Ronda sat in the passenger seat and tried to digest what
had just happened. She felt dirty and degraded. She must have
done something to arouse him, she believed. How could she have
allowed herself to do this? It was more urgent now than ever
before that she and Eddie wed. He had taken the choice away
from her. She believed no other man could want her now.

Ronda and Eddie sat around her parents' Thanksgiving table
with her brothers and their wives, and she never let on to any of
them that something was amiss, that she was a changed person
from the last time they had seen her.

Shortly after their return to Dallas, there was a second sexual
encounter at the Junius Street boardinghouse. Eddie asked Ronda
to come up to his room with him for something. Once there,
Eddie began to kiss her and, just as in the car, Ronda's protests
seemed minor obstacles to be overcome and not expressions
meant to stop him. Again, Ronda felt shock and disgust. He obviously viewed sex as an integral part of the courtship. Ronda
was too confused and fearful to reveal her feelings about the
sexual episodes; instead, she opted out of further confrontations
by announcing several days later that she had decided to return
to her parents' home to prepare for the wedding.

On December 18, Ronda bade Eddie goodbye. At home in
Colorado, she struggled with the memory of what had happened
on the highway in Texas and in the Junius Street boardinghouse.

She started to wonder whether she knew enough about this man to whom she was about to commit herself. In their phone calls and letters, they never had any discussion of their future together but rather just day-to-day things. Why did Eddie never speak of weightier matters?

After much reflection, however, Ronda decided the reasons for marrying Eddie outweighed the misgivings the sexual incidents provoked. Foremost, she really did love him. Despite the very short time they had known each other, despite the observations of Ronda's friends who counseled her to wait a little longer, Ronda felt a deep attraction to this man who had been through so much pain and suffering in his short life. His turnaround seemed to her miraculous. She wanted to reward him with the love of a faithful and caring wife.

Moreover, she could not bear the possibility of canceling the wedding. The dresses and gowns were all on order, invitations at the printer, reservations made. With dozens of friends and relations notified of the impending event, Ronda did not think she could survive the embarrassing questions that would surely be raised if she were to suddenly call the wedding off. Never very tolerant of an imperfect performance in herself, an admission of error at this point was unthinkable.

And finally, Ronda's dream of virginity until marriage was forever shattered by a ten-minute tryst in the front seat of a Volkswagen. Now she belonged to him. There was no way she was going to back out. Eddie was a very good man, she reassured herself; they could make the relationship work.

Eddie sent Ronda a special delivery package with her engagement ring, which arrived shortly after Christmas. When she saw the diamond, her belief that Eddie was making a true commitment to her, and not simply using her, was firmly bolstered. She went to a church service on New Year's Eve, and during the prayers she kept holding the ring up to the light, watching the reflections through its prism. Others saw her, and after the service they gathered around her to admire the ring and congratulate her.

Eddie's two brothers had planned to come to Colorado to be in the wedding. But as February approached, it became apparent that Eddie's mom would be the only family member who could attend. In addition, none of the couple's Teen Challenge friends had the time or money needed to make the long trip. There would be more than two hundred guests on Ronda's side of the aisle, and only Eva Wyatt on the groom's side. The guest list was ample evidence that Eddie Wyatt was a changed man who had almost no remaining ties to his past.

Eddie wrote constantly to Ronda during this separation, professing his love. Every two or three days would bring another thick letter. They bolstered Ronda through her remaining doubts. He kept her up-to-date on his search for their first apartment and with news of their Teen Challenge friends. But mostly, as in this letter he wrote on January 17, 1975, he wrote of his love for her:

Hi. I love you so much today. It's so wonderful to know you're mine. You've brightened my life so much, and so I want to make you happy the best way I can. I want to love you and take care of you with every ounce of my strength. I know we will be happy. We have so much going for us, but best of all we have the Lord. I know He brought us together, and He will never leave us. The Lord has been so good to me, but I could never thank Him enough for you.

It was very different for Eddie to be expressing his feelings. As a youngster, he had always stuffed them deep inside, usually because they were unpleasant. But now, Eddie reassured Ronda that they would always air their feelings to each other. In one of his last letters before coming up to Denver for the wedding, he told her she would never have to worry about talking over their problems with him.

That's part of being in love and learning to understand each other. It's always helped me so much to talk about things that bother me. I don't want to ever have to keep them inside of me, and I sure don't want you to, either. That's partly what we need each other for, to share our feelings, to feel free to come to each other about anything.

Ronda, the closer we get to seeing each other, the more I find myself unable to do anything, period. I can't do anything but think about you. I try doing things to keep busy and not worry about the time or how close it is. It's useless though. This dream is starting to come true. It's no longer months or weeks, it's down to days. I can hardly wait to see my bride.

Ronda's parents accepted Eddie as a son despite their initial misgivings about him. In the Green Acres Church of the Nazarene in southwest Denver on Valentine's Day 1975, they and their guests witnessed his wedding to Ronda. Eddie was dressed in black truousers and a formal white jacket trimmed with black lapels. He looked over at his mother, who brought her long, dark blue dress with her from Galveston. She wore a pink corsage near her left shoulder. She had met Ronda for the first time Wednesday night, only two days before the wedding.

Ronda felt so special as her father escorted her down the aisle. Her gown was tiered and lace-edged, with a ruffled skirt, high-necked chantilly lace bodice, and long bishop sleeves. Covering her head and face, she wore a long chapel mantilla trimmed with lace. A pianist accompanied her slow walk down the aisle, then a soloist sang "Your Tender Love." Ronda and Eddie wrote their own service, and it was full of references to the kind of love they hoped to share, one that was more giving than receiving. After they exchanged vows and rings, Ronda sang to Eddie "The Twelfth of Never." The service ended with the soloist singing "True Love Comes from God." The ceremony could not have been lovelier.

Eddie's schedule and finances allowed for only the most modest of honeymoons. He could not afford to miss much school because his welder's certification exam was coming up, and he needed that piece of paper to advance at Litton. Eddie drove Ronda's uncle's car only about six miles away, to a motel at the Sixth Avenue Freeway interchange with Kipling Street. While Eddie checked in at the front desk, Ronda bought a picture postcard of the motel to tape into her wedding book as a keepsake.

She had been by the place often while growing up. Ronda had dreamed about her wedding night since she was a little girl, but after they had gone to bed and made love, it seemed somewhat anticlimactic to her. Because of the sexual encounters in Texas, it was not the special night she had dreamed about. Afterward, she ended up stretched out in bed next to Eddie watching a television rerun of the show "Love American Style."

While they were dozing off, the telephone rang. Ronda picked it up and heard her brother Randy, who was giggling about having tracked them down. He asked her what she and Eddie were doing.

"We're watching 'Love American Style,' " Ronda told her little brother. She had always been protective of Randy, but now she felt like wringing his neck. Randy burst out laughing.

"You're not supposed to be watching it," Randy roared. "You're supposed to be doing it!"

On Saturday morning, Eddie and Ronda returned to her parents' house, loaded as many of their gifts into the VW as they could, and headed back to Dallas. Eddie had rented a one-bedroom apartment for them in a small complex on Bachman Boulevard, near a beautifully shaded park that was across Bachman Lake from Love Field airport. The six months that followed their wedding was the happiest time of their lives. Eddie and Ronda were loving and devoted. He had a job that had advancement opportunties and he seemed to shed all the low self-esteem he had carried around since boyhood. Ronda believed that the voice inside him that always told him he was a failure and a misfit had finally been silenced.

The two of them often crossed busy Bachman Boulevard hand in hand to stroll through the park on the warm summer evenings. Sometimes they would go for a drive, and park in a lot near Love Field to watch the planes roar overhead. Often, Eddie dropped over to Teen Challenge to see their old friends and to visit with new clients who could benefit from his counseling. What made those simple times all the more pleasurable was that they shared their experiences, each was interested in the other's day. They would talk about their work, Eddie at the plant or Ronda about the problems at the center. They would talk about having children. They both said they wanted a child right away, and Ronda was disappointed when she did not get pregnant during the first few months.

Ronda adjusted well to sex with Eddie despite her lack of preparation. She saw sex as something to be enjoyed freely within marriage. Ronda did not look on it as a duty, but as the very essence of expressing her love for Eddie. She looked forward to lovemaking, plus the before and after of snuggling and resting in each other's arms in bed. That was what made her feel especially loved. She cherished the security of placing her faith in Eddie, and in looking up to him as the stronger half of the relationship.

She had prepared herself well to be a wife, homemaker, and mother, and she was excited that her dream was coming true. Ronda had always found it soothing to keep a journal, to put her feelings on paper, particularly thc harshcr ones, so she could put them in perspective several days later. True to her nature, she was still very hard on herself when problems or mistakes came up. She often concentrated on the things she did wrong, and what Eddie had done right.

Three weeks into their marriage, she wrote:

> *My faults and failures bother me often. But do you know what? He put my mind at ease and I can be me. It feels good. At first it was difficult to give of me to him. So when he understood, he stopped and loved me with words. It wasn't hard anymore. When he's gone as he is tonight, my heart waits impatiently for him to come home. I long for him to be beside me.*
>
> *Forever and just beginning—that's how long it feels. I love him more today than yesterday.*

Eddie quit the job at Litton in late March to take a better-paying position at U.S. Industries Wyatt Division. While he earned only a nickel an hour more at first, by May he got a raise to $3.50 an hour. It was a little farther from home, but it was easier for Ronda to pick him up after work because it was on the way back from Teen Challenge. Usually, they were home by 4:00 P.M. and had the rest of the evening to themselves. Ronda was so focused on her husband, to the point of idealizing him, that she neglected to work on herself. In her secret writings, she easily subjugated her own self-image when it came to building up her husband. April 1, 1975:

> *Oh, am I ever, ever tired tonight. Eddie started his new job yesterday and he's tired too, and happy. Eddie's so kind and gentle too, Lord. Saturday, I was so tired and fell asleep. When I awoke he had washed the dishes left from lunch (and there was a* mess*) and then he took me out to supper. I love him. Lots of times he's my "little boy" when we play but there's no doubt he's my man in real life.*
>
> *Oh Lord, he's made me so happy. Thank you, thank you, thank you for him. Help me to make him happy, just as happy and more than he's made me. I've smiled more since we've been married than ever before. It's so wonderful now, it is hard to believe how wonderful it can possibly be in the future.*

Ronda trusted Eddie implicitly. All those nights he was away at school before he got his certification, and then when he worked nights, Ronda waited at the apartment with confidence that he would come right home, that he would never run around, and that he would never lie to her. Actually, it was beyond confidence. Ronda did not even think of such things, it was so inconceivable to her. Their marriage seemed so right and their relationship so close. She trusted Eddie's judgment and submitted to it just as she had been taught wives must. She confided to her journal on May 22:

> *I'm glad Eddie doesn't let me make final decisions about things. Don't get me wrong. I get to have a say, and sometimes we agree to do it. But sometimes he has to do the deciding and sometimes it's not what I want, but am I ever glad he doesn't let me change his mind. It makes me feel so secure knowing that once he has set his mind*

to do what is right, he does it. Some kind of man, huh?
My man—and I love him so!

By late summer, the young couple prepared to leave their apartment to move out to Grand Prairie, in the flats between Dallas and Fort Worth, where two other couples from Teen Challenge were also living. They moved into the El Presidente Apartments on a hillside north of Tarrant Road opposite Grand Prairie High School. From the apartment balconies were commanding views north over the Trinity River valley looking toward Irving. They traded in the old Volkswagen Ronda's parents had given them for a relatively new 1974 Volkswagen Beetle, also powder blue. They bought it in August from Steve Griffith, their good friend from Teen Challenge, who had gone on to become a car salesman.

First Assembly of God, their new church, was a short distance away on High School Drive. It was easy to fit in with the young congregation. The Reverend Don Gray, who had been one of Ronda's teachers at Southwestern in Waxahachie, was the pastor. The Wyatts were welcomed into all the activities of the church. They also began tithing out of their meager incomes, donating $520 in only three months.

Eddie had changed jobs again in late June, leaving Wyatt Division after less than three months to work at Glitsch Incorporated, which was located on Singleton Boulevard, a few miles from his old job. It was a quick jaunt and a jog down Interstate 30 from their new apartment to get to Glitsch. Eddie was constantly looking for better jobs and more money. And it was paying off nicely for him. He immediately bumped up $1.05 an hour at Glitsch over what he had been getting at Wyatt Division. Six weeks later, he got a raise. Three weeks after that, he got another raise, to $5.20 an hour.

After only ten months out in the working world, out from under the wings of Teen Challenge, Eddie Wyatt had increased his salary by 73 percent, and he had passed the test for certification that would open the door to more specialized welding and higher-paying assignments. Ronda was proud of him and glad that he could earn the money, especially after she became pregnant in May. Ronda was overjoyed. This was exactly what she wanted to give Eddie, a child of his own flesh, to seal their love forever.

When Ronda started showing, Eddie beamed with delight at the thought of becoming a father. Ronda marked the day on her calendar, September 30, when she first felt the baby kick. Several times when they were at services at First Assembly, Ronda would nudge Eddie and direct his attention to her expanding womb, where Eddie could actually see the kicks from the baby every time the choir burst into song, as if the baby was singing along.

Eddie changed jobs again at the end of September, his fourth employer of the year. He got only a two-cent raise in the move, but the new welding job at Peerless Manufacturing Company also held the promise of a lot more overtime, increasing Eddie's earning potential. There were weeks that fall that Eddie put in fifty-five hours and grossed $350, at the time an impressive sum for a young ex-convict who had absolutely no prospects a year earlier. The best part of the job at Peerless was that it came with an insurance package that would cover the costs of labor and delivery of the new baby.

Shortly after Christmas, however, Eddie was laid off from Peerless because of a lack of work. He was fortunate to get back on quickly at Glitsch. But with the change in jobs came the loss of the insurance coverage for the birth, now only a month or so away.

Ronda went into labor on a Sunday night, more than two weeks before her due date. Eddie twice drove her over to Presbyterian Hospital, a forty-minute trip each time clear across town. On the first visit, the doctor said it was premature labor. On the second trip, Ronda was taken to the delivery room. Eddie, left behind, listened over an intercom as his son slipped into the world and immediately christened the doctor by peeing on him. The baby, born on February 23, 1976, was named Paul Eugene Wyatt, after Ronda's dad.

*   *   *

Ten days after the birth of their son, Ronda got a call at home that there had been an accident at the Glitsch plant, could she come to the hospital. The shop foreman, aware that she had just had a baby, had told her it was a "little accident" so she would not get too upset. Ronda quickly dressed the baby and headed for the city. At the hospital, she was led into the emergency room. When Ronda first saw her husband, she felt a surge of panic that, with great difficulty, she was able to suppress. It looked like he was going to die right there. His face had swollen to an unbelievable size, and the color was a horrible mixture of deep purple, black, and red. He was still wearing his work clothes, and they were covered with blood. Eddie, she was told, had been driving a steel wedge between two ring sections of a large bulk tank he was preparing to tack weld when the wedge suddenly shot out under the immense pressure. In a split second, the hatchet-shaped wedge smashed into the left side of Eddie's face, barely missing his eye.

The fear that came over Ronda when she saw her husband was of an intensity that she had never felt before. She was filled with anguish over Eddie's pain. She also felt that she was going to lose him forever. In her mind, she cast herself as a widow with an infant son. This frightening vision gnawed at her even after doctors, and Eddie himself, assured her that he would make it through the injury. Coming so close to losing everything she had been building, Ronda realized how easily her bliss could be turned to tragedy. After this incident, she would always be aware how fragile life was. At any moment, something unexpected and terrible could snatch her beloved little family from her, as easily as that steel wedge almost snatched Eddie away.

Eddie remained in the hospital for ten days. For much of that time, his eyes were sensitive to light, and he had to sit in the dark until the sensitivity lessened. By the time he was released, the swelling had gone down considerably, but his entire head was still puffy and bruised. Luckily, there was little permanent damage to his vision, but he would have a discolored patch on the left side of his face for the rest of his life.

Ronda leaned heavily on the folks at First Assembly over the next few weeks. A couple from the church volunteered to care

for Paul so that Ronda could have her hands free during the day
and get rest at night. Ronda left Grand Prairie early each morning
and stayed at St. Paul Hospital until late each night. When Eddie
came home, he was unable to go back to work immediately.
Worker's compensation payments would not begin for a while,
and he had no savings on which to rely. The Wyatts applied for
food stamps, but it was not enough. Knowing of the young family's
plight, Eddie's coworkers at Glitsch took up a collection and
delivered about $100 to the couple for groceries. Then some folks
from First Assembly showed up at the apartment with armloads
of food that fully stocked Ronda's cabinets and cupboards. The
church also donated $100 to them.

Despite the financial hardship, Eddie seemed very content
during the two months he recuperated at home. He grew close
to his new son, Paul, even getting up at night to prepare bottles
and feed him. He changed Paul's diapers and gave him baths. He
rocked him in his arms until the infant went to sleep. He did the
things his own father had never done for him. He told Ronda that
he felt such a strong bond with Paul, it made his own father seem
all the more alien and impossible to understand. Eddie talked
little of his father, who was still alive but whom Eddie had not
seen since the day George Wyatt left the house for good. Eddie
told Ronda that it was beyond his comprehension how strong a
pull could have dragged his dad away from such a profound
happiness as the one he felt holding Paul in his arms.

While the workers' collection and the church offering helped
tide them over, the family faced a continuing financial crisis.
Because he had lost the insurance coverage with the layoff at
Peerless, Eddie had a $960 bill from Presbyterian Hospital and
the obstetrician, which he had no hope of paying. Although he
went back to work at Glitsch in May, the accident had dug Eddie
a money pit out of which he could not climb on his own. Upset
after being told he did not qualify for worker's compensation,
Eddie listened when a friend suggested that he sue the company.
He concluded that a lawsuit was the only way his family could
survive.

His resolve was bolstered when he visited an attorney, who
listened to Eddie's story and assured him that he would get some

money from the company. After notice of intent to sue was sent, Eddie returned to work and was surprised when a supervisor questioned his legal action. He told Eddie that he should not have gone to the lawyer.

"Y'all didn't act this concerned when I was layin' up in the hospital tryin' to figure out how we was gonna buy milk for the baby," Eddie replied, certain that right was on his side.

Nobody at Glitsch said anything more to Eddie about the lawsuit while he was working, but it soon became clear he had become an unwelcome employee. As the summer dragged on, Eddie became more and more restless, and it hurt Ronda to see him so unhappy. Teen Challenge friends who visited remarked to each other that Eddie seemed a bit more edgy since the accident, not like his usual self at all. One churchgoer from First Assembly, Fermon Tidwell, was a career navy man and had worked as a recruiter. He told Eddie he ought to consider joining the service if things didn't work out at Glitsch. Eddie admired Tidwell's bearing and tucked the advice away in a corner of his mind.

Ronda suggested they pack up and move to Colorado. She had been talking with her mom and the two believed that Eddie needed a fresh start. Ronda's brother Ron worked at the Coors brewery in nearby Golden, and they thought Eddie could get a welder's job there. Although hesitant to leave his native Texas, Eddie agreed to consider it. A few weeks later, he settled the legal action with Glitsch for about $5,000. It paid off the hospital bills and several other debts, and left enough for a new vacuum cleaner.

Ronda was anxious to move to Colorado, not only because she would be near her family, but because she saw the change in scenery as precisely what her husband needed to make a clean start after the trouble with Glitsch. Shortly after the financial settlement freed them from their bills in Grand Prairie, Eddie told Ronda he had given the move a lot of thought, and had decided to go along with it. At the end of August 1976, Eddie and Ronda said goodbye to Texas and to the tough times brought on by Eddie's accident. They flew to Denver on September 1, and spent the first few weeks with Ronda's parents while Eddie looked for a job. The prospect of working for Coors had by then faded.

Around the time of the move, Ronda took stock of her husband in her journal. She drew up a list of thirty-three "good qualities in my husband." Among them:

> *Kind and gentle with Paul.*
> *He has a sense of responsibility.*
> *He has determination which makes me feel secure. He has an inner drive which constantly pushes for him to strive towards bigger goals.*
> *He loves me, and he lets me know that he does.*
> *He is very helpful in the home even with "domestic duties." It means much when he does something (such as cooking a meal, helping with the dishes, etc.) without really having to do so.*
> *He's my very best friend.*
> *Slow to get angry, and when he does, he doesn't strike out verbally or physically at others.*
> *Excellent with children.*
> *Has goals that he is striving for—keeps him going forward and keeps him from becoming stagnant.*
> *Kindhearted. Sensitive.*
> *He's very trustworthy. It never enters my head to worry about what he is doing, or if he is going to the wrong places.*

Ronda Wyatt could tell that Eddie was unhappy. The young family stayed for more than a month with Paul and Erna Hunter while Eddie searched for welding jobs. Eddie did not like relying on the charity of his wife's relatives. Ronda sensed that his pride was hurting, and she felt compelled to shore him up whenever she had the chance. So when he landed a welding job at Arvada Steel Fabrication Company, Ronda took Eddie up to the Denver suburb of Arvada and they searched for an apartment of their own, even though his salary would be half of what he had left behind at Glitsch.

Eddie and Ronda moved into the Brookside Apartments in mid-October. Eddie enjoyed welding and was getting good at it. Ronda admired how her husband worked with his hands, and she told him how proud she was to be the wife of such a talented man. But the more Eddie worked at welding, the more he grew to question whether it was how he wanted to spend the rest of his working life. There were guys in the shop who frightened him with stories of injury and sickness from a lifetime breathing in the fumes, dust, and chemicals. Some of them looked as if they had just stepped out of a war. One old geezer looked as if he had been slashed head to toe with a razor blade from handling all the metal slivers. The man told Eddie how a beam had fallen on him and split him open at the shoulder while erecting Denver's Blue Cross building, nearly ripping his arm from his body.

Having had one close call with death on the job, Eddie began to wonder whether he should start looking for another career. It so happened that his daily commute through Arvada took him past a naval recruiting station, where the poster outside caught his attention. Eddie's conversations in Grand Prairie with Fermon Tidwell, and his favorable impression of Jim Jessup, who left Teen Challenge to serve on a navy submarine, had planted a seed in Eddie. One morning, more on a whim than with any firm resolve, Eddie stopped at the recruiting office. He wondered whether he could join despite his teen burglary conviction. The recruiter made sure Eddie got everything he requested, and answered all his questions quickly and with authority. As for the problem of the criminal record, he told Eddie that the navy could look it over and consider issuing a waiver of the general rule against enlisting such people. Eddie was intrigued.

When he returned to the Brookside Apartments after work that evening, he told Ronda about his visit to the navy recruiter. Ronda knew that Eddie loved the water. Her husband was an expert swimmer, and during their visits to Galveston he had shown her the spot on the Sixty-first Street Causeway where he had made innumerable jumps into the cool water of Offatt Bayou, just a few blocks from his mom's house on Avenue Q. Ronda discerned Eddie's homesickness, but she was also leery. The thought of her husband entering military service upset her. It was not only the exposure to physical danger or the fact that Eddie was almost eight years older than the typical recruit. Ronda knew that if Eddie joined the navy, there would be times when he would have to leave her and the baby for extended periods. Still, Ronda had a sense of deference to her husband. She would back him in whatever he chose to do. They agreed to pray on it.

Ronda knew that Eddie needed to break out of the cycle of failure in which the family had found itself since the accident at Glitsch. Ronda thought her husband somewhat restless when he jumped from job to job, but she understood. She believed that it masked a more laudable trait, ambition, since each move had brought with it a better salary and greater responsibility. But after the accident, Ronda sensed just the restlessness, not the ambition. That was why she was anxious to move to Colorado for the fresh start. But the Navy? Still, as much as she dreaded the thought of her husband in the military, she knew that if it calmed Eddie's restlessness and ignited his ambition once again, it would be the best thing for their family.

Ronda was eager for Eddie to find satisfaction on his job because she was becoming troubled by a lessening of sexual passion in their lives. Eddie's kisses were not lasting as long as they had when they were first married. And they were not making love as often, or as tenderly, as they had before. Often, when they went to bed together after getting baby Paul to sleep, in the midst of cuddling and kissing, Ronda would feel that Eddie was not really involved. One night after Eddie had entered her, Ronda wrapped her arms around him and stroked his back lightly with her fingernails while he moved. Yet she felt something was missing. The physical sensations were not building up, not pushing themselves higher. Eddie kept up his rhythmic movements for what seemed like an eternity without showing signs of approaching a climax. After about twenty minutes, when what should have been rapture had turned into ennui, Eddie withdrew from his wife and flopped onto his back. Ronda cuddled him, then gripped his penis firmly and rubbed him until, finally, he had an orgasm. Eddie then reciprocated for Ronda.

Is this what happens to married people, she wondered. Was

this the way it was supposed to be? It was a common joke that nothing slowed the sex drive like marriage. Did passion have to die that way? Hers was not dead, but the way things were going, she felt as if it was condemned to unfulfillment.

After they were finished, Ronda wanted to embrace for a while and fortify their closeness. As Eddie reclined, Ronda moved over and laid her head on his bare chest. She wanted her move to signify to him her submissiveness, and also to feel his strong and securing grip of protection around her, the way they used to hug back in that little apartment in Dallas. But Eddie was uneasy about it. He asked her politely if she would mind moving her head off his chest. He said the scratchy feeling of her hair bothered him.

She raised up and kissed Eddie goodnight. Then she rolled over and closed her eyes. She guessed that all marriages must be something like this, but she could not avoid the feeling of rejection and degradation that came over her, a feeling that she was being used instead of loved.

When winter hit, work slowed at Arvada Steel. Eddie was laid off right before Christmas, after working there for less than three months. Suddenly, the financial crisis was back at their doorstep. Eddie and Ronda had to refinance the Volkswagen to meet the month's rent. Eddie found a job in another metal shop, but it only lasted a short time. They had to move.

In February, they moved to a small apartment above a greenhouse in Denver's Washington Park neighborhood, at the corner of Louisiana Avenue and York Street, owned by Ronda's cousin. Eddie did some odd jobs in exchange for free rent, but there was a misunderstanding with the cousin over what other work was to be done, and it created some tension around the household. Still, Ronda was optimistic that something good would come of all this.

Family members pitched in to see that Ronda, Eddie, and baby Paul had enough to eat, and church offerings helped meet some bills. Along the way, Ronda put up with some joking remarks about her husband going nowhere fast, but she remained steadfast in her support of Eddie. The love was still evident in her journal, but it was tinged with defensiveness:

> *My uncle thought it comical that marriage is a happy thing for me. What a shame. It is happy, very happy, for me. There have been difficulties, but the good far outweighs the bad. Eddie is a terrific husband!*

Ronda enjoyed living above the greenhouse. Washington Park was one of Denver's prettiest places to live. In the early afternoon, she would put Paul in his stroller and walk him the six tree-lined blocks down Louisiana Avenue to the park. There, she wheeled him around Grasmere Lake while taking in the warmth of the late winter sun.

But occasionally, there were jarring reminders that despite the idyllic setting, danger lurked in the area. One day Ronda read in the newspaper about a woman who had been raped in their neighborhood. Although she had never felt threatened by rape before, the news of a violent sexual assault so close to home made her uncomfortable. Eddie's response to her anxiety struck her as unfeeling. He showed no concern or sympathy. He simply told her to stop reading the crime news if it upset her that way.

Ronda wanted to stay in Denver if Eddie could find the right job. But Eddie was still leaning toward going into the navy. He persuaded Fermon Tidwell to write a letter of recommendation for him, and that apparently carried a lot of weight with navy brass. Then, unexpectedly, Ronda and Eddie found themselves faced with what appeared to be a pleasant choice. Teen Challenge had an opening for a Christian couple to run its home up in the mountains near Conifer, only thirty miles southwest of Denver. It might be the perfect opportunity. In addition, he found a job in a welding shop. The Teen Challenge position would bring with it a lot of responsibility.

Several times in the past, during times of crisis or difficulty, or simply when he sought guidance from the Lord, Eddie fasted and prayed for a day or two. He did that once again, trying to discern what he was meant to do. Ronda was ready to follow Eddie wherever he chose, but she hoped it would be with Teen Challenge. They had never been happier than during their time there. She wrote in her diary on March 16:

> *Eddie went to work Monday. We are grateful for the answer to our prayers. Sunday night brought to a head one of our decisions. We decided not to go into the Navy. After prayer and fasting Monday, Eddie called Royce Nimmons, director of Teen Challenge in the Rocky Mountain area. Doors are opening so quickly. Tuesday we met with Bro. Nimmons, talked, and we agreed to consider position of directors at the mountain home. One other couple is to be interviewed for this job. We feel God is leading us in this direction.*

But in a matter of a week, the Teen Challenge position went to the other couple. This setback was decisive for Eddie, who settled on pushing full-bore to go into the navy. He and Ronda packed up all their things, and put what little furniture they had in storage. He told Ronda he wanted to move back to Texas and stay at his mother's house in Galveston until the navy clearance came through. He would work for his older brother's construction company to earn some income while they waited.

They spent two months in Galveston before the navy waived Eddie's burglary record and cleared the way for him to enlist. Ronda returned to Colorado with her baby to stay with her parents while Eddie flew off for basic training in Orlando, Florida. Ronda was sure things were looking up, even if it meant being away from her husband for a time. Her journal entry on June 27:

> *I miss Eddie so much, but I'm so proud of him. The decisions he has made have been difficult for him to make, but he made them feeling that they were for our best. It's really odd how much more secure I feel now after having seen some more of his wonderful attributes. I love him with a love deeper than any I've ever known.*

*   *   *

Ronda watched through her mom's front window for the mailman each day, hoping to hear from her husband, who was down in the flatlands of Florida at naval basic training. Once Eddie decided to pursue a naval career, he seemed as excited about the future as he had been when they first met. Getting out of that greenhouse apartment, where he was relying on the kindness of strangers, and moving into his boyhood home in Galveston was rejuvenating. It filled Ronda with joy to see it. Life was back on track.

When basic training ended in July, Eddie had a week of leave before he was due at the Naval Air Station in Millington, Tennessee, for his first classes in aviation structural mechanics. He was going to learn how to repair jet airplane bodies. Ronda welcomed him back to Colorado for the short vacation, and was awed by the sight of her husband in his crisp new uniform.

The fresh start also gave a lift to their sex life, and Eddie was more animated. It was the only time Ronda drew the line. Eddie wanted to experiment with different forms of sex, and suggested that they try anal intercourse. Ronda balked at it, finding it distasteful. They had vaginal intercourse instead, and Eddie soon reported back to duty.

Within a month, Ronda discovered that she was pregnant again, and she realized how fortunate she was to have had that brief time with Eddie on leave. She longed to join him in Millington so they could be together during her pregnancy, even though his assignment there was temporary. She felt an urge to be at his side to share their happiness, so she arranged to move with the baby. All the things they owned could be packed into a small, one-axle trailer Paul Hunter built for his daughter that attached to a hitch on the back of the powder blue VW bug.

Ronda's parents drove her down to Millington on October 1, and she moved into military housing with Eddie. But within a month Eddie got orders to go to San Diego for four more weeks of classes, then across the continent one more time for his permanent assignment in Norfolk, Virginia. Ronda could not accompany him to California because of finances, so once again, she returned to her parents' home in Denver while Eddie struck out on his own, taking their Volkswagen to San Diego. Despite the upheaval, the long moves, and the weeks spent apart, Ronda felt that all was for the better. The increase in Eddie's self-confidence had put her at ease. All of the pain of separation, when she yearned to be with Eddie to share their newfound successes, were worthwhile because Eddie finally seemed to be truly happy, and that was what mattered most of all to Ronda.

Eddie was in San Diego for a month taking advanced training in corrosion control, and Ronda counted the days until she would see him again. Late on the night before Eddie was due to arrive back in Denver, the telephone rang at the Hunter house, and Erna called her daughter over after answering it.

"Hi, honeybun," Eddie said when Ronda got on the line.

"Eddie? Where are you?" she asked. His voice was always soft and hard to hear, and Ronda wondered for a second whether he might be in trouble. She hoped he was not calling to say his return was being postponed.

"I'm in New Mexico, at a motel along the highway," he answered.

"Is something wrong? Are you okay?" Ronda sounded worried. At that, Eddie chuckled.

"No, I'm fine," he answered with a lilt in his voice. "I'm all done training, and I'm halfway home to my honey for a week of leave. I got tired and decided to stop here for the night."

"Why did you call?" Ronda asked. "Are you okay?"

"I just wanted to hear your voice, Ronda," Eddie said with a touch of longing. "I've missed you so much."

Ronda let out a sigh of relief, then felt a swelling of affection for her husband. How sweet it was for him to call just to say that. She could hardly wait until the next afternoon to see him.

But when the road-weary Volkswagen pulled into the curving driveway at the Hunter house the next day and Eddie stepped out, Ronda stopped short for a second. Her husband's smile was bright, but his body was drawn and undernourished. He must have dropped fifteen pounds, which he could scarcely afford, from his already slender frame. She had sent him off to serve his country well fed and healthy-looking; in return, the navy must have starved him to death with all that basic training and hard work.

"C'mon in," Ronda said while holding Eddie in a tight embrace out in front of the house, "and let's get some food in you. Hasn't the navy been feeding you at all?"

CHAPTER 4

QUIET BETRAYAL

Our time together lately has been sparse, but oh, how I love the times when he holds me in his arms, calls me his "little wife," and tells me "I love you." It has to be close to what God intended marriage to be when we are together, sharing our love. Lord, help me please to be the kind of wife Eddie needs. —*from Ronda's diary*

The Wyatts packed the homemade trailer to the gills with their belongings a week later, hitched it to the back of the VW bug, and waved goodbye to Paul and Erna Hunter. Ronda wrapped her arms around baby Paul, since they had packed the rear too full to hold a car seat, and Eddie started the car off east on the long road trip to Norfolk. The drive put Ronda in mind of her happiest times with Eddie. Along the way, they got lost making a wrong turn and ended up in Muskogee, Oklahoma. Ronda and Eddie had to laugh because it was a wrong turn that had initially brought them together.

Eddie was very attentive to Paul, who spent most of the trip on Ronda's lap. The boy, not yet two, was starting to talk, and seemed fascinated with the passing scenery. Eddie enjoyed doting upon him, and Ronda loved to watch him spend so much time with their son. He had helped Paul learn to walk. He changed his diapers and fed him. He took Paul along on nearly every errand he ran. Eddie told Ronda that he was determined to be a good father. Having a son made him proud, he said, and he was going to be the kind of father that he wished he had had. There was a sadness mixed with Eddie's tone as he said it.

The couple and their baby arrived in Norfolk late in the evening on the day before Eddie was to report to the huge U.S. Navy

base, where the wide James River flows into Chesapeake Bay. It
was a slate-gray December day. Eddie rented an inexpensive
apartment for his family in a rundown complex called the Robin
Hood. It sat alongside the freeway on the east side of Norfolk.
The upstairs unit Eddie rented was a bit dumpy, but Ronda was
glad to have a place to call home after spending the last ten
months living in other people's houses.

The Wyatts' unit at the Robin Hood Apartments was up a
dark, interior stairway. The apartment had no carpeting and no
central heating. All of the tile-floored rooms were warmed by a
space heater in the hallway. Situated under one of the approach
paths to Norfolk International Airport, Eddie and Ronda were
bombarded with noise on a regular basis as jetliners roared overhead on takeoffs and landings. Sometimes at night when the huge
jets rattled the rickety building down to its joists, Ronda's bed
vibrated like one of those coin-operated beds at a cheap motel.
It lacked the romance of living near Love Field, but it was home.

It took several weeks for the Wyatts to find the right church.
They sampled several of the surrounding Assemblies of God
churches each week, looking for the best fit. When they finally
attended Ocean View Assembly, up near the bay, they felt they
had found their place. The fact that the church was packed ap-
pealed to Ronda, even though it was a five-mile drive from the
Robin Hood. The preacher gave a stirring service, and the singing
was filled with joyful praise. The people around them seemed
warm and genuine. Afterward, the pastor picked out the young
couple as newcomers, and made it a point to greet them. About
90 percent of his congregation came from military families and
he was used to seeing new, young faces every Sunday. Eddie and
Ronda Wyatt had moved into a company town, dominated by the
navy but with other branches of the service represented as well.

It did not take long for the Wyatts to become friends with
their downstairs neighbors, Don and Sue Rosenbaum. From the
day she moved in, Ronda suspected they were churchgoers. Their
little girl, a well-mannered eight-year-old with bouncy blond hair
and glasses, spent much of her time at her electric organ playing
Christmas hymns for the upcoming holiday. It made Ronda feel
homesick listening to it.

The Rosenbaums were Baptists by background. Don was a self-employed carpenter, an older fellow of forty-three whose light brown, wavy hair was starting to go gray on him. Sue was twenty-seven, a tall, pleasant, and easygoing brunette. Within a week or so, Don and Sue were helping the Wyatts fix up their threadbare living quarters. The Rosenbaums had gone through their things and found some old pictures, curtains, and other housewares that they gave to Ronda.

Eddie had not been in Norfolk for much more than a month before he went out to sea for the first time. It was a short trip, about a week, but it gave Ronda a taste of what it was going to be like once Eddie shipped out for six-month cruises of the Mediterranean. The recruiter had downplayed the possibility of long stretches at sea, which pleased Eddie because he did not look forward to spending months away from home. But it appeared likely that Eddie was going to be assigned to the aircraft carrier U.S.S. *John F. Kennedy*. He was placed in corrosion control, and would be a part of a unit that inspected and repaired jet airframes. When the carrier went out to sea for a week or so to qualify pilots, Eddie would sometimes have to go, other times he could stay ashore.

Ronda met several of the friends Eddie had made in the service, and they grew close to a few of them. There was a young couple from Georgia, Dave and Peggy Houser, who had entered military life as a family the same as Eddie and Ronda. What's more, they were practicing Christians, so even though Dave and Peggy were about eight years younger than the Wyatts, the two couples had plenty in common. The Housers also had a baby, Matthew, and the two families frequently socialized together with trips to the zoo or picnics at the park. It turned out that Dave Houser and Eddie were assigned to the same unit, and so their fates were often entwined. They were usually together on shore duty and on cruises, and spent a lot of time together talking about life, about Jesus, and about the navy.

When Eddie left on those short work-up cruises, Don and Sue Rosenbaum looked after pregnant Ronda to make sure she and the baby were all right. When it got cold in January, Don came upstairs and crafted makeshift storm windows from a wooden frame and plastic sheeting for Ronda's windows. He or Sue generously baby-sat for Paul whenever Ronda needed to run to the store or to church. Over those first few months, the Rosenbaums got to know Ronda well, and Eddie only a bit less so, since he was away every so often. Sue became Ronda's best friend. Frequently, they took their children on walks together to feed the ducks at the Norfolk Azalea Gardens. Ronda recruited Sue to go with her to the ladies' prayer group meetings on Tuesday mornings at Ocean View Assembly, and even though Sue was going to a different church, she readily fit in.

Sue admired Ronda's way with children. Ronda would take time to talk to Paul or to other children, and patiently explain in little-kid terms everything that they did together. Sue told Ronda that she wanted to pattern her own mothering after Ronda's. Sue also admired how Ronda found time to practice her talents in arts, crafts, and music. Sue had never met anyone as outgoing and caring as her new friend.

Sue and Don found Eddie to be a pleasant but reserved young man. Ronda had told them about Eddie's head injury, and they figured that it somehow must have made him more prone to stay to himself, perhaps more introverted. But still, Don enjoyed talking about religion with Eddie, sharing their experiences while they worked on car engines, fished, or tinkered around the apartments. There were several good fishing spots in the area where the two men went off for a day. Eddie made a few runs at trying to get Don to go to Ocean View Assembly instead of the Great Bridge Church of God, which Don and Sue attended.

Eddie shared with Don the fact that he had been a dope addict before he met Ronda, and that marrying her and being saved by Jesus had transformed his life. In Don's estimation, Eddie Wyatt was a solid and very likable young man who seemed to have it all together. He appeared to have a firm grip on his life.

Eddie was fortunate to be on shore in mid-April when Ronda went into labor—it was a circuitous route from Norfolk to the Portsmouth Naval Hospital, where the baby was to be delivered. They had to go through a tunnel under the Elizabeth River, which separated the two cities. Ronda had horrible visions that the tunnel would be jammed with traffic. The Rosenbaums took Paul, so Eddie and Ronda would not have to worry about him. It was a difficult labor, stretching over twelve hours, but this time Eddie was able to be in the room with Ronda when the baby, a girl, arrived on April 15, 1978. They named her Diana Lynn Wyatt.

By this time, Eddie had traded in the Volkswagen bug they had bought in Dallas for a darker blue Plymouth Valiant, a used 1974 model with a white top. It had a lot more room for his growing family. Within two months of Diana's birth, Eddie got his orders to ship out on the *Kennedy* for a six-month cruise through the Mediterranean Sea. Ronda did not want to be alone for that length of time. So she decided to go back to Lakewood with the children and stay with her parents. It would be nice to have the children with her in the place where she had grown up so happy and secure.

They held on to their lease at the Robin Hood, and after Eddie left, Ronda handed the keys to the Valiant over to Don and Sue Rosenbaum. She welcomed them to use the car while she was gone to make sure it kept running. Then Don drove Ronda and the two children to the Norfolk airport. The family boarded a plane, and soon it roared off the runway and banked over Ronda's ramshackle apartment house on its way to Denver. Eddie and Ronda had often talked about how they hated being apart, yet it always seemed that they wound up being separated.

Still, judging from the first few letters Eddie sent home, it did not lessen their love for each other.

Ronda quickly learned that even with Eddie earning a regular paycheck, it was very expensive for the family to be spread so thin while keeping a vacant apartment in Norfolk. It also cost Eddie money to keep himself while aboard the *Kennedy*. Every month Ronda sat down at her mom's kitchen table in Lakewood and wrote out checks to keep up payments on the Valiant, to pay the rent on her vacant Virginia apartment, and to handle some of the other bills. Usually, the letters from Eddie contained little if any money. It came in dribs and drabs, along with an excuse.

Eddie felt bad about the financial squeeze, and wrote to Ronda on July 8, shortly after the *Kennedy* had gotten under way and was headed for port in Spain:

> *I've only got 6 dollars and some change so I don't know if I should go off [in Rota] or not. It's my fault though 'cause I didn't save my money. I keep spending it on junk. Like candy and them Cokes they have in the machines. I needed other things too like stamps and stuff. Anyway, next time I'll save it.*

As usual, when she needed help, Ronda turned to her parents. Any time she was short of money in her checking account, Paul Hunter stepped in to make sure the checks did not bounce.

Ronda looked forward to reading Eddie's letters, which, aside from his excuses for sending no money, were often very expressive in a way he could never seem to muster in person. In them, Eddie told of how much closer to Jesus he felt. But he also confided that being out to sea, and being away from her, was making him feel that joining the navy had been a mistake. He was not prepared for the rigors of shipboard life, the hostilities and paranoia that breed in such close quarters. Soon, he told Ronda he wanted to get off the *Kennedy* more than he had wanted to be paroled from prison.

Eddie confessed to anxieties about potential enemies on the ship. There were men lost at sea, presumed overboard from the *Kennedy*, and the rumor among the sailors was that some of the toughs on board had tossed those missing over the rail at night. Eddie was gripped with the fear that if he inadvertently upset the wrong man, he might be the next target. It was not long after he had set sail that Ronda received another letter, written from the middle of the Mediterranean, that filled her with anxiety over Eddie's safety:

> *We've been out to sea nearly three weeks now. The pressures and tension is so bad I'm afraid to even look at someone the wrong way for fear I'll be in a fight with them. Everyone hollers and screams at each other. I just*

stay out of the way. If someone loses their temper I just walk away. I've never seen people so uptight. It was never this bad even in prison.

Eddie had always been a quiet and rather shy person, and Ronda could feel that he was uncomfortable being jammed into a bunk on the aircraft carrier with hundreds of men, many of whom it was certain would not share Eddie's way of life. Then, after Eddie had been gone for nearly three months, Ronda received a letter from him postmarked September 17. No sooner had she gotten past the first few words than her heart leaped into her throat. The letter read:

Hi, Honeybun, how are you and the kids? Fine I hope. I'm OK, but not so OK. I'm kinda bugged about something that happened yesterday. Our shop worked late that day again as usual. When I came in the compartment our aisle was packed with guys so I started to turn around to leave, but then decided it was just as much my aisle as it was theirs. So I squeezed back to my rack and was about to get ready to take a shower. Houser was there beside me and we were talking. Two master-at-arms passed by and saw all the people back there so they came in and started asking everyone questions.

He came up to me & Houser and started looking behind our racks & even searched us. Houser asked him what he was doing and he pulls out this little pipe and asked if it was ours. I told him I didn't use one, so he said this one is different in that someone he thought was smoking some kind of drugs out of. I told him I don't use drugs. I'm a Christian and so is Houser. Anyway, they took everyone's security card in our aisle and said we would all have to explain it to the captain. We haven't heard anything else about it so hopefully they will leave me alone.

I don't know what was all going on, but I don't like anyone saying something like that about me. He says he found that pipe in our aisle and so he is going to find out who it belongs to. I said good but just leave me alone because I don't know nothing about a pipe. I feel awful funny about this whole situation, like they're trying to push something off on me & Houser. Hopefully it is all over. I just don't like him accusing me of something like that.

The rest of the letter said that he and Dave Houser were getting into Bible reading together, and he closed by saying they were headed down to the chapel to watch a Christian movie.

In subsequent letters, Eddie kept Ronda abreast of the shipboard situation. Eddie was taken before the ship's captain on drug charges based on the hash pipe that was found near his bunk. He was dropped in rank and pay grade, and fined several hundred dollars. Eddie vowed to pursue an appeal of the unjust accusations, and Ronda encouraged him to push it. Eddie seemed almost bewildered by his predicament. He asserted that a man like himself, who had suffered through such a lonely and unhappy adolescence, would never return to using drugs. Drugs had taken his life to the brink of complete ruin. Ronda was upset that she could not be at Eddie's side at that moment. They had both worked at Teen Challenge to turn young people away from the self-destruction of drugs, and the injustice of Eddie being accused on the basis of a pipe found near his bunk made Ronda shudder with a feeling of helplessness.

A breakthrough came when Eddie found a superior officer to vouch for his character, and he wrote Ronda that there was a chance his rank would be restored, his pay increased, and the fine dropped. It was the answer to Ronda's prayers. Eddie had not been able to send any money home before Christmas and bills were mounting. Happily, his commanding officer went to bat for him and his pay was restored, although the fine remained and was deducted. The entire incident compounded Eddie's disillusionment with the navy. He wrote to Ronda in November:

The only time I've truly been happy in my work is when I was at Teen Challenge as a counselor. I'm restless, not satisfied, unhappy. It seems everything I've tried ended

*the same way. If I'm doing what God wants, why can't
I be happy? I don't want to leave the Navy, I really don't.
I hate changing job after job, which is what I've been
doing. That's one reason why I came in the navy. I
wanted this to be my last job. I wanted to stay in and
retire from the Navy, and I think we both felt it was
God's will for me to come in. It bothers me so much,
Honeybun, that I feel the way I do 'cause I still have so
much longer to serve.*

Although Eddie was back to receiving his regular pay, he was
still not sending money home. He explained that he had to pay
back some of the guys from whom he'd been borrowing during
his ordeal. He also thought that with his financial situation, two
children were all he was going to be able to afford. Consequently,
he informed her, he wanted to have a vasectomy. Ronda understood Eddie's feelings on the matter but she did not share them.
She would have preferred to stay on birth control pills and be
able to change their minds later. But if Eddie needed that permanent margin of safety, it would be his decision and she would
abide by it.

Eddie had been at sea for eight months before the *Kennedy* slowly
sailed up Chesapeake Bay in February 1979 and docked at Norfolk
Naval Base. Ronda had arrived back to unlock the apartment at
the Robin Hood just the day before. It was an exciting time in
Norfolk when a carrier was due back from an extended cruise.
Spouses of seafaring mates excitedly told of the times their husband, after six months out, could not even wait to get home with
their wives but simply pulled into the nearest motel to celebrate
their reunions. Ronda wondered how Eddie would feel when he
saw her and the children again after their longest separation ever.
She had not told him she was returning to Norfolk a day early
to greet him on his arrival, preferring to surprise him.

When Ronda spotted Eddie pulling his duffel bag from a car
in which he had hitched a ride over to the Robin Hood, she
straightened her skirt, fluffed up her long, brown hair, and went

to unlock the door. Paul and Diana waited in the living room while their mother walked out onto the landing of the upstairs apartment entrance.

Eddie was about halfway up the dark staircase toward his apartment door, thinking he would open it up and clean in the morning in anticipation of his wife's return, when he heard the door ahead of him open, and the landing was splashed in light. It jolted him when he saw Ronda standing above him, her face beaming with a big, bright smile.

"Welcome home, Eddie!" Ronda said with an eager tone of expectation in her voice.

"Well, hi, honeybun," answered a startled Eddie. He hesitated for a second, then awkwardly brushed by her waiting arms and stepped into the apartment, making some small talk about his trip as he tossed the bag into a corner of the room. With quick motions, he gave the children a squeeze and, still talking about minor aspects of his cruise, went into the bathroom. There he began to brush his teeth. Ronda was stunned by her husband's indifferent response to her. She had anticipated this moment with great joy, expecting to be swept up in a welcoming embrace. Instead, a powerful pain of rejection flushed through her. Eddie's return had no more magic to it than if he had just come back from taking out the garbage.

Eddie left a stale breeze in his wake, and Ronda waved it from her nose with a few passes of her hand. It seemed like a strong body odor. She figured that must be why Eddie sidled by her so quickly and ran in to brush. As best she could reason, this was the smell one acquired from living several decks below the top of an aircraft carrier, in cramped quarters with hundreds of men. Eddie was badly in need of a shower. Why could he not have freshened up before the ship docked, she wondered?

Later, when they finally got to bed and made love, Ronda's sense of rejection was eased. But the long anticipated reunion was nothing like the romantic scene she had envisioned. Her whole sense of self was wrapped up in being Eddie Wyatt's wife and the mother of his children. It was very threatening to sense that there might be cracks in the facade. Appearances were very critical to Ronda, and Eddie was not playing the role of the overjoyed, love-starved husband that the other military wives had written for their husbands.

Over the course of the spring and summer following his first Mediterranean cruise, Eddie grew more withdrawn. He became depressed on occasion, but he dismissed Ronda's inquiries about it by insisting it was nothing serious, just unhappiness over having to go to sea so often. Then the moods began to affect their sex life once again. Until that summer, Ronda thought she had a happy marriage. She was no prude when it came to sex, and enjoyed making her husband happy in the bedroom. When sex with Eddie produced no fireworks, Ronda thought it was up to her to improve things.

As the frequency of their lovemaking diminished, Eddie joked that if a couple put a penny in a jar every time they made love during their first year of marriage, they could spend the rest of their lives taking them out. Ronda understood that Eddie's increasing unhappiness with navy life was having an effect on their marriage. Yet she believed it was within her power to change that. She did not like the fact that it was becoming the norm for her to masturbate Eddie to orgasm, rather than to complete intercourse. She could not understand what it was about her that turned him off. She began to question her looks, her figure, her personality, and any other aspect of her being that Eddie might be finding unattractive. There had to be something that she could improve upon, she believed. She was always the fixer, and with this she would be no different.

Sexual problems were not all that confronted Ronda after Eddie's homecoming. Despite the fact that he was on shore duty and was not spending money away from home, their finances were still very tight. Ronda never seemed to have enough left over after the rent, car payment, phone, and utility bills to stock her pantry. Good-hearted Don and Sue Rosenbaum felt compelled to help out whenever they could, even though Don was having a difficult time as a carpenter during a local building slump. They were folks who believed that it was in giving that they would receive, and Ronda was grateful for their help.

Ronda was good at stretching their budget to cover necessities, and the kids had never gone hungry. But now, even with a steady paycheck coming in, they were back to accepting occasional charity from family and friends, the way it had been in Grand Prairie and Denver when Eddie was out of work. Ronda knew that they were not going to live like royalty on the navy's start-up pay. With Eddie's prospects for advancement, better days were ahead. Still, what she could not understand was just where all the money was going.

Ronda always thought Eddie looked good in a uniform, especially when he dressed in his navy blues and the smart-looking white cap that went with it. But the light brown Royal Rangers uniform was very special to her, because it signified her husband's commitment to their church and his eagerness to work with the children. Royal Rangers was the Assemblies of God program for young boys, akin to scouting but leaning heavily on Bible lessons. It was the male equivalent of the Missionettes, the church's program for young girls, to which Ronda had belonged in her childhood. On a typical Wednesday evening, prior to the midweek services, Eddie and Ronda would gather Paul and Diana and head off to Ocean View Assembly. While Ronda went into the service with Diana, Eddie took Paul into a community room for the Royal Rangers meeting, which went on concurrently with the service and helped keep some of the noise of the children from disrupting the preacher's sermon. The preteen children in the Ocean View's Royal Rangers program delighted in Eddie's leadership in their crafts and outdoors activities, while their parents attended the services.

The more Pastor Alvin Hall got to know Eddie and Ronda Wyatt, the more he regarded them as a model Christian couple. He had heard about Ronda's piano playing and singing, and asked her to help lead the congregation in song. Eddie would often stop by the church during his free time just to see if there was something he could do for the pastor. Together, the couple volunteered to help out with the children's church program. There was nothing Pastor Hall could ask of Eddie or Ronda that they would not cheerfully set about doing. While working closely with Pastor Hall, Eddie told of his past, from reform school through Teen

Challenge. Hall was moved by the tale, and it made him admire Eddie all the more to realize just what a victory it had been.

While at the church, Ronda heard about a half of a duplex that a military couple was leaving, on Military Highway near Azalea Garden Road. It had more living space and a yard where Paul and Diana could play. The Wyatts quickly took the apartment.

The small development sat behind the Military Highway commercial strip, a mile from the Robin Hood. In some ways, however, it was no improvement. The floors had a visible tilt toward the northeast, and Ronda had to put shims under two legs of her kitchen table to keep the soup from sloshing out of the bowls. In the bathroom, the wall was separated from the floor, and when Ronda got down on her knees to scrub, she could see daylight through it. The view from the fenced-in front yard was of the white-washed cinderblock rear of the Farm Fresh supermarket, a Mexican restaurant and lounge called El Toro, and a laundromat that Ronda used to dry her wash when the weather was too cold to hang clothes on the line.

They had not lived there very long when Eddie said he had decided to have the vasectomy. Ronda wondered whether it was necessary. More and more, they were practicing the surest form of birth control, abstinence. Eddie was scheduled to ship out for the Mediterranean again the Sunday after Thanksgiving, on a different carrier, and he wanted to have the operation before then. On November 1, he went over to the naval hospital in Portsmouth, where Diana was born, and a navy doctor performed the simple procedure on him as an outpatient.

The aircraft carrier U.S.S. *Forrestal* would be cruising the Mediterranean for six months, through the winter. The Wyatts spent Thanksgiving together, then the following Sunday, Eddie left by plane for Jacksonville, Florida, since the carrier sailed out of nearby Mayport. Ronda flew back to Colorado with the children at the invitation of her parents. Diana was older now, and Ronda found herself with more time on her hands than the year before. So she busied herself with teaching a ladies' Bible study in the neighborhood.

While at sea, Eddie received word through the Red Cross that his father had died. He felt no immediate sense of loss because, for all purposes, George Walter Wyatt might as well have died when Eddie was five. He told Ronda how several years after his dad had left, they learned he was living only about an hour away, with another woman. Eddie had written off his father. In twenty-three years, not once had the man come back to see him, or called on a birthday, or sent a Christmas card. Eddie did not shed tears for him now.

Eddie wrote home less frequently on this Mediterranean cruise than he had on his first. Ronda could go for a month without a letter. But when he did write, he kept his letters upbeat and filled with faith. Sometimes, Eddie sent packages with religious articles he had bought, once sending Ronda a statue of Jesus. Infrequently, he sent money. Once again, Ronda had to rely on her parents for car payments and rent on the vacant duplex in Norfolk.

When Ronda confided to a friend in Bible study that she missed Eddie's touch and the sexual closeness they had before he went into the navy, the friend suggested that Ronda write Eddie a deeply personal letter confessing to her yearnings. Ronda sat down one evening and wrote the most intimate letter she could. She wrote frankly and openly about how she enjoyed sex, and how his touching and loving made her feel wonderful. She dropped the letter in the mailbox with the expectation that it would arouse a passionate response from Eddie.

But the next time he wrote, Eddie never mentioned Ronda's love letter, and it crushed her. Something must be wrong with her, she thought, if she couldn't get her husband interested in sex after several months at sea. It never occurred to her that the problem might be with Eddie. She had admired him for so long, she was sure the problem was with her.

The *Forrestal* headed back to Mayport in April 1980. Eddie was scheduled to be flown back from Florida with his squadron to Norfolk's naval air station. Ronda planned to meet him there, and returned with the children a day early so she could retrieve their car, which they had left again with the Rosenbaums, and freshen up the duplex on Military Highway, which had been vacant since Thanksgiving. Eddie's plane was due in around midnight, so Ronda dressed Paul and Diana in their pajamas and put on one of her nicest dresses.

The squadron was treated to a welcoming reception on the base, and Ronda waited anxiously for Eddie to appear. She beamed with pride when she caught sight of him in his formal uniform. Eddie was smiling and looked happy to set foot on the same ground as Ronda for the first time in six months. He strode over to his wife, and greeted her with a quick hug and a peck on the cheek. The perfunctory welcome flustered Ronda. A feeling of embarrassment followed when she looked around and saw all the other wives being greeted with passionate kisses and risqué embraces.

With money as tight as it was, and without the possibility of having more children, Ronda decided it was time to return to work. She had not worked since leaving Teen Challenge, four and a half years earlier. So in May, Ronda began an eight-month course of evening classes at the Professional Medical Institute in Norfolk to become a medical assistant.

Ronda noticed how depressed Eddie had become since returning from the second Mediterranean cruise. Both of them came to realize that it had been a mistake to go into the service. It took Eddie away from the family too often and robbed them of the chance to grow closer. Ronda figured that Eddie was upset over his dad's death. Any time Ronda reached out to him and tried to draw him out of his malaise, he pulled back. This had become his standard reaction when he was hurting emotionally, to bottle up his feelings and not give others access to him.

When Eddie was writing to Ronda before their wedding, he seemed so open, and in fact he had stressed how important he felt it was for the two of them to always talk things out. Ronda always thought that she was the one who had trouble doing that. But when she tried to get Eddie to discuss things with her, he insisted there was nothing wrong that he could not handle on his own. "You wouldn't understand it," he often told her in what became a familiar refrain around the house. "I don't understand it myself, but I can handle it."

Ronda asked a male friend of Eddie's at Ocean View Assembly to take her husband aside for a man-to-man talk. The friend agreed, and one Sunday after services, he went off with Eddie for part of the afternoon. Eddie told his friend about being upset over unresolved feelings stemming from his father's death, and about being unhappy in the navy. He said that he was having a hard time staying in the church because of how depressed he felt over the situation. But Eddie said he thought it would pass once he worked it all through. The friend reported back to Ronda that she simply needed to give Eddie some space, that all men go through a period when they veer away from the church, and Eddie was just depressed. She was making too much of it, he told her. Eddie was a thoughtful and intense person, the friend said, and sooner or later he would pull out of it.

Pastor Alvin Hall also noticed the change in Eddie after he came back from the *Forrestal* cruise. Hall had heard from some of his military sources that fully one-third of the *Forrestal*'s sailors had come back from the cruise hooked on dope. He did not know if this was Eddie's problem, but he was troubled when Eddie cut down his attendance at services. He had known Eddie as a good and caring Christian man, especially good with the children he supervised in the Royal Rangers. Hall was especially eager to help Eddie through a crisis. He felt indebted to Eddie, for when Hall was new to Ocean View Assembly and having a difficult time adjusting to the new congregation, Eddie Wyatt was always the first one to come up after services with an encouraging word or a warm embrace.

Hall arranged to have a few long talks with Eddie, but he ended up with the same basic conclusion as the male friend who had spoken with him earlier. Hall wound up thinking that Eddie was going through a rough period, triggered by his dad's death, but that he would surely grow out of it. In the meantime, Hall handed Eddie a key to the church building, and told him to feel welcomed to come in and pray whenever he felt the need.

Unable to reach her husband's problems through his male friend or the pastor, Ronda took the initiative and found a Christian sex manual that addressed common problems in marriages, such as impotence, birth control, and reluctance. It was written with the purpose of increasing the mutual sexual pleasure of both husband and wife, and contained quite frank discussions of problems and the ways to deal with them, along with illustrations. Ronda began to follow the book's advice and established a regimen of exercises meant to tighten her vaginal muscles, so that she would better grip Eddie's penis when they had intercourse—if they had intercourse.

Ronda kept up the exercises, hoping it would make her a better partner whenever she was able to break through Eddie's wall of indifference. She read that depression was a common trigger for a man's sexual "inability," but that it was most often temporary. Ronda could tell that Eddie was bottling up a terrible amount of frustration, and she guessed that if she could get him to talk about his dad, she might be able to unlock some of that depression and set it free. Then they could pick up where they left off.

But it was hard to break through Eddie's wall when he kept turning away from her, and when he kept insisting it was something he could handle. Often, when opportunities arose for Ronda and Eddie to talk, he avoided it by saying she wouldn't understand, then leaving the house for a drive or a walk to clear his head. On the night of July 2, 1980, after Ronda came home from midweek services, Eddie seemed particularly restless. When Ronda was getting ready to go to bed, he kept his clothes on and retrieved the car keys. He said he needed to get out and walk around. He was feeling depressed and wanted to get out into the night air and think.

Steve Thomas lived in a tranquil neighborhood on the other side of Azalea Garden Road from the duplex development where the Wyatts lived. He had cut short his graveyard shift as a Norfolk police officer Wednesday night because he was scheduled to be in court to testify all day Thursday. He returned to his house on Burrell Avenue shortly before midnight and was starting to undress for bed when, in the quiet of the night, he heard a noise that sounded like the backyard fence rattling. His police instincts triggered, he grabbed his handgun and went out toward the backyard.

Previously, Thomas had found evidence that someone had been skulking around his yard. In fact, off and on over the past year, many of the homeowners in this subdivision of single-family homes known as Azalea Acres had reported prowlers to the Norfolk police, and some burglaries had occurred that were being blamed on local teenagers. Persistent reports of a Peeping Tom were also coming in. A couple of stewardesses who worked out of the nearby airport and boarded at a home in Azalea Acres had reported a peeper several times. No one had been caught yet, and they started to pin their curtains together at night so no one could see through the tiny slit from outside.

Officer Thomas shared an L-shaped, one-story house smack in the middle of the block with his mother, stepfather, and a sixteen-year-old brother who was recuperating from a motorcycle accident and stayed in a hospital bed set up in the den. The brother's girlfriend, also sixteen, was staying with the family to tend to her injured beau through the night while his mother slept. Thomas was concerned about their safety, especially when he worked the overnight shift and could not be at home. Thomas did the yard work, and on a couple of occasions he found that a few logs from the woodpile over by the chain-link fence had been brought over and set up like a pedestal right under a window out back. Once he found a lawn chair had been left under a window. And another time, Thomas found shoe prints on his mother's central air-conditioning unit, right below the kitchen window. He tried to keep his senses sharp at night so he could hear if an intruder came into the yard.

Because of these signs, Officer Thomas was more alert than usual when he went outside to investigate the noise, handgun drawn, hoping to surprise whoever might be there. He went out the front and quietly made his way along the side to the back of the house. When he poked his head slowly around the corner, he saw a man of medium build, dressed in dark clothing, standing on top of the air-conditioning unit. The man was peering in through the kitchen window, where he could watch the teenage girlfriend working at the counter.

"Freeze!" Thomas yelled at the man, who suddenly bolted upright. He grabbed the man and frisked him, finding the stranger was carrying a buck knife in his pants. Thomas led the man into his front room and pushed him into a chair. He then sent his brother's girlfriend to the bedroom for his handcuffs and to call the police. Thomas had seen hundreds of criminal faces in his work but rarely had he seen such a cold and emotionless expression as the one he saw on his prisoner.

Within seconds, Thomas's elderly mother came storming out from the back of the house, where the girl had awakened her. She charged up to the intruder, intent on taking it out on the man on behalf of all the residents of Azalea Acres.

"Why are you doing this to us!" she demanded. "How dare you! You stay away from my house!" Thomas turned slightly to back his mother away, and when he did, the prisoner jumped out of the chair, shoved the older woman into her son, and bolted through the front door. Thomas ran after him and saw him enter the yard of a neighbor who kept a Great Dane.

"Get him, son! Get him!" Thomas yelled. The big dog began to bark loudly, and the fleeing intruder dove to the ground, where Thomas quickly collared him. He took the prisoner downtown to the police station, where he was booked for suspicion of trespassing. Asked by a detective to give his name, the man provided identification showing that he was Edward Eugene Wyatt.

Ronda was awakened by the ringing of her telephone. As she roused herself to answer it, she noticed that it was after midnight.

"Hi, honeybun. I've got a problem," Eddie started. "I'm at the police station. Some guy says I was trespassing on his property." Ronda swallowed hard. She had no experience at all with the police, except for a speeding ticket she got in Dallas. Eddie had been so smooth and forgiving about that.

"What happened, Eddie?" she asked him.

"I parked the car and went for a walk, and I lost my bearings and couldn't find the car again, honey. And I thought it was over the next block, so I was just cutting through this guy's yard, and he comes out and chases me with a gun. They're making a big deal out of it."

"What do you want me to do?" Ronda asked him.

"I need $100 to bail out," Eddie replied.

Ronda knew there was no way they could scrape together $100, not on their own at least. She felt panicky.

"I'll work on the bondsman, honeybun," Eddie continued. "Don't worry. Everything will be all right." Eddie talked a reluctant bondsman into taking a postdated check for $100, claiming he would make good on it when payday came. The bondsman handled the bail and then gave Eddie a ride from the police station to the duplex on Military Highway.

Once he was back home, Eddie elaborated on his version of events, telling Ronda he had become so absorbed in his thoughts while walking off his depression, he didn't realize where he was. It was so simple, Ronda thought, what was so hard to believe about that? She lived with his depression and was upset that this big misunderstanding could cause more problems, like the time he was accused of using drugs aboard the *Kennedy*.

The preliminary hearing was held July 22, a Tuesday morning, in criminal court. Pastor Alvin Hall, who had been counseling Eddie in the weeks since the arrest, showed up as a character witness. One of Eddie's supervisors from the navy also came to attest to his fine work record and relationships on the base. Their testimony about Eddie's character, his work with the church and children, and about his young family was so effective, even Thomas's mother began to have second thoughts. Maybe he really was only cutting through their yard while he was lost, she began to think.

Eddie's trial was set for August 15. Prior to that time, the city attorney looked over the case and told Officer Thomas he was inclined to drop the matter because of Wyatt's church involvement, his character witnesses, and other circumstances. Thomas was livid. He had seen a side of Eddie Wyatt that no one who knew him had ever seen. He knew who was standing on his mom's air conditioner that night. Wyatt was a potential sex offender, Thomas believed. But no one would heed his warning.

Eddie's trial was on a Friday morning. He and Ronda dressed up and drove downtown where they met their lawyer; they then went to the courts building on St. Paul's Boulevard. The courtroom was filled with people Ronda didn't know. They sat together on a bench near the back of the room. Ronda was unfamiliar with courtroom procedures, but she knew that Eddie had experience. So she kept asking him to explain what everything was, and why certain things were happening, until Eddie turned to her.

"Cool it," he said nervously.

After waiting a while through some other cases, Ronda heard the bailiff call Eddie's name, and he went up to the defendant's table with his attorney. While the prosecutor recounted the case for the judge, Ronda saw Steve Thomas looking over at Eddie like he was some pervert. He had no right to do that, Ronda thought indignantly. He was the one making the mistake. She felt like standing up in the courtroom and pointing her finger at the man, and accusing him of butting in and complicating their lives at the worst possible time. Now she understood the feelings Eddie often expressed about being victimized.

Ronda could not hear the proceedings very well. Everybody talked quietly, fast, and in a jargon difficult to translate into everyday English. But at the end, she had no trouble hearing the judge. He found Eddie guilty of trespassing, and sentenced him to two days in jail, plus one year on probation. He would do the jail time the next weekend. Ronda was shocked. Eddie, however, seemed to be relieved that it was over.

Four days later, Ronda was attending her Tuesday morning class with a group of women from Ocean View Assembly, and when the session reached the time when special prayer intentions are solicited, Ronda spoke up.

"Eddie's going to be working downtown this weekend, and I'm a little nervous about it," she said to the group. "I'd like to pray for him so he's kept safe."

For some reason, that did not set right with Joanie Sargent, one of the women who had been involved in the group for a long time. She knew that with Eddie's navy work assignment, it was highly unlikely there was anything for him to do downtown. The thought of the Norfolk jail popped into Joanie's mind as the group started to pray, but she shrugged off that uneasy feeling for the moment.

Ronda's immediate problem was what to tell the children. Paul was four and inquisitive about everything. Eddie seemed particularly anxious that his son not know where Daddy was going to be spending the weekend. That Friday afternoon, August 21, Ronda put the kids in the backseat of their Valiant, and drove Eddie the five miles to downtown.

"I don't want Paul to know what this building is," Eddie said when the jail came into view. Eddie used to take his little boy everywhere with him, and Paul liked nothing more than to tag along with his dad, but lately, after the *Forrestal* cruise, Eddie had been distancing himself from Paul, leaving him home more often when he ran errands, even if the boy begged to go along. Eddie jumped out of the car to check into the jail, and Ronda started to pull back into traffic.

"Where's Daddy going?" Paul asked.

"He has to work downtown for a few days, Paul," Ronda told him. "He'll be back on Monday."

That evening, with a stew of different thoughts and emotions running through her mind, Ronda decided she needed to get it all down on paper so as to put it in perspective. She wanted to show that her commitment to Eddie was good for the difficult times as well as when times were easy. It took the form of a letter that she would give him when she picked him up on Monday:

Eddie,

Do you want to know one lesson that's been mine over the past few weeks? That my love for you reaches depths I never knew possible. When you've hurt, I've hurt! When you've been despondent, it touched my soul too. When you felt fear, I felt it too. And isn't that what love is really about? We've shared our joys, and our lonely hours, and some of our dreams, and now we've shared some of our

*pain. I love you, darling, and I see in you what I've
always wanted in a man. You've done great under all of
the pressure. I need you and your kind of love. How
fortunate for me you are there.*

Ronda went to the Sunday evening serving at Ocean View
Assembly of God that weekend, and in due course she went up
to the piano to sing a song that was particularly meaningful that
night. In her beautiful and clear voice, she sang "No One Ever
Cares for Me Like Jesus," an old, slow spiritual that touched many
in the congregaton, including Joanie Sargent. At the end, Pastor
Hall issued a prayer call. At that, Ronda got up in front of everyone
and, with her head lowered, said she had been to the ladies' Bible
study the previous Tuesday, the day she asked for prayers for
her husband.

"When I was there," Ronda continued, "I was really depressed.
I mean, I was down about as low as someone can be. All I needed
was someone to hug me, to say some words of comfort to me.
And no one did." At that point, Ronda began to cry before the
entire congregation.

Joanie, remembering her odd premonition about the Norfolk
jail, jumped up and went over to Ronda, gathering her in a tight
hug as others moved close.

"You'll never feel that way again," Joanie whispered to Ronda.
"Never." Over the next few months, they became very close
friends as they worked together to try to lift Eddie out of his
depression.

Pastor Hall called on Eddie in jail over the weekend in order to
witness and minister to him. He thought he had something to
offer Eddie that might help lift the black cloud of depression his
good friend was dwelling under. But when he got into the visiting
room, Alvin Hall was confronted with an Eddie Wyatt he scarcely
recognized.

Eddie sat facing his pastor, arms folded, a blank look on his
face. It was as though there was no soul left inside the shell. It

was a glacial expression that offered little hope of melting, a stone statue of the Eddie Wyatt he used to know.

Hall started by offering testimony of hardship in his own life, hoping Eddie could identify. He was careful to be nonjudgmental, instead reminding Eddie that in Jesus there is forgiveness for all things that a person might confess. He recounted some remembrances of the troubled childhood that Eddie had revealed to him earlier, and reminded him how he had overcome it. He went on about Eddie's loving wife and two beautiful children. "The Lord," said the pastor, "is able to forgive you for any sin, and cleanse you from any unrighteousness."

Hall was becoming frustrated. Eddie had not said a word. He had hardly blinked his eyes, instead fixing his gaze on something far beyond the visiting room wall. Finally, Hall was struck with the idea to stop what he was doing and to just pray over Eddie. So he reached in his pocket and pulled out a small Bible he carried, and opened it to Psalm 23. While Eddie remained deathly still and stared into the distance, Alvin Hall read the psalm.

"The Lord is my shepherd; I shall not want," he began. "He maketh me to lie down in green pastures: he leadeth me beside the still waters. He restoreth my soul: he leadeth me in the path of righteousness for his name's sake. Yea, though I walk through the valley of the shadow of death, I will fear no evil: for thou art with me; thy rod and thy staff they comfort me. Thou preparest a table before me in the presence of mine enemies: thou anointest my head with oil: my cup runneth over...."

When he finished the short recitation, Pastor Hall looked up toward Eddie. There was no change. He looked back down at the text and began to read it a second time, still with no change. He read it again and again. The fifth time he read it, after he uttered the final verse—"Surely goodness and mercy shall follow me all the days of my life: and I will dwell in the house of the Lord for ever"—he saw Eddie crack. A tear that had welled in Eddie's left eye spilled over and down his cheek. Quickly, more tears followed as Eddie's face tightened convulsively, until he let out a mournful wail and began crying. He slowly loosened his crossed arms, and they dropped to his side. Then he leaned forward and collapsed into Hall's waiting grasp. Eddie draped his arms around the pastor's neck and sobbed heavily.

"I'm so sorry," Eddie cried. "I don't know why I'm doing this. I need Jesus to renew my heart." He asked Pastor Hall to pray with him. The pastor, who had seen a great deal during his twelve years in the ministry, had never seen anything as startling as that abrupt personality change in Eddie.

CHAPTER 5

DON'T LOOK AT ME AND I WON'T HURT YOU

See what kind of person Eddie has to live with? No wonder he's bored. I see myself as easy to be forgotten, worth forsaking, angry, ugly and boring. I hate myself. I think that I should spare everyone my presence. So where can I go? I can't leave my babies. But maybe they would be better off with a pretty, patient mom. How would it affect Eddie? I don't know. How can he love someone like me anyway? There has to be a solution somewhere. I'm so tired, and dear God, how my head hurts. Is there anyone, anywhere, who cares?

—from Ronda's diary

Eddie was in his element with his rod and reel, relaxing at the water's edge or out in a boat. All of his friends knew how much he liked to go fishing. It started as a childhood passion and was probably the one diversion he enjoyed the most when he was on shore duty. So when Don Rosenbaum invited Eddie to go along on an overnight fishing trip with a men's group from the Great Bridge Church of God, shortly after Eddie did his weekend in jail, he jumped at it.

A group of a dozen men from Don's church were going to a campground and fishing area at Bay Haven Ponds, just over the state line in North Carolina. Don and Eddie often fished together, and sometimes Eddie worked on Don to try to get him and Sue to go to Ocean View Assembly. Don liked Eddie's religious countenance, and knowing of his recent difficulty with depression and his problem in court, he figured Eddie needed some caring support to regain his spiritual foundation. After they had worked together on their cars and the apartments at the Robin Hood, and after Don had taken little Paul under his wing while Eddie was out to sea, Don considered Eddie to be one of his best friends, even after the Wyatts moved a mile away to the duplex on Military Highway.

Don drove his van over to pick up Eddie, and soon they were on the highway south out of Norfolk headed for Bay Haven Ponds. Don quickly noticed that Eddie was more withdrawn than usual, and assumed it was related to having spent the recent weekend in jail. After getting some initial pleasantries out of the way, Don decided to try to draw Eddie out of his shell. But no sooner had his jailhouse tears with Pastor Hall dried up than Eddie went about rebuilding that momentary breach in his defenses.

"Eddie, what's wrong with you today?" Don asked him.

"I can't really talk about it, Don," Eddie answered.

"That's all right, Eddie. You don't have to tell me anything you don't want to," Don said. Then he turned and looked at his passenger. "But would you like to talk about it?"

"No, not really. I can't," Eddie replied.

"Does it involve you and Ronda?"

"No," Eddie told him.

"Well, you know, Eddie, there's no problem so big that the Lord can't help you," Don offered.

Eddie looked down at the floorboard for a moment.

"There's one thing the Lord can't help me with, Don," Eddie finally said. "This one he can't solve."

Don was struck by how firmly Eddie resisted. Don was not the sort to push a man into something he was reluctant to do, but he wished that Eddie would open up. Don sensed a desperation in his friend that he attributed to some great inner conflict in Eddie's soul. During the two-day trip, Don continued to offer his ear to Eddie. But Eddie would not budge. While he found it easy to talk about their cars, their jobs, or their children, Eddie kept his feelings tightly bottled up. He could share his past, but he found it impossible to share his present. He would only tell Don that it was too personal.

*   *   *

It was late, about two-thirty in the morning, when Ronda was awakened by Eddie's restless tossing and turning next to her in their bed at home. She was still coming out of her sleep when Eddie turned toward her and wrapped her up in a tight embrace. Without warning, he moved on top of her and began kissing her, hard and passionately. He said nothing as his hands held her down forcefully and roamed over her body.

Not that Ronda wanted to escape his clutches. Ronda wanted nothing more than for Eddie to break out of his cage of listlessness, and to become again the caring husband she had known before. When Eddie amorously sprang to life in bed, Ronda was eager to respond. She had felt as if she were walking on eggshells around the house since Eddie came back from those few days in jail. He did not want to talk about anything with her.

But suddenly, Eddie was strong and confident as he proceeded to make love to her. It had been weeks since they last had intercourse, and Ronda had felt it too degrading to ask for it. This was more to her liking, something initiated by Eddie that made her at last feel desired by him.

In fact, Eddie's actions were so forceful that Ronda could not have gotten up if she had wanted to. A fleeting thought came to Ronda that if this were not her husband and she were not more than willing, this would be what it was like to be raped. She was completely at Eddie's mercy, watching him exercise control and power over her body. She had felt that way once before, in the VW bug off the highway in Texas before they were married.

Then, abruptly, Eddie withdrew. Ronda opened her eyes and looked up at him. It was as if some unseen hypnotist had snapped his fingers, ended the trance, and instantly brought Eddie back to the real world. Eddie slowly rolled over and, with his back to Ronda, went back to sleep. Ronda was devastated.

In the morning at breakfast, Eddie said nothing about the late-night sexual encounter until Ronda mentioned it. Eddie was apologetic, as though he had done something wrong and was caught at it. He was embarrassed. On the contrary, Ronda told him, it was okay. She wished he had finished.

On another night when they were in bed together, Ronda got Eddie to talk a little bit about their sex life. Eddie offered no reason for his lack of interest, other than his depression. Then he began talking about his dad dying while he was out to sea. Eddie began to cry, and that surprised Ronda, who had not seen him cry in a long time. It was a sign that she was reaching his pain and finally getting him to talk about what was bothering him. The more he talked about his dad, the more he cried. As they continued talking, Ronda asked why Eddie had been distancing himself from little Paul in recent months.

"I don't want to get too close to Paul," Eddie said. "I always lose the things I love." It was such a gloomy thing for Eddie to say. Ronda was struck by its sadness.

By the terms of Eddie's probation, he was forbidden to enter the Azalea Acres subdivision, which was ticklish because it was right across the street from where he lived. He and Ronda still walked together sometimes, and they started to take their strolls in another neighborhood, behind their duplex. They took the children along, and it was during these times that Ronda thought she might be more successful in getting Eddie to talk about why he was so depressed. On one such walk, after Ronda asked Eddie to open up to her, he said that he felt as if he were backsliding from Jesus. This upset Ronda because the foundation of their marriage, she believed, was their unshakable faith that God would carry them through any crisis. Who could stand against them if God was with them, she believed.

"If we keep going on this way, Eddie, our home is going to end up in the same shape your parents' home was in," Ronda warned him. "I would give us about one more year."

"I can handle it," he said. "I just don't want to talk about it. No one would understand."

Ronda took the microphone in her hands and waited for the accompanist to begin. It was one of Eddie's favorite songs, "Whatever It Takes," but he wasn't at Ocean View Assembly this Sunday in November to hear his wife sing it for the congregation. Eddie had it on a tape of the Lanny Wolfe Trio, which he played over and over at home, letting the soft country rhythm drift into his mind so relentlessly it became an obsession. As Ronda sang it, she thought of her husband and how she would give up anything to restore his spirits:

"Take the dearest things to me, if that's how it must be, to draw me closer to Thee . . .

"Take my houses and lands, change my dreams and my plans, for I'm placing my whole life in your hands . . .

"I'll trade sunshine for rain, comfort for pain, that's what I'll be willing to do. For whatever it takes for my will to break, that's what I'll be willing to do."

If Eddie felt he was backsliding, Ronda resolved to do whatever she could to reinforce him. She had already run the course of her "tightening exercies," without discernible impact. Now she set about to improve Eddie's outlook. She had confided to several of her friends that Eddie was very depressed. Joanie Sargent got the idea of throwing him a surprise welcome-home party when he got back from a short work-up cruise. They wanted to boost Eddie's ego and let him know that there were a lot of people who loved him and were behind him all the way. Joanie planned the party for mid-December in her big house on the navy base. Someone produced a long computer print-out banner that said "Welcome Home, Eddie. We Love You." Joanie, who like Eddie was an expatriate from the Lone Star State, prepared Mexican food, since Eddie was part Mexican. She hoped it would measure up to what his mother used to make.

Ronda got Eddie over to the Sargents' house on a pretext of visiting them on his return home. But there were seventy-five people, almost all of them from Ocean View Assembly, waiting inside. When Eddie walked in the door and the folks yelled, "Surprise!" Eddie was stunned. A big smile grew across his face and his eyes welled with tears. Although he looked a little awkward, Ronda knew that that was how Eddie always reacted in such social settings. He was a loner by nature.

Soon after, Eddie's commander asked him if he wished to extend his enlistment two years. Eddie, who hated going to sea, thought that the guy had to be joking. But then the commander explained that by extending from four to six years, Eddie could get a guarantee that he would spend the entire time on shore duty. Along with that, he could have his pick of several decent assignments. There were three naval air stations down in his native Texas from which Eddie could choose his next base— Kingsville, Corpus Christi, or Beeville. The promise of not shipping out any more made Eddie take this very seriously. He had just under a year to serve, but he was desperate not to go to sea again.

Dave Houser, the navy friend and fishing buddy on whom Eddie often unburdened his sense of failure and his growing restlessness, suggested they extend their enlistments together. They could continue to commiserate while fishing in the bountiful salt waters of the Gulf of Mexico. Dave was going through some of the same dissatisfaction as Eddie, and they could feed off each other's misery while they kept company.

It was more than Eddie could resist. He was so desperate not to go to sea again that he readily agreed to extend for two years in spite of his conviction—and Ronda's concurrence—that the navy was the wrong place for him.

Another big party was thrown for the Wyatts, this one over at Ocean View Assembly, just before the young family left for Texas. It was after a Sunday evening service in February. Nearly everyone stayed behind to wish the couple well. Pastor Hall said he would miss the Wyatts, and hoped that Eddie would find the change in scenery enough to help him deal with his depression over the death of his dad. He thought Eddie was one of the finest young men he had ever met, and he prayed that the Lord would bring him back to happiness and peace with himself.

The Wyatt family prepared to move down to Texas after three years in Norfolk. One afternoon about eight weeks before the scheduled transfer, the telephone rang and Eddie, who was alone in the duplex, quickly answered it.

"Put it in the bag," said a woman's voice. Eddie was momentarily startled. The words were so familiar, it threw him for a loop. Put it in the bag? Could it be?

"Patty?" Eddie asked incredulously.

The woman began to laugh heartily. It was a sound Eddie had not heard in, what, maybe fifteen years.

"Patty? Is that you? My God!"

"How've you been, Eddie Wyatt?" she said.

"Oh, all right, I guess." Eddie was still stunned by the sound of her voice. "How about you? How did you ever find me up here in Virginia?"

"It was easier than you think. One of your friends told me you married some gal from Colorado, and they had her parents' number there. So I called Denver and I guess it was your mother-in-law answered. I told her I was an old friend of yours, and asked her for your new number."

At that precise moment, Erna Hunter was dialing her daughter's number in Norfolk. She had become suspicious of the long-distance dialer who had asked for Eddie's telephone number. She got a busy signal. She kept redialing for an hour without getting through.

Eddie had not spoken with Patty Battaglia since the tear-filled day at Gatesville when she came to the reform school for a visit and he told her not to write any more. Eddie was fifteen then. He was so in love with her, but too hot-headed for his own good. Hearing their childhood code phrase, "put in in the bag," unleashed a flood of unrequited desires. Patty was the one great, unfulfilled love of his life. He had never spoken to anyone about it, but he was never able to stamp out the embers of those burning bonds of attraction, spurred by the painful memory of something that should have happened and never did. He thought of her often over the years, and the memories of her made him smile, even though she had never allowed him between her legs.

Patty brought her old beau up to date, telling him that she had married a rather well-to-do Galveston man, but she was bored with it. She had toyed for a while with her craving to track Eddie down until she finally gave in. Once she heard his soft voice on the phone, she teased him with the line he had heard her toss indignantly to the candy shop owner so many years ago. Eddie and Patty talked for an hour, and it was the most he had laughed in a long time. She was about the only woman on the planet Earth who could have drawn him out that way.

"Listen," Patty finally said, "if you ever find yourself down near Galveston, look me up. I'd love to see you."

"Yeah, I'll do that," Eddie replied. "Don't be surprised if it's not too long from now."

"What do you mean by that?" Patty asked.

"Never mind. Just don't be surprised."

No sooner did Eddie hang up the phone than it rang again. This time when he picked it up, it was Erna Hunter.

"Hello, Eddie," she said. "Is Ronda there?"

"No," he told his mother-in-law. "She's out with the kids."

"I've been trying to call but your line's been busy," Erna said.

"Oh, that was my mom," Eddie replied. "I hadn't talked with her for a while and just decided to call her."

The sprawling rangeland of Kleberg County, Texas, was so flat, Ronda thought it looked like a taut drumhead. For mile after mile on U.S. 77, Ronda drove the family's silver Dodge Aspen, loaded with clothing and other necessities, and absorbed the landscape. She kept her eyes fixed on the bumper of the blue Valiant up ahead, which Eddie was driving south. The children had shifted back and forth during the long ride, but Paul rode most of the time with his dad. Diana was seated next to Ronda during this last leg into Kingsville.

Welcome back to Texas, Ronda thought, scene of much greater happiness in her past, and now holder of her hopes for a fresh beginning. She inhaled deeply that fresh air as she drove, feeling free of the oppressive weight that had descended on her relationship with Eddie those final months in Norfolk. She could see a big lift in Eddie once they made the decision to transfer.

This was a part of Texas with which Ronda was unfamiliar. It looked a little barren to her. Kingsville, their new home, was originally grazing land. It was still surrounded by the 825,000-acre King Ranch, at one time the world's largest. But the Kingsville area's economy had become fairly well diversified, including Texas A&I University, several petrochemical and gas processing plants, and oil fields. Of great importance was the Kingsville Naval Air Station, a single-base training site where both basic and advanced training was given to military aviators. The base was producing two hundred trained navy and marine jet-fighter pilots every year.

As Ronda crossed the city limit, she found Kingsville itself a pleasant little burg. A small business district lined Kleberg Avenue, which was bookended on the west by the old Henrietta M. King High School and eight blocks east by the Kleberg County Courthouse and Jail. The courthouse, a traditional light-brown brick building with white trim, sat in a grove of mesquite, palm, and pecan trees on a town square. The palm trees that lined some of the other streets gave Kingsville a tropical feeling that Ronda had not experienced in Norfolk. But she liked it.

The city's population was mostly Hispanics, including American-born Mexican-Americans and those who came in from Mexico for the job opportunities. A small but significant black population was concentrated in the southwest corner of town. The diversity of the town's economy had brought about a more highly mixed population than Ronda had expected. She and Eddie, a military family with two young children, were anxious to become part of this small and transient community.

Most of the people were religious folk, supporting more than fifty houses of worship in and around the city. Ronda soon discovered that one of the growing churches in the city was the First Assembly of God. It was a thirty-six-year-old Pentecostal congregation pastored by the Reverend James Fields, a blind minister, in partnership with his wife, Dolores. Their church and fellowship hall was located on Angle Road at Highway 77, on the way to the main gate of the Naval Air Station, and it was one of the first places Eddie and Ronda visited.

A one-room apartment in transient housing on the sprawling Kingsville Naval Air Station served as home for Eddie, Ronda, and the two children for the first week after they arrived in south Texas. They lived out of suitcases because their belongings were being shipped by the navy. Ronda experienced a bit of culture shock adjusting to Kingsville. Norfolk had a nice downtown area, a vital waterfront, and yards and parks with bright flowers. Kingsville had a small-town pace, and brown was the color that dominated the landscape. When Ronda took Paul and Diana outside the housing to play, she passed a sign at the door warning her of snakes and scorpions on the grounds.

When their week in transient housing was used up and their furniture was still nowhere in sight, Eddie decided to take a bunk in the enlisted men's quarters while Ronda and the children went to visit a couple they had known at Teen Challenge. Ralph and Sandra Spruill, who had since moved to Waco, used to live two doors down from the Wyatts at the El Presidente Apartments in Grand Prairie. They, like the Wyatts, were among the seven Dallas Teen Challenge couples who married in the same short span of time.

Sandra was quick to discern that something was bothering her friend. Ronda soon confided in Sandra that Eddie had changed since they had last seen him, the day the Wyatts moved to Denver. He had become very depressed since his dad died, she said, and so withdrawn that she was powerless to reach him. When Sandra asked Ronda how it was affecting her marriage, Ronda told her friend that Eddie appeared to have lost all interest in sex. Whatever was left of their physical relationship was primarily up to her.

"He can take it or leave it, and he'll usually leave it," Ronda said. "Sometimes I think he'd be happy if he never had sex again."

Soon after, Eddie got some leave time and joined Ronda in Waco. Ralph Spruill, who ran a small construction outfit, arranged it so Eddie could earn a few extra dollars on his crew. Back at Teen Challenge, Ralph had enjoyed talks with Eddie in which they would share their life experiences, and how they had been saved. He remembered how Eddie would lead his wife in home devotions. He recalled how his friend lived for Sundays so he could go to church, and worked at breakneck speed on Wednesdays so he could make the midweek services, too. Ralph thought Eddie was just like him, a former renegade who had turned to Jesus, and for whom there was no turning back.

But now when Ralph tried to talk to Eddie on the job, Eddie was generally unresponsive and somewhat withdrawn. In fact, it seemed to Ralph that his old friend didn't even want to be around the Spruills, as if Eddie was uncomfortable in their presence. At the house, Eddie spent most of his time in the room where he and Ronda were staying. And on the job, whenever Ralph tried to start a coversation, Eddie would deflect any inquiries with perfunctory answers.

After working with Ralph for four days, Eddie announced he was returning to Kingsville, hoping to find a place for the family before he had to report back to work. Whatever was troubling Eddie, Ralph figured, was something spiritual that he had to work out with the Lord.

In mid-March, Eddie found a bungalow for rent at 418 West Mesquite Avenue, several blocks east of the Texas A&I campus. Ronda returned to Kingsville a few days later and began to set up her household.

The house was a white, two-bedroom modular unit. Like most of the houses along the low-lying coastal plain, it sat up off the ground on stumpy concrete stilts. The front yard was a mixture of sand, gravel, and the stubble of ancient bluegrass some previous tenant had foolishly tried to grow in this climate. A young mesquite tree twisted out of the ground to about twenty-five feet in height. Vertical panels made up the exterior siding on the house, and there was a low-slung asphalt shingle roof that sloped to the sides of the house. There was a single carport with a door at the back end leading into the kitchen. Directly behind the carport was a storage room accessible from both the kitchen and the backyard. Two concrete steps led up to the front door, covered by a beat-up storm door. At the curb was a small wooden corral that held two garbage cans.

Inside, the house was fairly spartan. It was split straight down the middle, front to back. On the left side was the living room and kitchen. The living room was compact, with a set of double windows on the front wall looking out toward Mesquite Avenue and a single window looking west through the carport. The room had a boxy feeling to it because it was paneled all the way around in faux-walnut sheets. It had a short-hair gold carpet. The kitchen was straight back, separated from the living room by two short walls on either side. The kitchen floor was tiled with a diamond pattern of brown and gold. Eddie and Ronda's bedroom was in the front, and the children's room was at the back of the house. Eddie bought a water bed for the master bedroom.

The first Sunday the Wyatts were together in Kingsville, they went to the First Assembly of God. Eddie seemed a little uncomfortable but Ronda loved the church. Pastor Fields struck her as a level-headed, practical preacher with a positive approach to life. He always asked newcomers to raise their hands so the congregation could meet them. He and his wife followed up with a home visit. When the Fieldses visited the Wyatt house, Ronda and Eddie impressed them as a happy young Christian couple, as Eddie could always charm one-on-one. James Fields looked forward to having them become involved at First Assembly.

But after a few weeks in Kingsville, it became apparent to Ronda that Eddie's depression was as strong as it had been in Norfolk. She felt extremely alone without his companionship in this new town. She could not turn to people she did not know well and tell them her troubles. Quite the opposite, she had to work twice as hard to disguise her unhappy state from the people at First Assembly. Her only hope was that her love for Eddie would anchor him as he rode out the storm raging inside him.

Eddie worked days for a few weeks after he got settled in Kingsville, but soon, his commanders put him on a late shift to keep pace with all the airframe work on the T-45 Goshawk jet trainers. Eddie ended up supervising a group of men on a 6:00 P.M. to 2:00 A.M. shift. It was good work, but it was hard on the family. Eddie would share dinner with them, but then he would have to hurry to clean up and report to the base for his shift. Ronda heard Eddie come in late at night—the sound of his Valiant with its sick muffler would usually be enough to rouse her. But instead of coming to bed, Eddie would stay up in the living room to unwind. He would respond briefly to Ronda's greeting and then switch on the television.

When Ronda complained of her solitary existence, Eddie suggested she look for work. They could use extra income to pay off their bills, he reasoned, and she would meet people that way. Ronda had not finished her classes at Norfolk's Professional Medical Institute when it came time to move, but she had pulled all A's in those she had completed. So by mid-April, Ronda was out visiting doctors' offices with her résumé seeking an office job. The initial rejections were hard to take, since she was already feeling rejected at home. Ronda wrote in her diary on April 24:

I feel inexperienced, old, and unwanted. You have to be beautiful and forward to work with people. I'm neither. Obviously, Eddie doesn't even think I'm pretty anymore. What's happened to those long, impassioned kisses? All I get anymore is a dutiful peck on the cheek as he goes out the door. To my husband, I am unattractive—just a stick in the mud—useful for scrubbing floors, bathing kids, boosting an ego occasionally. That's it. Who am I? Does anyone even care that I exist?

What is going on? Dear God, what is going on? I've asked you and asked you to make Eddie more free in his love for me—toward me. And nothing happens. It only gets worse. I don't want to find fulfillment in another man. I want it in him. Why won't he love me? I feel so ugly and unlovable.

There were a few rays of hope. One day, Eddie surprised her with a sewing machine. She loved crafts, especially sewing.

"How could you ever pay for this, Eddie?" Ronda asked, knowing they had little money to spare.

"Remember that guy I was helping paint his car?" Eddie answered. "He didn't have any money to pay me anything, so he asked if I would take this sewing machine as payment for my work. I know how you like to sew."

Ronda did not know these friends, because they were people Eddie met on base. But she was happy to see him break out of his shell once in a while to make friends, be industrious, and do the things he really enjoyed. And for him to accept a sewing machine in payment showed Ronda that he really was thinking of her.

By mid-May, two months after they had settled into their new house, Ronda found a job as a receptionist at the Angle Medical Center, just off the busy, five-way commercial intersection of South Fourteenth Street, Caesar Avenue, and Angle Road. She went to work with about a half dozen women in the clinic that was staffed with three doctors. For the most part, Ronda enjoyed working and liked most of her coworkers.

Ronda found day care for Paul and Diana with a woman from First Assembly, Sharon Lawson, who had two sons the same ages as the Wyatt children. Ronda was becoming more familiar with Kingsville and its people. Pastor Fields had begun a home fellowship program on Wednesday evenings, in place of the mid-week service, to foster more intimate bonds among his congregation. Ronda found herself placed in a group of about a dozen folks who met each week in the home of James Crowell, a supervisor at the Exxon gas plant on the King Ranch, and his wife, Barbara. For the first time since the move, Ronda finally felt she was beginning to put down roots.

Over on the west side of Kingsville was a pleasant, tree-lined, middle-class neighborhood of older single-family homes. It was here that Pastor Fields and his wife lived. Across Wanda Street from them and several doors south was a white clapboard house with four big trees in the front yard. Twenty-nine-year-old Sue Wilson lived there. She went to bed late on the night of Saturday, June 13, wearing a light blouse and loose gym shorts. She slept fitfully. The neighbor's dog, which stayed outside during the hot summer nights, yapped at the slightest noise, and it disturbed Sue's sleep. Around 2:30 A.M. there was a rattling noise from the backyard chain-link fence, and the dog's barking caused Sue to stir; she then rolled over and fell immediately back to sleep.

Scant minutes after that, Sue was startled awake by a sudden crush of someone landing full on her back, shoving her into the mattress. It was difficult for her to catch her breath because of the weight. Then she heard a man's voice, low and hoarse.

"Don't look at me and I won't hurt you."

She started to scream, but the intruder grabbed her roughly. From behind her, he extended his hand around to her face and brandished a buck knife. She saw its shiny blade close to her eyes.

"Don't holler again, bitch," her attacker ordered. That was

enough to stifle her screaming; utter panic began to immobilize her. The man grabbed a piece of cloth—it could have been a T-shirt or a pillowcase, it was diffcult for Sue to determine—and tied it around her eyes from behind so she couldn't get a look at him. The man then lifted her by an upper arm, and pushed her toward the living room. He forced her down onto the couch, on her back. Sue could hear him breathing more and more heavily. He insisted he was not going to hurt her, but Sue could not believe that.

The man inserted his fingers inside the elastic waistband of her shorts and quickly tugged them down her legs. At that, he undid his own pants and climbed on top of her. He forced her legs apart and, with some effort, managed to penetrate her. Repeatedly commanding her to tell him that she liked it, he seemed more intent on making her obey than on sexual gratification. Sue did not resist, hoping that by doing as he instructed, he would not hurt her. She felt the rage of her assailant and was terrified that he would kill her. He called her bitch and whore, and climaxed quickly.

After a short time, he grabbed Sue's naked hips and rolled her off the couch so that she was kneeling, still blindfolded and wearing her blouse. He gripped the back of her head and shoved her face down onto the cushion. From behind he began to assault her again, this time anally. It was much more intense and painful than the first assault. He made her tell him that he was good and that she liked it as he worked his way to another climax.

After the second assault, the man rummaged through the house. Sue remained as still as she could until she realized that her rapist had gone. Then she ran to a neighbor's house for help.

CHAPTER 6

BURYING THE SECRET

If someone were to pick up this notebook and read it just at random, they would think me to be a terribly pessimistic person. That's not so. Everyone has bad days. It just seems that the bad days have been running close together lately, and when my heart really hurts it's just easier for me to write down how I feel. You know that for a long time we have been hurting. Our physical relationship has been the pits for a long time. Eddie won't talk about it—he just seems to ignore that the problems are there. I don't like me anymore. If I cannot please Eddie, I have failed.

—from Ronda's diary

The kind of offense that had traditionally dominated the crime-watch column in the twice-weekly *Kingsville Record* would have been too commonplace for big-city papers to report. When someone ripped off a few letters from a portable advertising sign on the Fourteenth Street business strip, it led to a story in the *Record* about the loss of $14.40 worth of alphabet. The headline on another crime brief read "Nuts Missing," about the apparent theft of a jar of peanuts from a woman's kitchen.

It was not that Kingsville was immune to serious crime. It just did not happen that often, even though the narcotics trade was threatening to change all that. The little city of just under thirty thousand people straddled the Missouri Pacific Railroad line coming north from the fertile Rio Grande valley growing fields. Highway 77, following the rail line, came straight up the Coastal Bend from Brownsville and Harlingen right through the center of Kingsville, while to the west, Highway 281 paralleled the same course from McAllen. They were pipelines for illegal drugs being smuggled across the Rio Grande from the Mexican state of Tamaulipas through Matamoros and Reynosa. And like a slow leak in a hopper car plying the Missouri Pacific, drugs were dropped off along the pipeline by the couriers.

During the late 1970s and early 1980s, Kingsville grew into a heroin hotspot. Addicts from Robstown, Alice, and even Corpus Christi would come down to Kingsville to shoplift, burglarize, or rob, and then turn the stolen items over for money or drugs. It was difficult enough to apprehend these commuter criminals, but even among the townspeople, there were new faces all the time. From King Ranch cowpunchers to naval aviator trainees, oil and gas roughnecks to college students, a substantial portion of the population changed over completely in three to four year cycles.

But while the burglary rate soared, a more disturbing thing began to happen in Kingsville. Police began to get more reports of break-ins occurring while the residents were home. In some of them, robbery was not the motive. Rape was. In all of 1979, there had been six reported rapes in the city of Kingsville. But in 1980, the number of reports doubled, and continued into 1981. Some of the cases involved known assailants. The unsolved cases accumulated gradually, before investigators were able to spot similarities among them. At the time Eddie and Ronda Wyatt left Virginia to make Kingsville their new home, there had been a number of other sexual assaults in and around the small Texas town that obscured the budding emergence of the pattern rapes.

On February 3, 1981, over on the southwest side of town, three boys, aged nineteen, eighteen, and seventeen, grabbed a fifteen-year-old girl, forced her into a vacant house on West Caesar Avenue, and raped her. Later that month, after a late-night party on Valentine's Day near the Texas A&I campus, a twenty-one-year-old student told police she was raped by a man holding a knife on her outside her house about 5:00 A.M. She had minor cuts on her neck and back. At about 3:00 A.M. on February 26, an intruder entered a bedroom where a woman was sleeping and tried to yank her T-shirt over her head. She struggled with him, and he fled before he could do anything else. Later that same day, two men tried to abduct a thirteen-year-old girl on East Caesar Avenue.

Shortly after midnight on April 15, a Chinese student at the university got off work and was walking home when she was attacked and raped by a Hispanic male. Police later arrested a suspect, but the woman declined to press charges. In her culture, she told police, the victim was stigmatized, and a trial would make her shame worse. She wanted to put the crime behind her.

Ten days later, a woman was stranded at night on a back road near Bishop, a couple of miles north of Kingsville, after her car broke down. Three men came along and raped her several times over the next four hours.

On East Kenedy Avenue in Kingsville, a forty-one-year-old woman was asleep in her bedroom about 11:30 P.M. on June 8. She was abruptly awakened by a man who jumped on her bed and threatened her with a knife. He started to attempt to rape her, and she struggled. Unnerved by her screams, the attacker fled back through the window from which he had entered.

Five days later, Sue Wilson was raped.

Judy Hayes wanted to be a cop even if it meant leaving her home in central New York and migrating to south Texas. She had been a juvenile counselor for the police department in Syracuse, but there were very few opportunities to become an officer. After counseling for two years, she was told it would still be a hefty chunk of time before she could be sworn into the ranks. In south Texas, there was so much turnover, police departments advertised monthly with job openings. Generally, it was the low pay or the lack of pension benefits in the smaller towns that helped feed the flow of talent up into the Texas Rangers, U.S. Border Patrol, or the higher-paying big city departments.

Judy Hayes came down to Kingsville in February 1980, and several weeks later, she was hired onto the Kingsville force. In the history of the Kingsville Police Department, no woman had made it past probation to become a permanent member of the sworn service, although several had tried.

But Judy had a very firm determination around her soft-spoken manner. By that summer, she had made probation and had become Officer Hayes, Kingsville's first full-time female officer. She was assigned to the patrol division, day shift. Judy wore her brown hair short and spoke with a deliberate and businesslike manner when she dealt with the public, the way she thought it should be. As a groundbreaker, she felt there was more pressure on her. When a male rookie did something wrong, it was blown out of proportion about tenfold. Hayes found that when she made a rookie mistake, it was magnified a hundred times.

She had been on the force exactly six months and four days when she handled her first sexual assault case. It was a burglary and rape on September 7, 1980, at an apartment building just a few blocks south of the police station. Just after 1:00 A.M., she got a call from a fellow officer who told her they had a distraught rape victim who wanted to tell her story to a female officer. Judy got dressed quickly and hurried down to headquarters at Sixth Street and Yoakum Avenue. Hayes interviewed the victim and was assigned to write up the complete report, staying up into the early hours of Sunday morning to do it. When she came in for her patrol shift Monday morning, she found herself summoned to the captain's office. She figured she had made a mistake on the report and was about to be chewed out.

Captain George Gomez was a gruff career cop with wiry salt-and-pepper hair. He took his duties seriously, and usually found he was most effective when he bypassed the niceties. He was about as subtle as a two-by-four upside the head. He liked to get involved in his squad's investigations, whether they invited him or not. At this point in his career, Gomez sported a girth that was a little greater than his rookie days, and his lungs were a lot blacker from years of sucking on cigarettes. But still, Captain Gomez enjoyed his work as much as he did his first day on the job.

Hayes walked over to meet with Gomez, wondering where she might have tripped up. This was the first time she had taken a sexual assault report, and she hoped she had not done something that jeopardized the case, about which she found herself taking an intense personal interest.

Gomez was lost in a slow-moving cloud of cigarette smoke, reading through the report, when Hayes got to his office door. He told her to take a seat.

"Why did you end up doing this report start to finish?" Gomez asked her, in a way that betrayed no motive for the question.

"I got a call from the detective at home, and he said the victim wanted to speak with a woman," Hayes told him.

Gomez looked unsmilingly straight at her for a second, then spoke without changing his expression.

"You got poked in the eyes, Hayes," he said.

Judy looked at him, puzzled about what he meant.

"He didn't want to do the paperwork, so he dished off the whole thing to you," he explained. "The victim didn't ask for a woman officer."

Gomez quickly went back to reading over the paperwork. Hayes found that she was not at all surprised at her captain's revelation, once she reconsidered the previous morning's circumstances. If the men in the department were squeamish about interviewing a woman who had just been emotionally devastated by the crime of rape, Hayes knew she would step right in. They could only imagine how those women felt; Hayes knew. She didn't know many women who could honestly say that they had never been gripped by the threat of rape even in some of the most innocent settings, something men could never live with day to day. But it was a recurring reality in women's lives.

Gomez asked Hayes a few questions about her report, asked her to define a word she had used, and then set the papers aside. Lighting another cigarette, the captain finally looked Hayes straight in the eye again.

"Hayes, we have an opening here in detectives," Gomez told her. "Put in for it."

"Yes, captain," Judy replied with a touch of surprise. She smiled now. She took his attitude as a compliment, his statement as an order. Soon after, Hayes was put on half time as a detective, and half time on patrol. After two weeks of that, she became a full-time detective.

Over the next eight months, Hayes was dismayed by the amount of experience she gathered interviewing sexual assault victims, about ten in all not counting women who managed to frighten off intruders in their homes. Most of these cases were taking place in the few hours sandwiched on either side of midnight. Many of them were also burglaries. After filtering out the cases where the victims knew their assailants, or cases that were cleared by arrests, the detectives looked at what remained and saw that the same methods were being used, and similar words were being said.

The early cases seemed to indicate a Hispanic suspect. The women thought their attacker, whose face they never saw before their eyes were covered, spoke with a Mexican accent. But after the new year kicked in, victims began to report that the assailant sounded like a black man with an odd accent. Because many of the victims were Kingsville newcomers unfamiliar with the nuances of local accents, police did not know whether there were in fact two rapists—a Hispanic and a black—or one man with a weird accent. Judy Hayes was assigned to take statements from nearly every one of the women of Kingsville who had been raped. And the most recent, Sue Wilson, hit close to home. Hayes lived in the same neighborhood.

With a couple weeks of leave due him in July, Eddie decided he wanted to get away from Kingsville for a while. It seemed like a spur-of-the-moment decision to Ronda.

He called his brother in Galveston and asked if there was some extra construction work he could do for him to earn some money on the side. The family needed some financial breathing room. His brother was happy to accommodate him and arranged some work. When Eddie told Ronda about his plan to go to Galveston, he made it very clear that he was speaking in the singular. He did not say, "We're going." He said, "I'm going."

Ronda was feeling pretty lonely in her new town, and she began to yearn to go along, even if Eddie was planning to work most of the time. But she had only been on the job at Angle Medical Center for about six weeks, and did not think she could get a week off so soon. She kept dropping hints around Eddie, however, that she would ask the doctor to let her off so she and the kids could go to Galveston with him. But every time she said she was thinking of asking for the time off, Eddie changed the subject.

Ronda was angry at Eddie for wanting to go alone, but she

decided not to fight. After spending so much emotional energy trying to cheer up her husband, helping their friends throw parties and barbecues for him, sticking by him through that big misunderstanding about the trespassing charge, she had lost the will to stage a big stand. The stress level around the house on Mesquite Avenue was high enough. Maybe, Ronda thought, it would be good for her and the kids to have some time without Eddie.

One thought that had not yet occurred to Ronda was that her marriage itself might be dying. Ronda was not ready for that. Whatever it was that was keeping her husband from touching her, from kissing her passionately, from making love to her, it was something she believed could and would be fixed. If she had nothing else, Ronda had faith. It was what made her such an optimistic and pleasant person to be around.

South Texas was gripped by heavy humidity and heat when Eddie left for Galveston on Wednesday, July 8. So he took the Dodge, which had air-conditioning. That left Ronda the Valiant and its disintegrating muffler. Her telephone had been out of order for nearly a week, and a repairman was not expected to arrive until the weekend. That would prevent Eddie from phoning after he got to Galveston.

After Eddie departed, Ronda took the children to their day-care home and went on to work, hopeful that things would go smoothly while her husband was away. At least this time, she thought, he would not be gone for six or eight months like he was on the Mediterranean cruises. She soon discovered, though, that this would be a very trying period.

At the end of the day, Ronda started to draw a cool bath for her little girl Diana to escape the sticky weather. When the water was high enough, Ronda turned the valve, but the bathtub faucet would not shut off. She rousted a neighbor, who cut off the main water line to the entire house until it could be fixed. The next day, while trying to turn the water back on, a family friend accidently shut off the natural gas line. The landlady told Ronda she would have to wait until Monday to have the water fixed. On Saturday, the phone company repairman did not show up as promised.

In just four days' time, Ronda had accumulated enough frustration in her husband's absence to make up another six-month cruise. It reminded her of how much she needed Eddie, who if he were home would have had everything shipshape in short order. She felt lost without Eddie there to take care of these things, and it reinforced for her just how dependent she had become on him as a provider. As she and the children sweltered in the heat that weekend, she wondered what Eddie was up to in Galveston. Probably having a good time without her, she figured.

Eddie returned to Kingsville on July 16. Ronda thought he might have felt a little guilt over spending that "vacation" away from his family, because he suggested that they pack up the kids and head over to Padre Island National Seashore for some time at the beach. The time away seemed to have brightened his outlook, Ronda sensed. For a brief time, they were a happy family again. Whatever frustrations had been building up in Eddie, they appeared to have been washed away during his absence, and Ronda noticed how easily a smile came to her husband's face as he let Paul and Diana bury him in the sand on Padre.

Several more sexual assaults occurred in Kleberg County while Eddie was away in Galveston, and the resulting news coverage started to rivet the community's attention on the growing problem. On July 9, a man out in the county south of Kingsville tried to rape a sixty-year-old woman who was confined to a wheelchair. She struggled and he was unable to get her out of the chair, so he fled. That touched off a huge search involving the Kleberg sheriff, U.S. Border Patrol, Texas Department of Public Safety, and the Texas Rangers. On Sunday, the front-page headline in the *Kingsville Record* brought the terror of rape right into people's living rooms: "Manhunt fails to find suspect in rape attempt."

On the same day that headline appeared, another rape took place. Down on Highway 77, which shoots south-southeast like a beeline out of Kingsville for fifteen miles until it bisects the town of Riviera, nineteen-year-old Julie Brooks was headed home late at night when her car broke down just a few miles south of Ricardo. Julie had been standing by her car for a while, watching headlights whiz by in both directions, before a southbound car pulled to a stop behind her. But it was not a roadside samaritan at the wheel. Instead, the man who stopped forced Julie into his car, took her off the main road, and raped her. This crime, being nearly five miles south of the Kingsville city limits, fell to the Kleberg County Sheriff to investigate.

The rapes and attempted sexual assaults that had been taking place over the previous ten months had been chronicled mostly through small news stories printed on inside pages of the *Record*. But little by little, awareness was growing around Kingsville that there was a serious sexual assault problem in their quiet corner of Texas. Women on the Texas A&I campus began to walk around in groups at night for safety. Rape had finally hit the front page.

The Wyatts did not subscribe to the local paper, which perhaps had added to Ronda's feeling of isolation in the community. Her church activities—the women's Bible study, the home fellowship, and her singing—were Ronda's touchstones for what was going on around her. Among the churchwomen, little was said about the rapes, so Ronda was only vaguely aware of the growing problem. She was much more concerned with the continued deterioration of her relationship with Eddie, whose animation after returning from Galveston had quickly given way to depression. One night shortly after they had come back from the beach, on a rare occasion when Eddie went to bed at the same time as she, Ronda wanted to make love. Their rare sessions of lovemaking in recent months had consisted almost exclusively of Ronda masturbating Eddie. But this night, Ronda wanted to have intercourse. Eddie usually took a long time to climax, but this night, after trying for a half hour, he stopped. He simply quit and rolled over to his side of the bed.

Ronda was devastated. She felt degraded and used. Why was he bothering to go through the motions of intercourse when there was no apparent desire behind it? She began to believe that Eddie was with her not because he loved her but because he was married to her, trapped with a woman he evidently felt was not even attractive enough to have sex with twice a year. She made up her mind that she was not going to ask him to make love again, not out of some sense of retribution, but out of a compelling need to avoid facing up to her own unworthiness. The rejection simply hurt too much.

It was sometime during the winter months that Judy Hayes first began to realize that a serial rapist was prowling Kingsville. There was a grouping of assaults that fit together by virtue of their similarities. Usually, they appeared incidental to a home burglary in the late night or early morning hours. But perhaps rape was the primary motive for the break-ins.

Other aspects tied this particular group of assaults together: the man used a similar method to get into the house; a weapon was used, usually a knife; and the women reported the same words being said by their attacker. All of these were indications that there might be one man developing a set pattern for his rapes. The women had not seen the man's face because he attacked swiftly when they were not looking, but some of them had a clear impression from hearing him speak that he was Hispanic. Some saw his arm or his leg, and said he was a caucasian.

As spring unfolded, two distinct strains emerged in the evidence. Some victims began to give different accounts of the words being said by their attacker. At one point, women who were raped began to tell police that their attacker sounded like a black man, not a Hispanic. Some said his voice sounded like a black man with an odd accent. Finally, one rape victim told police that she saw the attacker's arm around her neck, and it was definitely a black man. Hayes and the other detectives came to the alarming conclusion that not one but two serial rapists were working the town. They began to regroup their unsolved cases under either the black or the Hispanic assailants.

After investigating the rape of Sue Wilson, police tentatively lumped her case with those they believed were being committed by the Hispanic rapist. Many elements were the same. The late-night burglary through a back or side window, the swift attack, the knife, even the general tenor of the attacker's words were similar to the modus operandi of the earlier cases attributed to the Hispanic rapist. One major element, however, was different.

She was raped anally. While this was a new twist, it was not unusual for serial rapists to evolve new methods during the course of their crimes. The urgent thing to police was that the Wilson rape was number fourteen. They had to come up with a war plan.

Captain Gomez gathered his detectives, and they decided that the problem was greater than six detectives working eight-hour shifts could address on duty. Nearly every rape was occurring around the midnight hour. On their own time, the detectives decided to flood the west side with overnight surveillance. Most of the assaults were taking place on the west side of the Missouri Pacific tracks, where the college campus was located. Generally, they were occurring south of Texas A&I. The Wyatts lived four blocks east of the campus's northeast corner, yet none of the assaults had taken place in that neighborhood. Campus police had jurisdiction on the grounds, although Kingsville police worked closely with the private security force.

Based on partial descriptions of the Hispanic rapist, police put together a composite sketch and placed it in the newspaper. Almost immediately, calls started coming in. Men who had the misfortune of resembling the sketch were dragged in for questioning. One luckless soul's resemblance was so uncanny, he was reported eight times by alert citizens.

When the sheer volume of information became too great to manage, Gomez went out and got a wide roll of butcher block paper. The detectives unraveled a fifteen-foot-long section of it, tacked it up on a wall at the station, and used it to build an information matrix. They pored back over the records of each case. Then, on the paper, they listed each crime and broke out its many elements. They noted the time each occurred, the day of the week, the locations, the progression from one neighborhood to another. They listed attributes of each victim, such as their ages and whether they were blond, brunette, or redhead. They recorded how the rapist got into the house; whether he had a knife or a gun, or was unarmed; what sexual acts he used in assaulting the victim; whether he was Anglo, Hispanic, black, or unknown.

Gomez even told his investigators to find out the phase of the moon at the time of each crime. He firmly believed that the full moon brought out the kooks.

The matrix helped establish what they knew, but it was also a visual reminder of how much more they did not know. With this information, crews of detectives and a few patrol officers regrouped at the squad room about 9:00 P.M. on most nights, talked about where they might station themselves based on what the matrix revealed, and headed out for lonely and tiring nights of waiting and watching. Gomez put out requests for special equipment for the surveillance effort. The King Ranch provided a huge telescopic lens mounted on a rifle stock. Texas A&I contributed a special-frequency, voice-activated radio system, so the officers could talk quietly with each other through the night without fear of being picked up on a police scanner. They had standard binoculars, plus a night-vision scope that could pierce the darkness to enhance images in the shadows.

The detectives paired off for the grueling schedule of late-night stakeouts. Judy Hayes's partner was Detective Hector Treviño, a brawny south Texas native and ex-marine with a degree in criminal justice from Texas A&I. He had worked part-time with the Kingsville Police Department while he went to school, and stayed on full time after he graduated.

Police expected to see people at all hours, especially near the college campus. But the reality was they found few places to station themselves without looking conspicuous. So the spotters got up on rooftops, hopped on bicycles, padded around on foot, and found other ways of quietly keeping watch over their town. They climbed into alley garbage bins, using their binoculars to scan through the little slit between the lid and the rim. They usually stayed out until three or four in the morning, the latest that any of the rapes had occurred. They would then report for their regular shifts, Judy Hayes at eight, and the rest of the squad at nine.

The results were surprising, but not in the way they had hoped. They saw some weird goings-on at the oddest hours, and caught a good number of Peeping Toms. Hayes and Treviño were doing a stakeout near the Harrel Elementary School, down the street from where Sue Wilson was raped, and caught three window peepers in that neighborhood on the same night. It was typical for window-peepers to develop into rapists. But police caught no rapists during the stakeouts. In fact, several times when citizens called police to report suspicious characters crawling into trash cans in the alleys, the uniformed patrol officers ended up "busting" their undercover colleagues. A few times residents themselves challenged the plainclothes detectives when they found them wandering around late at night.

How come these people spotted the cops so quickly, Gomez wondered, but no one had ever spotted the rapists?

Seeing Eddie mired in his depression, with nothing she could do or say to relieve him, Ronda suggested that he get counseling with Pastor Fields. Eddie had firmly resisted Ronda when she asked him to consider going to a professional therapist, telling her the last thing he would do was go to a "nut doctor." Ronda thought Eddie would consider talking to the pastor as a compromise. But again, he said no. He liked James Fields, he told her, but he simply felt that his depression was something he would have to work out on his own. He could handle it, he insisted.

At that, Ronda decided to take a more active approach. She went over to visit Pastor Fields and asked him to befriend Eddie and counsel him.

Fields was aware that the Wyatts were among many young families in his flock in which the husband was staying away from church. He told Ronda he would be happy to call on Eddie. Ronda was relieved. If one thing stood out in the partnership that was the ministry of James and Dolores Fields, it was their utilitarian approach. They were able to see their people's problems, dissect them, and find biblically based solutions to them. If James Fields could break through Eddie's wall, Ronda knew, he would be able to hand him the tools to build himself up again.

After Ronda's visit, Fields called on Eddie socially, as his pastor. He tried to learn as much about him as he could. The young man struck Fields as shy but also deeply troubled. Eddie

lapsed into his familiar plaint about the painful years of his childhood, finishing with the death of his dad prior to either the father
or the son developing the will to reestablish contact. James heard
about Eddie's father abandoning the big family and about the
father's alcoholism and gambling. In the course of their conversation, Pastor Fields discovered that they both were in love with
the water. Eddie had been considering underwater welding as a
specialty, to match his career with his childhood love of swimming. The pastor had a passion for scuba diving, which had grown
greater as his eyesight began to fail and the underwater magni-
fication effect allowed him rare vision. So they loaded the pastor's
scuba gear into Eddie's car and drove over to the South Park
Apartments, where the Wyatts' friends Dave and Peggy Houser
were living. The complex included a small swimming pool. There,
James showed Eddie how to put on the equipment, and they
spent a good part of the afternoon submerged.

As James found Eddie laughing and smiling with the activity,
he wondered what it was that troubled the young man so. If Eddie
could enjoy himself so much without that cloud of depression,
what was it about being around Ronda and his children that
seemed to make the task so impossible? Gut instinct told James
Fields that Eddie Wyatt had something troubling him that went
beyond simple sorrow over a father he never knew.

Returning from a night out for dinner, a Kingsville couple opened
the front door to their west-side home one night late in July and
found they had been burglarized. They called the police and, after
taking a quick inventory, gave the officers a list of things that
had been stolen. The police did a check of the area for clues,
and out in the alley and down a bit from the house, they discovered the homeowners' television set had been stashed in an out-
of-the-way place, with a blanket thrown over it. Apparently, the
burglar could not carry off everything at once, and planned to
return later for the television. After completing their investigation
at the scene, most of the officers left. But two stayed behind and
hid in the alley to keep watch on the television.

After hours spent crouched in the shadows, the detectives

were rewarded. Shortly after dawn, they heard footsteps nearby. The person's pace sounded hesitant, but eventually he made his way into the alley. Soon, the sequestered detectives spotted a black man approching. They watched as the man scanned the area, then went over to the blanket. He pulled the blanket aside and began to lift the television.

"Freeze!" one of the detectives yelled. The man stopped short, obeyed, and was handcuffed and arrested.

Down at the station, the suspect, Billy Joe Garner, was fingerprinted, photographed, and booked on suspicion of burglary. A nominal bond was set. Garner raised it and was released in quick order.

Police continued their west-side surveillance campaign as August approached. Then, on the very first night in August, a Saturday, a call came into the station at about 4:00 A.M. from a twenty-year-old woman on West Alice Avenue, up near the college campus. The rapist had hit again. Hayes, Treviño, and others hurried up to the house to gather as many details as they could.

The victim, Mary Mosher, told Hayes that she was asleep in her bed when she was attacked at about 3:00 A.M. by a man who pounced swiftly on top of her and covered her face with a pillow. He then tied her hands behind her back. She did not get a look at him. Over the next forty-five minutes, the man raped Mary twice before leaving through the window screen he had sliced to gain entry. Mary told Hayes that her impression was the man was Hispanic.

The facts from the Mary Mosher case went up on the butcher block paper matrix, and the detectives went back out into the streets and alleys of the west side. They felt intense pressure to crack these cases, stemming more from their own sense of professional pride than from the public outcry over the rapes. The longer the cases remained unsolved, the more their egos were bruised.

Subscribers read about the Alice Avenue rape in the *Record* when the next semi-weekly issue hit the streets on Wednesday. But even before they got to read about it, that very morning a rapist struck again in the same neighborhood. This time the victim was another twenty-year-old woman, asleep in her bed, and with three children asleep in nearby rooms of the apartment on North

Third Street. The rapist cut his way through a window screen in the room in which she was sleeping. Amy Hume did not sense the man's presence until she awoke at about 3:40 A.M. with a knife pressed to her neck. As in most previous cases, the rapist quickly covered the victim's face before he sexually assaulted her.

Judy Hayes was beginning to reel from the volume of pain and suffering she encountered while interviewing the city's rape victims. Her superiors declined to classify the several women whose screams had frightened men out of their bedrooms, as in the June 8 case on East Kenedy Avenue, as victims of an attempted sexual assault. But Judy Hayes felt those women had been violated also, and should be interviewed as such. At least, even if a rape had not been committed, she felt police should be obtaining the facts of those cases to compare with the successful assaults up on the matrix. She believed the attempts could contain a clue missing from the rape cases that could lead to the suspects.

But her hands were full enough with the victims who had been raped. Whether she first met them at the scene, at the hospital, or at police headquarters, she did her in-depth interrogation in a small closet of a room off the detective squad office. It was a cold and uninviting place for her to try to draw out the details of such a horrible crime. She never knew how any of the women, with their unique personality traits, their own fears and problems, was going to react. She sat in the Kleberg Memorial Hospital emergency room with one victim, only hours after the rape, and the two of them became giddy and told jokes. She had been with women who remained hysterical the entire time, even though she tried to assure them that they were out of danger. She had been with one who was so traumatized by the experience that she absolutely blocked everything from her mind, and for an entire day could remember nothing about what had happened to her.

The detectives did not have to wait long for Billy Joe Garner to stumble back into their clutches. On a weeknight in the second week of August, Garner slipped his way into a west-side house where he thought the woman inside was sleeping. She was not. In fact, Donna Fair was very much awake and alert. She had a small lamp on her desk, which did not give off much light, so to the outside it appeared the entire house was dark. She was reading a book there very late one evening when she thought she heard a noise in the house. It sounded like it came from her kitchen.

Garner, making his way through the kitchen, moved a glass from the kitchen table to the sink counter. That was the noise Donna heard. She craned her neck toward the hallway when suddenly Garner came into view. She screamed at him to get out of her house, and having lost all element of surprise, Garner obligingly zipped out of the window.

Plainclothes police were nearby on their nightly ritual of alley and trash bin checks, so they quickly made it over to Fair's house to interview her. While relating the events to Hayes and the other detectives, she glanced over at her countertop and saw the drinking glass on it.

"I left that glass on the table," she said, with a puzzled tone of voice. Another detective walked over and put his face close to the glass. The swirly lines were clear.

"Bingo!" he said. It was a great, big thumbprint, as distinct as in the police textbooks. Back at the station, a technician lifted the print while detectives pulled the files on known black burglars. There were not that many in Kingsville, and because of Garner's recent arrest, his was one of the first they examined. It was a perfect match.

Garner ran when the cops came after him, but he was quickly caught and charged with another burglary. There had been no attempt at a sexual assault on Donna Fair, so he was not charged with any sex crime. But in interviewing him, detectives noticed a funny accent. Garner had come from Louisiana, and there still was an edge to his Cajun accent. That jibed with the accounts of victims who said their attacker sounded like a black man, but with a weird accent. Also, the way he had gotten into Fair's house, the time of night, the neighborhood, and other clues on the matrix told Gomez and his squad that chances were good this was their black rapist. They had no proof of it, but their police instincts told them it was so.

Now they believed that there was only one more guy to get.

CHAPTER 7

GREEN TAPE

Surely my prayers of late have been unacceptable. What should be done? Eddie so obviously needs help. He is just being pulled downstream by the current, often he goes under, and each time the struggle to come up again is weaker. Surely it is not wrong for me to want someone along the way to throw him a lifeline . . . or better yet, to go in after him. I love him so much, and it is a helpless feeling to watch the one you love drowning in the waters of his own life. I am so weary, I don't even know how to pray. My heart is crushed so badly because the man given to me is hurting. He just seems to be existing.
—from Ronda's diary

With the jailing of Billy Joe Garner, two quiet weeks went by with no reports of any sexual assaults. But in the dark morning hours of August 24, a woman called police to report that she had been raped, and Judy Hayes was summoned to interview her. There were sixteen cases strung out on the detectives' matrix, and Hayes found a personal reason to make this seventeenth case the last. The rape occurred in twenty-two-year-old Kim Sullivan's house on Lantana Drive, only two blocks from the house where Sue Wilson was raped in June. Both of those houses were in Hayes's neighborhood.

Much of the story Kim Sullivan told Detective Hayes was familiar. She said that she had gotten into bed about one-fifteen and was going to sleep when a man pounced quickly on top of her. He apparently had gotten into the house by slicing a window screen. All she saw was a figure rushing at her, face concealed by a ski mask. In his right hand was a gun. He succeeded in penetrating her vagina and he angrily thrust into her, quickly achieving climax. Then, after only a short interval, he turned her around and raped her anally. He warned her not to go to the police, or he would return with his gun and rape her again.

There were two crucial differences in Kim's account from those already drawn out on the matrix. First, Kingsville's burglar-rapists had always covered their victims' faces with whatever happened to be handy—pulling their shirts up over their faces, throwing the bedclothes over their heads. This time the rapist came prepared. Moments after he jumped on Sullivan, the attacker began to wrap tape around her head. It was a strong, duct-repair type of tape, about an inch wide. He encircled her head several times, covering her eyes completely. The tape was a new element. It could indicate another rapist, perhaps a copycat spurred on by news reports of the increasing sexual assault problem. Or it could be the Hispanic rapist evolving a more sophisticated routine, bringing his so-called rape kit along with him instead of relying on whatever material might be available.

But that was where the second major difference threw a twist into the investigation. Kim Sullivan was emphatic that her attacker was an Anglo male, not a Hispanic. Up on the matrix, there were other cases in which the victims described their rapist as "possibly" an Anglo, judging purely from the voice. But many of the victims were from outside of south Texas and were unsure of the local accents. Kim Sullivan was from down the road in Riviera. She knew the local accents. When she said Anglo, not Hispanic, she had credibility. The detectives looked for ways to reconcile the differences in the Kim Sullivan rape with the other cases.

The latest rape escalated the news coverage in the *Record*. On Wednesday, August 26, the story hit the front page under the headline: "Lantana Street woman third rape victim." It was unheard of in Kingsville to record three rapes in the same month.

There was not much time to investigate the new case before detectives had to move again. Four nights after Kim Sullivan was raped, an intruder broke into another house on the same block of Lantana Drive. A forty-four-year-old woman was awakened by the noise, saw the man, and screamed. This time, he ran off. When the woman told police about the intruder, she gave the same description as that of the man who had raped her neighbor down the street four days earlier. This marked the fourth time that particular two-block area near the Harrel School had been targeted.

Four days after the last Lantana Drive break-in, Kingsville was socked in with heat and humidity. Cheryl Palmer was feeling hot and sticky, but on her limited budget she could not afford an air conditioner. The eighteen-year-old Texas A&I student lived near the campus in an inexpensive alley apartment, located off busy, noisy Santa Gertrudis Avenue. It was 2:00 A.M., and Cheryl lay naked in her bed, sleeping too soundly to hear the man who came in through the alley door. Cheryl awoke only when he jumped on her bed and placed his hand over her mouth to stifle her screams. She felt something sharp against her neck.

"If you scream," the man said, "I'll shove this ice pick right into your throat." Cheryl was too terrified to scream. The man grabbed her torso and roughly turned her over onto her stomach. Then he pulled out a roll of silver duct tape and wrapped it around Cheryl's head several times so that her eyes were covered.

Then, as she lay helpless on her bed, the attacker stripped off his clothes and straddled her on his haunches.

"I want you to suck me," he ordered her, lowering his penis near her mouth. Cheryl tried to remain calm and keep her wits about her, aware that he might carry out his threat to stab her.

"All right," she obeyed. "Tell me how long you want me to do it." Cheryl could hear the man moaning as she fellated him. When he had had enough of that, however, he moved her down on her back and put himself flat on top of her. He moved her legs and forced himself into her vagina. A stream of filthy epithets poured from him while he built to an orgasm.

"You whore!" the man said angrily as he spasmed.

Things quieted for a short time, but Cheryl could hear that the man was still in her apartment. Then he returned to the bed and ordered her to her knees. Pushing her over so that her buttocks were thrust upward, he penetrated her anus and proceeded to rape her in that fashion, climaxing again after several minutes. Afterward, she lay in pain on the bed, his semen dripping from her body, as he retrieved his clothes and got dressed. Before he left, he threatened to come back and get her if she called the police.

As soon as she was certain the man was gone, Cheryl ran to her phone and telephoned the police. She was one of the strongest victims the detectives had seen, offering detailed information about the attack almost with detached thoroughness.

Gomez's detectives felt besieged. The frequency of the attacks had increased to four rapes in the last month. In the next edition of the *Kingsville Record*, on the streets only thirty-six hours after Cheryl Palmer was raped, Chief of Police Gerard Gutierrez tried to keep the public informed without arousing panic.

"Latest rape not believed related to others," the headline read. Gutierrez was quoted as saying that more than one of the rapes over the summer may have been committed by the same man, but there were enough differences in the latest one to believe there may be more than one person committing them. He warned women that all the information detectives had developed indicated that the rapists were window peepers. "So the women should be a little more careful about how they are dressed when their windows are open," he said—as though the woman's state of undress rather than the man's predispositon was the reason for the attack.

The rest of the summer after Eddie's return from Galveston was a lonely time for Ronda. She did a lot of thinking, reassessing her relationship with her aloof husband. As summer went on, Eddie seemed to cut back even further on the time he spent with his family. Ronda tried to be understanding about it. She reasoned that he was upset at his lack of sexual appetite. That, combined with a general sense of failure in his life, made him feel inadequate not only as a husband but as a father as well. He was spending less time with the children, particularly with Paul.

Dave Houser seemed to be the only person with whom Eddie could talk. The two navy buddies frequently went down to the deserted shoreline, along the Cayo del Grullo or the Laguna Salada, where there was an abandoned naval airfield site where

they could cast their lines. They got to know many of Kleberg
County's back roads. It was lonely territory, and these two men,
who had shared much of their misery since joining the navy,
could talk things out. Dave was hardly in a position to offer
constructive advice, but he seemed to understand Eddie. Or
maybe it was just the mellowing effects of stretching out in the
grass near their fishing lines, drinking a couple of six packs of
beer, and smoking several joints that made all their problems
seem a little less intimidating. They never caught many fish, but
that didn't matter, for this was the only time Eddie appeared to
be free of his frustrations.

When September came, Paul was enrolled in kindergarten at
Harrel Elementary, near the scene of four of the attacks. Ronda
threw herself more ardently than ever into her church activities.
She found a special refuge in those Wednesday home fellowships
that Pastor Fields established earlier that year. It helped to foster
strong emotional bonds with which Ronda compensated for the
absence of love at home. It gave her a sense of worth that was
missing in her marriage. Ronda was comfortably matched in the
group that met in the home of James and Barbara Crowell. The
Crowells exhibited the same kind of loving acceptance and counsel that Ronda had found in Pastor Fields, yet she could not tell
them the full story of her domestic situation. While she confided
to her fellowship group that her husband was very quiet and
sometimes got depressed, she could not tell them that he seemed
deeply troubled, that it was making her feel terribly inadequate
as a wife, and, even more specifically, that she and Eddie had
not experienced true sexual intimacy in over a year.

She made friends, but Ronda's need to maintain appearances
ensured that they were only skin deep. Ronda appeared to be a
typical, young, working mother of the 1980s, harried by a seemingly unmanageable schedule and frazzled by the demands of a
dual-career life, but no more or less than many other wives. Inside,
however, Ronda seethed with frustration, hoping that someone,
just once, would see through her self-defense and reach the confused and hurting child within.

Ronda's days were full. Before leaving for work, she drove
Paul to school or put him on the bus. Then she took Diana, aged

three, over to Sharon Lawson's house for day care. Even when Eddie worked the night shift, and was home during the day, he was either too tired or had other things to do, and so was not enthusiastic about watching the children.

One day late in the summer, Ronda happened to come home for lunch and smelled a sweet, smoky odor in the house. Although she had never smelled marijuana before, friends had described it to her and she knew instantly that's what it was. Eddie blamed it on some friends who had dropped by the house that morning. Ronda told him she did not approve of it, and Eddie said he would see that they stopped. Then one morning a few weeks later, Ronda smelled the odor again, this time in the utility room off the kitchen. When she confronted Eddie, he admitted he had used it a few times because it helped him get through the day. Ronda begged him to stop, saying it would make his problems worse. Eddie once more promised her that he would stop.

At around the same time, Ronda began to smell alcohol on Eddie's breath. It disturbed her that he was returning to the destructive behavior of his teen years. When she tried to talk with him about it, he again claimed to need the alcohol to deal with his depression. He was concerned that she not tell the children about it.

Late one night, Eddie and Dave Houser were drinking in a private club near the naval station when Peggy Houser stormed through the door. Peggy, more aggressive than Ronda in handling her husband, apparently had gone to the trouble of tracking Dave down.

"Just what do you think you're doing in here while I'm sitting at home waiting!" she demanded.

"Man, your wife ought to be a detective," Eddie whispered to Dave. As he watched his contrite friend being hauled off home, Eddie thought of his own wife, slammed down the rest of his drink, and hurried home. When he got there, he told Ronda the story of Peggy storming into the room full of men and dragging Dave out, tail between his legs.

"I can't believe she would do something like that," Eddie declared, shaking his head in wonder. "She must've followed us or something."

"Well, maybe I should do something like that," Ronda answered. "I've thought about following you to see just what you do with all your time."

"Have you, uh, have you ever done that, honeybun?" Eddie stammered.

"No, Eddie, I haven't," she replied. Eddie seemed relieved, and changed the subject. Ronda knew it was something she would never do. Amid her confusion over why Eddie was so depressed, so lethargic, she still trusted in his good judgment.

On Thursday night, September 3, with the news of Cheryl Palmer's rape only a day old, Shelly Polk put her young daughter to bed and waited until she went to sleep. Shelly's husband, Jim, was going to be home late, about midnight, after closing up the fast-food restaurant he managed. Shelly decided to shower and wash her long red hair before Jim got home. The Polks had only been in Kingsville about three months, following Jim's transfer to the Kingsville franchise. Shelly, twenty-seven, was from the Midwest, and south Texas was a strange new place to her. Their house, a blond-brick rancher, was a good two miles south and east from the center of all the west-side rapes. It was close to the South Park apartment complex where Dave and Peggy Houser lived, where Eddie and Pastor Fields had played with the scuba equipment in the apartment pool.

On the rear wall of the Polk house was a set of glass patio doors giving out into the backyard, which ended at a waist-high chain-link fence along the alley.

About 11:00 P.M., as Shelly got ready for her shower, a man entered her yard by hopping over the fence from the alley. He sneaked up to the back windows of the house and looked inside. Shelly was beginning to undress in her bedroom. The man walked over to the sliding patio doors and jimmied them open. Shelly put on a robe, and after she turned on the shower to warm the water up, she heard a door open. Thinking it was Jim, she turned and started for the doorway.

In an instant, the stranger was on her. The man's head was

covered by a dark ski mask, and he had a gun in his hand. At first, Shelly reached out and grabbed the gun barrel.

"Don't fight me, or I'll hurt you," the man threatened her. Shelly immediately released the gun. The man grabbed a tight fistful of her red locks and yanked her toward the living room, where he shoved her down on the couch. He began to wrap colored duct tape around her head several times so that the inch-wide tape covered her eyes completely. Then he pulled Shelly's wrists together behind her back and taped them as well.

Leaving her helpless on the couch, the intruder rummaged around the house. She heard him going through her purse and rifling her jewelry box. Soon he returned to the couch and grabbed her hair again, pulling her back into the bedroom, right past her sleeping daughter's room. Flinging her onto the bed, the man turned loose a stream of filthy names aimed at the frightened woman.

The man then parted Shelly's robe down the front, exposing her. He bore down on her naked body and forced his erection into her, pressing her into the bed as she cried in pain. He cursed her with every thrust while coming to a quick climax. When he pulled out of her, Shelly was convinced that he was about to kill her. The man had seemed to get angrier during the rape. She waited in silence a short time before the man came back to the bed and turned her over onto her stomach. He ordered her to draw up her knees, and Shelly felt the man's renewed erection attempting to enter her from behind. With great pain for Shelly, the man succeeded in getting into her anus, and he raped her again. Shelly pictured herself being murdered by this man, in her own bed. She was also terrified to think that he would kill her young daughter.

The rapist finally withdrew from her after his second orgasm. Instead of killing her, he issued a vile succession of threats aimed at her and her family should she be stupid enough to go to the cops. The threats were so severe that after the man made his escape, Shelly blacked out from her memory all that had happened in the previous half hour.

*   *   *

When Jim Polk arrived home a little past midnight, he found his wife bound and half-naked on the bed, unable to talk. He first checked on his daughter, then he called the police to report that he believed his wife had been raped.

Captain Gomez alerted the entire detective squad. If Shelly Polk had indeed been raped, it was the fourth incident in just ten days, each showing an escalating level of brutality. The rapist was getting physically rougher with his victims, but he was also becoming psychologically crueler. Not only was it so soon on the heels of the Cheryl Palmer rape, but there was an added twist to the new case. If indeed it was a break-in and rape, it would mean that the detectives' concentrated efforts on the west side had all been in vain. The rapist was not geographically locked into the neighborhoods west of the tracks. Now it would be impossible to predict with any reliability when or where the next rape might occur.

Judy Hayes was the last detective to arrive at the house. Her colleagues were having a hard time trying to establish what had happened based only on the vague clues available. Hayes tried to prod Shelly's memory, but without success. She was taken to Kleberg Memorial Hospital for examination and treatment, and it became evident that she had been sexually assaulted. Hayes stayed with Shelly, in the hope that she would remember something. But that evening she did not. Hayes brought her back home for the night.

Before she had a chance to return to the Polk house the next morning, Judy Hayes got a phone call at the police station from Shelly Polk. It was 9:30 A.M.

"I need to talk with you," Shelly told her. "I woke up this morning and I started to remember things."

"I'll be right over to get you," Hayes told her.

Hayes interviewed Shelly Polk for five hours in the small interview room at detective headquarters. As she drew more and more information from the victim, she found that Shelly's memory kept improving. She remembered the man grabbing her as she emerged from the bathroom, thinking she had heard her husband. She remembered waiting, blindfolded and with wrists bound, on her couch while the man rummaged through personal belongings.

Hayes stopped her there for a minute.

"Do you know whether he took anything?" she asked Shelly.

"I'm not sure. I haven't checked," she replied.

"First thing I want you to do when you get home is go through your things to see if anything is missing," Hayes said. She took Shelly home about 3:00 P.M.

Chief Gutierrez, who had tried to project calm only days before, finally acknowledged that the sexual assault problem was out of hand. Early on Friday morning, he put out a call for a meeting later in the day at Kleberg First National Bank, which had a community room large enough for his purposes. He invited all police agencies in the area, making sure that Texas A&I campus security was notified. Naval security officers also came. The Kleberg County Sheriff sent detectives, along with the district attorney's office and the county attorney. State law enforcement officers came from the Department of Public Safety. The Kingsville office of the U.S. Border Patrol sent someone. In addition, the King Ranch sent one of its security people, and there were representatives there from the police departments in the nearby towns of Bishop and Alice, as well as the sheriff from neighboring Jim Wells County, where there were also several unsolved rapes.

Gomez brought over the roll of butcher block paper that outlined the cases to date. There now were eighteen women listed on the matrix. The detectives taped the fifteen feet of possible clues to the meeting room wall. Judy Hayes showed up for the meeting after returning from the interview with Shelly Polk. As she walked in, nearly two dozen men stopped their discussions of the evidence, and turned to her.

"Do we have another rape?" Gomez asked.

"Yes, we do," Hayes replied.

"Fill in what we need," Gomez directed Hayes, handing her a marker pen. Hayes added the new information under the name of Shelly Polk, rape victim number nineteen. Gomez crossed off the cases in which the victim reported the suspect as a black male. "We got that one," Gomez said. "Let's concentrate on the others."

Shelly Polk called Judy Hayes back later on Friday and told her that she had gone through everything in the house, and could come up with only one thing that was missing: a diamond ring valued at about $1,500. It contained a nice-sized diamond in the center, surrounded by a circle of smaller diamonds. The rapist must have taken it.

On Sunday, the Polk rape and the stepped-up investigation was the lead story in the *Kingsville Record*. The large headline read, "Sixth rape sparks session of lawmen." The newspaper count only went back as far as the Sue Wilson rape that kicked off the long summer of sexual assaults.

Gutierrez told the reporter that the meeting was held to trade information with the other law enforcement agencies. "I simply wanted to make everybody as fully aware of the rapes we're having as possible," he said. Gutierrez added that he was almost certain the rapes were being committed by more than one person. But he also tried to keep the community calm in the face of the evidence.

"There is no need to panic," Gutierrez was quoted in the paper, "but women should take precautions and report any suspicious activities. I don't think we have a fiend going around town, but the women should be careful."

Townspeople were not so certain. It seemed apparent to them that there was at least one fiend, if not more, eluding police. Many women in Kingsville were determined not to let it happen to them. Gun store owners reported an increase in couples and single women coming into their shops to pick out small-caliber specials for the ladies to handle.

Geraldo Nuñez, twenty-three, was a convicted burglar, out of jail on five years of probation. He had heard some talk on the streets that a certain apartment on the west side might contain valuable coins and jewelry. He had cased the second-story apartment and figured out how he would do it. Then, on Friday night, September 11, he saw the residents leave for a night out. Nuñez broke into the apartment, found some of the jewelry plus valuable coins, stuffed them into his pockets, and ran off.

Sergeant Mike Jones was on a routine patrol in the west side when he spotted Nuñez and called him over. Anxious to appear cooperative, Nuñez approached the cruiser. The officer asked Nuñez who he was and asked to see his identification. After the officer called in to dispatch, he was informed that Nuñez had a municipal warrant out for him, for a minor traffic citation he had ignored. So the officer cuffed Nuñez, put him in the backseat of the cruiser, and took him down to the station for booking.

Knowing that he would be searched thoroughly when he got to headquarters, Nuñez quietly reached into his pockets during the short ride, pulled out the items of jewelry he had just stolen, and shoved them deep down into the crack between the rear seat and seat back of the police car. Nuñez was processed on the traffic warrant, and quickly posted a $37 bond so he could leave.

During this time, the residents of the west-side apartment came home and discovered the burglary. They called the police, and another officer was dispatched to take the report. After Nuñez left the station, the officer who took the burglary report returned and mentioned the case to Jones. The sergeant had a hunch. He went to his patrol car and ran his hand down into the rear seat, pulling out jewelry matching the stolen items. In quick succession, the burglary victims identified the items as theirs, the police wrote out an affidavit for an arrest warrant, and the district attorney got it signed by a judge. It was the easiest arrest they would ever make, because Geraldo Nuñez soon walked back into the police station, claiming he had just been assaulted and wanting to file a complaint. Instead, he was arrested for the second time in two hours, and this time bond was set at $5,000. His family petitioned for a lower amount, and a judge cut it in half. The next day, Nuñez walked out of jail on bond.

Soon enough he was back at work. About 11:00 P.M. on Monday, he slipped on a pair of work gloves, snuck up alongside a house on the east side of the tracks, and worked the bathroom window open. Lifting himself up on the windowsill, he went inside. Marleen Grimes was in her back bedroom when she heard a sound like a door closing. Then she heard her dog begin to growl. From her bedroom door, Marleen saw a shadowy figure of a man dashing back into her bathroom. Quickly, she returned to her bed and grabbed a .38-caliber derringer she kept handy because of all the rapes.

Suddenly, Nuñez rushed into the bedroom and grabbed her. He wrapped one arm around her midsection while he shoved his hand into her face to block her view of him and to shut her up. Marleen started to yell.

"You keep quiet and you won't get hurt," he warned her.

Marleen cocked the pistol, jammed the muzzle into Nuñez's gut, and pulled the trigger. Nuñez felt a sharp, searing pain run through him. Instinctively he jumped back, grabbed his stomach, and bolted for the bathroom window. Marleen, meanwhile, fled from the house and ran to a neighbor's place to call police. Nuñez, bleeding from the stomach, stumbled west through the alley, crossed Seventh Street, stripped off his gloves and threw them into a nearby grassy area, then collapsed in the alley in the next block.

Police rushed to the scene. As Marleen told her story to some of them, others went out to search the neighborhood. Two officers came across Nuñez. He was in a lot of pain, and when he saw the officers, he begged them to finish him off right there. He was rushed into surgery at Kleberg Memorial, and doctors found the small bullet lodged near his spine. During surgery, Nuñez lost one of his kidneys, and the bullet remained stuck near his spine.

Nuñez matched the description of the Hispanic rapist. During an unsuccessful attempt earlier in the year, a woman got a good look at the suspected rapist when he broke into her house in the mistaken belief that she was asleep.

Unfortunately, there was no physical evidence placing Nuñez in Marleen Grimes's house. All they had was her word. Because Nuñez immediately ran, not a single drop of his blood had spilled until he reached the alley, well off Marleen Grimes's property. Police knew that a decent defense attorney would argue that Nuñez had been walking innocently down the alley late at night when this hysterical woman shot him for no reason. If carried to the extreme, Nuñez might even succeed in having the woman charged with attempted murder.

Judy Hayes examined the windowsill where Marleen said the burglar had gotten into the house. In the dirt and dust, she could make out a regular series of impressions, small dots lined up in rows. Marleen insisted the man she shot had been wearing gloves, but when he was found, Nuñez was bare-handed. It was Hayes who found the gloves, right where Nuñez had tossed them. They were work-style gloves with hundreds of small rubber beads on the palm-side surface. They lined up exactly with the impressions on Marleen's windowsill.

Confronted with this evidence, Nuñez later pleaded guilty to burglarizing Marleen Grimes's house and received a sentence of fifty years in prison. The bullet that remained lodged near his spine was thought by many Kingsville residents to be more than just.

Although they lacked specific evidence to link him with the unsolved rapes, detectives believed he was their Hispanic rapist. The particular way he had broken into Marleen's house was identical to the methods described by many of the rape victims. His manner, his attack, even some of his words were the same. It was plausible that the man now in custody was responsible for the crimes that had not already been checked off with the arrest of Billy Joe Garner. Kingsville police drew a deep breath and crossed their fingers. Maybe, they hoped, the nightmare was over.

When the story hit the *Kingsville Record* a day and a half later, the town erupted. "Intruder shot; condition fair," read the headline. Gun sales, which had quickened during the summer, exploded. Over the next month, police watched as incidents of sexual assault and burglaries virtually came to a halt.

Down at police headquarters, there was a pervasive feeling among the detectives that they were out from under the crisis. They looked up at the matrix and saw the nineteen women listed on it, and they clicked off the rapes they thought Billy Joe Garner had committed, then the ones they thought Geraldo Nuñez had done, and they somehow managed to fit all of them in, with the one nagging anomaly of Kim Sullivan's insistence she had been raped by an Anglo back in August. Because of the sudden cessation of the rapes over the following weeks, the nagging suspicion that another rapist was out there faded.

Judy Hayes felt relief. With the arrest of Nuñez, she was confident that Kingsville's serial rapists had finally been brought to justice. Hector Treviño felt it, too. Captain Gomez was slightly skeptical, but he hoped it was true. The proof would come with time, and it would be purely circumstantial. If the rapes ceased, then they would know they had won. When two weeks passed and the calendar turned to October without any more attacks on women, George Gomez decided the fifteen-foot-long sheet of butcher block paper could be folded up and packed away. The files were put back in drawers, and the detective operation started to return to normal.

One afternoon in late September, as Eddie was getting dressed to go to the base, Ronda walked into the bedroom and sat on the edge of the water bed. Eddie had been quieter than usual that day, and Ronda just sensed that he might need some reassuring words from her. Ronda recalled their early days of marriage, those times on Bachman Boulevard in Dallas when she looked up to Eddie so much. Then, he was the stronger of the two in their marriage, caring and affectionate, and even poetic in expressing his love. He had accepted her with all her faults, Ronda believed, and it had made her feel wonderfully secure. Now she thought that was what Eddie needed to feel, security. She knew that throughout his life, he had been abandoned by people, by his dad and his friends. Ronda was determined that Eddie would know she was not that way.

"I've been thinking a lot about us, and how depressed you've been," Ronda told him. Eddie looked uncomfortable, as he always did when Ronda started trying to draw him out. As he finished buttoning his shirt, Ronda continued. "I remember how I had a lot of doubts about myself when we were first married, and you really helped me feel good by just accepting me and loving me."

"You know, that was a real happy time for me," Eddie said.

"I know you have a lot of worries," Ronda continued, "but there's one thing I don't want you to have to worry about. That's me leaving. I'm going to be here for you. I would never walk out on you. I love you. It's difficult for you now, but I know you'll work out your depression and we'll make it."

Eddie got choked up, and tears started forming in his eyes.

"I love you, too, honeybun," he said softly. "Sometimes I feel like such a failure, and I just let it get to me. I keep it all inside of me, even though I know I shouldn't. It's good to know you're there for me."

After Eddie left for work, Ronda felt more peace than she had since midsummer.

It was well before midnight on Halloween and all the little ghosts and hobgoblins were tucked into their beds, stuffed full of candy they had received going house to house in their neighborhood. It had been nearly seven weeks since Marleen Grimes fired the shot heard 'round Kingsville, and all had been quiet since then.

Near the center of Kingsville, just west of the tracks, was an older gray building that contained eight small apartments on two floors. On the northwest ground-floor corner, a large window was lit; from the outside could be seen a young, attractive Oriental woman scantily dressed, relaxing on her sofa in front of her television set.

Kyung Ellis, twenty, was the Korean bride of navy man Bobby Ellis, who was assigned to the Naval Air Station. On Halloween night, in anticipation of her husband's return from his late shift at work, Kyung put on her sexiest nightie, a short and loose-fitting piece of lingerie that was held up by thin shoulder straps. About fifteen minutes after midnight, while she was watching a late-night movie, Kyung heard the sound of the window blinds rattling in her bedroom, and she went back to investigate.

Pulling the bedroom blinds aside, Kyung gasped in fright when she saw a man's right arm on the sill, a long-barreled gun in his hand. She screamed and ran out of the room to her front door, where she fumbled trying to open three locks to escape. The intruder was through the window in a flash and charged at her, head down so she couldn't see his face. He grabbed her and yanked her away from the door, pushing her onto the floor flat on her stomach. Kyung screamed again.

"Don't holler!" the man ordered her. "Stop yelling, bitch!"

"Okay, okay," she answered nervously, hoping that if she cooperated with him, he wouldn't harm her. Producing a roll of green tape, the assailant began to wrap it around Kyung's head until it covered her eyes completely. When he was finished, he pulled her up from the floor and told her he was taking her into the bedroom. Once there, he stood her in front of him.

"Is there anyone else in the apartment?" he asked her.

"No, I'm here alone," Kyung answered. She was fearful, standing blindfolded in front of this aggressor in nothing but that skimpy nightie, but she continued to be cooperative in the hope that he would not hurt her.

"Are you married?" he asked.

"Yes."

"Well, where's your husband at?"

"He's at work. He'll be home soon," Kyung said.

"Where does he work?"

"Down at the Naval Air Station," she answered.

If the man thought her husband might be home soon, Kyung thought, then he might leave in order to avoid confronting him. But instead, it triggered a more aggressive reaction. Spotting the woman's clothes, the man handed them to Kyung and told her to get dressed. Kyung complied.

"Where's your money?" he barked at her as she was putting on her clothes.

"In my purse, over in the corner," she replied.

The man grabbed the purse and rifled through it. It was pitiful. Inside, the woman had a few crinkled dollar bills. As he picked them out, Kyung began to cry.

"Please don't take my money. That's all I have," she sobbed.

"I don't want your money," the assailant responded. He put the bills back into the purse and tossed it aside. "Let's get out of here."

Kyung was dressed now, but still had the tape around her head. The man led her to the front door, unlocked it, and took her outside. But then just as abruptly as he seemed to be deciding everything else, he turned and pulled her back into the apartment.

"Get those clothes off, you whore," he told her once they returned to the bedroom.

"Please, don't kill me," Kyung pleaded as she stripped naked. She heard the man unzipping his own pants at the same time.

When she was finished, he forced her to her knees in front of him.

"I want you to suck me," he said angrily, pulling her head toward his penis. Kyung began to cry.

"I can't! I can't do it!" she sobbed.

The man relented, and told her instead to lay down on her bed. Over the next three-quarters of an hour, the man raped her vaginally and then, forcing her onto her stomach, he raped her anally as well. All the while, Kyung pleaded with him not to kill her.

"I'm not going to kill you," he repeated as he pushed into her. "I'm not going to hurt you." But when he finished, he warned her not to go to the police. If she did, he would come back and harm both her and her husband. Then the man fled through the window from which he had entered.

Kyung was so frightened by the threat that she and her husband, who came home shortly afterward, put off calling the police for twenty-four hours.

By the time Kingsville police were called to the Ellis apartment on Monday, any hope of gathering much in the way of physical evidence had been washed away. But Detective Treviño was intrigued by what he saw. Kyung handed over the green tape with which her head had been wrapped. It was similar to the tape that had been found on three of the victims from that ten-day stretch in late August and September, right before Nuñez was shot.

Judy Hayes realized that they did have an Anglo rapist all along. The police had been premature in thinking that the string of rapes had come to an end with the shooting. And for Hayes, the location of this latest rape brought a very ominous feeling. It was the same apartment building where the September 7, 1980, rape had occurred, the one that Hayes felt sure had kicked off the long string of sexual assaults that now numbered twenty. It was in the same, weathered gray building in the center of town where her career as a detective began and now she was back, starting over.

The records on all the rapes were pulled out again. The detectives grouped the cases involving tape blindfolds, of which there were now four. Then they reviewed other factors from the Kyung Ellis rape that might be present in the previous ones, such as the type of weapon used, the things the rapist said, the method of entry, and, most important of all, the type of assault. When they looked at all the evidence with a fresh eye, a third pattern clearly emerged, and they set those cases apart from the others. Although Sue Wilson was not one of the victims whose eyes had been wrapped in tape, she shared one important thing in common with the four whose eyes were taped. All five had been raped anally.

When those five cases were culled out of the pack, they clearly indicated to Judy Hayes that the perpetrator was becoming gradually rougher both physically and psychologically with his victims. Hayes believed it was a matter of life and death that the rapist at large be stopped quickly.

Treviño took the green tape, which was a distinctive type, around to Kingsville's hardware and department stores, trying to find out where it might be sold. None of the local stores could match it. Treviño was not concerned by this. Instead of thwarting the investigation, he realized that failure to match that particular tape with any mass-marketed tape would eventually narrow his possible suspects. It would be of little help if the tape had been available everywhere. If Treviño could find the place where this rare tape was obtained, it would help pinpoint the rapist.

With a short gasp, Ronda awoke in her dark bedroom late one night in mid-November. She did not know what had jarred her, and as her senses adjusted to the environment, she strained to listen for any noises. It was deathly quiet in the house and outside as well. Ronda had no idea what time it was, but it must have been very late. She couldn't even hear the usual faraway whine of truck tires out on the bypass two miles away, which was often audible in the still of the night. Turning her head slowly to her left, Ronda checked on Eddie. He was lying on his side with his back toward her. His rhythmic breathing told her that he was asleep.

Ronda looked the other way, toward the front window, half expecting to see a face looking back at her. A small amount of light filtered through the glass. There wasn't even a breeze to stir the fragile mesquite tree outside the window. Was something outside? No, worse; her sense was that something was in the house. Ronda turned her head back and looked over Eddie toward the bedroom door, only about three feet from the side of the bed. The door was partially closed, and she could not see out into the hallway toward the children's room. She stared at the back of the door for a few seconds. It did not move. But still, she had an overpowering feeling that there was someone else in the room. Or some thing. A palpable sensation of evil settled over Ronda and started her stomach to churning. She could not suppress the premonition that something terrible was about to happen.

Ronda clamped her eyes shut and prayed.

"Jesus, protect us," she said to herself, her lips moving silently to the words. She repeated the pleading over and over as the sensation seemed to suck the fresh air out of the room and replace it with a stench of ruin. "Jesus, protect us." Ronda prayed for deliverance from whatever was in the room. She had never been so frightened before in her life, and she did not even know what was causing it.

Gradually, as she continued praying, the oppressive crush began to lift. It was slow at first, but she could feel the evil sensation begin to subside, and she started to feel that she was safe. Finally, after what seemed like an intense struggle, but one that only lasted several minutes, Ronda felt that whatever had awakened her was gone from the room.

After a short while, she was able to fall asleep again.

In the morning, while Ronda was getting ready for work, Eddie got up from the bed and began to get dressed. Then he walked into the hallway to the bathroom door and looked in at Ronda, who was inside brushing her teeth. Eddie leaned against the door jamb, a concerned look on his face.

"Did you sense something in the house last night?" he asked her. He used the word *sensed* instead of asking her if she heard or saw something.

Ronda, suddenly wide-eyed, quickly rinsed her mouth to answer. "Why, yes!" she told him urgently. She had been disturbed by the experience and had kept it to herself, until she was relieved to hear Eddie speak of it.

"What did you feel?" Eddie asked.

"It was just like an evil presence that woke me up and started pressing in on me," Ronda told him. "It felt like it was right in the room with us."

"I felt that same thing happening to me," Eddie said. "It was like some kind of demonic spirit was in the room."

"You were awake?" Ronda asked.

"Yeah, but I didn't want to move," he said. "I was trying to listen. Then I just kept saying the name of Jesus over and over in my mind, and it went away."

"That's what I did, too!" Ronda replied. They discussed the coincidence for a while, but they could not come up with a mutually acceptable explanation for what had taken place in their bedroom. The fact is that both of them had been repressing some very strong emotions in the past few months instead of confronting them, and it might have been the overflow of too many unacknowledged feelings flooding forward from their subconscious minds.

Still, both Eddie and Ronda believed in spirits and their ability to demonically possess a person. Ronda had only heard and read about the experience before this, but the feeling in the bedroom was similar to descriptions she had heard of what happens when a person surrenders to Satan and is taken over body and soul. Ronda could not believe that an evil spirit was trying to take her over. And Eddie seemed to be his usual quiet self, piqued only by the same curiosity about the night. In the light of day, it was easy for both of them to dismiss it as an oddity, due perhaps to the buildup of tensions in their marriage over Eddie's withdrawal and depression. They decided to get away as a family for a while, and go to Colorado for Thanksgiving. But the mysterious event continued to haunt Ronda for some time.

Ronda and Eddie piled the kids into the silver Dodge Aspen on the Monday before Thanskgiving and headed out Texas 141 toward Alice, the first leg of a long drive to Denver to spend the holiday with Paul and Erna Hunter. Eddie had not gone fifteen miles before a cop pulled him over for speeding. Eddie was a good driver who rarely got into traffic trouble. It was a simple matter, and the cop let him go with only a warning. But the sight of the police officer terrified the children in the backseat. Diana started to cry, and Paul kept asking if the police were going to take his daddy away. Eddie and Ronda smilingly ressured them that everything was going to be okay. Daddy was not going to leave them.

A hard day of driving got them to Abilene, where they spent the night in a motel. They finished the trip on Tuesday, pulling into the Denver suburb of Lakewood late in the afternoon. Ronda's brother Randy and his wife and their two boys came up from Waco, where Randy was stationed with the air force, and her older brother Ron lived nearby with his wife and children. So the entire family was together, including all six grandchilden, for the first time in several years. Eddie and Ronda spent Tuesday evening socializing with her parents, and Paul Hunter showed Eddie around the family room addition he was putting on the house. Eddie was quiet, which was not unusual for him. But Paul Hunter felt that his son-in-law was much more depressed than the last time he had seen him in Norfolk.

On Wednesday morning, after breakfast, Ronda wanted to take the children up to Lookout Mountain west of Denver for some sightseeing. Eddie drove and Erna came along. During the drive, Erna was aware of how much more withdrawn Eddie had become. When they got back to the house, Ronda was surprised when Eddie said he was going out again—alone. He had seemed bored and distracted during the ride.

"Where are you going to go?" she asked her husband.

"I don't know, just for a drive," he answered. "I just want to get away for a while." He went out to the family car, fired the engine, and started off.

"Where's Eddie going?" Erna asked her daughter when she looked through the window and saw her son-in-law pulling out of the gravel drive onto Newland Street.

"Just out," Ronda said with a hesitant tone of voice. "That's

all he said, out for a drive." Eddie showed up later in the afternoon, and when he walked in the house, Ronda did not even ask
him where he had been.

Because all of the children and grandchildren were together,
when Paul Hunter came home from work Wednesday evening,
they all got dressed up and went over to a portrait studio for a
family photograph. Thanksgiving dinner went off without a hitch
the next day. The conversation carried itself around the table,
but Eddie stayed in the background most of the time, and the
family sensed that he was feeling low. No one pushed him to talk
if he did not feel like it. But later, both parents expressed their
concern to Ronda. They noted that Eddie had lost weight, and
his appearance was haggard. Ronda told them that her husband
had become more withdrawn from the family since summer, and
she was feeling depressed over her own inability to help him.
Ronda could not bring herself to tell her parents that she had
recently caught Eddie smoking marijuana.

Then, on Friday morning, after Eddie got showered and
dressed, he abruptly announced to Ronda that they were leaving
for Texas after lunch that day. It took a few seconds for the
statement to sink in. Their original plan was to leave on Saturday,
stay overnight in a motel halfway, and get back to Kingsville on
Sunday, in plenty of time for work on Monday.

"What do you mean we're leaving?" Ronda said incredulously.
"I don't want to leave yet."

"I want to get back," Eddie replied.

"Well, why can't we stay? Why do we have to get back?"

"We just have to," Eddie said.

Ronda could not get him to give a specific reason. Eddie was
insistent about leaving that day. Furthermore, he intended to drive
straight through without stopping overnight in Abilene, the halfway point. It would be a full twenty-four-hour drive, including
food and gasoline stops.

After eating lunch, Eddie and Ronda strapped the children
into the backseat, said goodbye to a disappointed Paul and Erna,
and took off for Texas. Ronda did not speak much to her husband
on the trip back. She felt dead tired by the time they got to San
Antonio Saturday morning, and begged Eddie to pull over for a

Ronda Jean Hunter grew up in Denver, the middle child and only daughter of a deeply religious family. When this photograph was taken on her eighth birthday, Ronda had a life-threatening brain tumor, which subsequently disappeared after a prayer session by members of the church to which her parents belonged. Partly as a result of this faith healing, Ronda grew to believe that anything could be cured through faith.

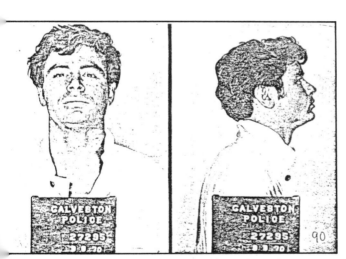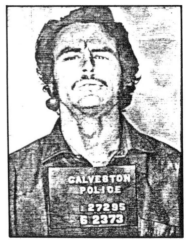

Eddie Wyatt's childhood could not have been more different from Ronda's. His father left home when Eddie was 5, and the boy early turned to drugs and petty crime, which eventually led to reform school and then prison. Eddie is 18 years old in the 1970 mugshots at left, taken when he was arrested for burglary. The one at right is from a 1973 arrest when, on parole from the burglary conviction, he robbed a convenience store and was sent back to jail. Eddie's life had reached a dead end when he became a born-again Christian in prison. Upon release at age 22, he decided to start his new Christian life in Dallas. (*Galveston, Texas, police photos*)

Ronda met Eddie while they were both volunteers at the Teen Challenge program in Dallas. Her work with underprivileged inner-city youth had convinced her that anyone could turn his life around with the help of the Lord. Eddie seemed to be living proof of this potential for redemption.

Although she felt some misgivings about Eddie because of his aggressive sexuality, nevertheless Ronda's faith in him outweighed all other considerations. After several months of dating, they were married on Valentine's Day, 1975.

The first year of their marriage was the happiest time of their lives. Ronda remained a Teen Challenge counselor for another year while Eddie worked as a welder. Three months after the wedding, Ronda became pregnant.

Within days after the birth of his son Paul, Eddie was injured in an industrial accident that cut short his welding career. Here, his eye is swollen from the blow by a steel wedge. The only bright side was that during his time away from work, he became very close to his new child. He proved to be a good father in those early years.

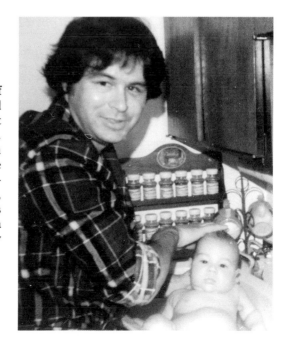

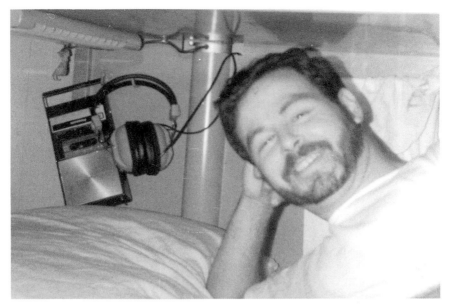

Increasingly unhappy after the accident, Eddie moved with Ronda to Colorado where, unknown to her, he started drinking. When he was unable to find work in Colorado, Eddie decided to join the Navy. On board ship, as in this photograph, Eddie escaped Ronda's watchful eye and resumed some bad habits.

After two extended overseas cruises and a pattern of lying, Eddie's marriage to Ronda had become strained. Although he now had a daughter, Diana, who made him happy, his hidden drug abuse and sexual frustration were causing Eddie to withdraw from Ronda both physically and emotionally.

Ronda hid her sense of failure as a wife by busying herself as a mother. Between her dedicated work for the church and her devotion to her children, her friends all considered her the ideal mother and woman.

Sixth rape sparks session of lawmen

Eddie extended his enlistment and was transferred to shore duty at the Naval Air Station in Kingsville, Texas. A series of rapes had been terrifying the town of Kingsville, and after the Wyatts moved there, more rapes began to occur. (*Courtesy of Kingsville Record*)

From the Kingsville Police Department, police officers extended their net to capture the rapist, working around the clock to break the case before more rapes could be committed. (*Photo by Kevin Flynn*)

Three days after he raped Allison Shaw in this spot beside the Christmas tree, Eddie sat there to assemble a new bicycle for Paul. What he didn't realize as he prepared this special Christmas present was that 17-year-old Allison had been able to see through her blindfold and had told the police the story of her kidnap and rape ordeal.

Allison told the officers that the rapist had transported her in the trunk of a blue sedan with a white top. The police traced the car to Wyatt, and in it found evidence of the kidnap. They also discovered a mutilated cassette tape hidden in an eggnog carton in Eddie's garbage, which proved to be a recording Eddie had made of his rape of Allison Shaw. (*Kingsville, Texas, police photos*)

Abduction, rape suspect nabbed
Navy man charged in Kingsville case

Eddie was arrested on December 28, 1981. The evidence against him was too strong to deny. Rather than face a trial he would surely lose, Eddie pleaded guilty to burglary with intent to rape, and was sentenced to 30 years in prison. After serving 9½ years, Eddie was released in July 1991. (*Kingsville, Texas, police photo; article courtesy of* Kingsville Record)

She did not want to believe it, but after he admitted his guilt to her, Ronda was forced to face the truth that her husband was a rapist. Devastated by the collapse of her marriage, and struggling with intense emotional pain, she moved back to Colorado to begin a new life without Eddie.

Although she had doubted if she could ever love or trust anyone again, she and her children found new happiness when she met Rob Knuth. This photo was taken on their wedding day, which unintentionally fell on the third anniversary of Eddie's arrest.

All photographs courtesy of Ronda Knuth except as noted.

while. He wouldn't. They were less than four hours from home and he did not want to stop. Ronda was hurt and upset, but by this time Eddie had refused to answer any of her questions, so she stopped asking them. She felt confused and belittled, with no say in what was going to happen to her. Early in her marriage, nothing made her happier than to defer to her husband, because he seemed to be headed somewhere. But now Eddie was directionless, confused. She believed he was a rudderless ship, and the storms were gathering around their marriage.

The Wyatts arrived in Kingsville at midday on Saturday and retired to bed early that evening to rest up from the lengthy drive. On Sunday morning, Ronda got up for church and roused Eddie. It had been a while since he had attended First Assembly, although he enjoyed the company of Pastor Fields during their sessions together. Eddie declined to go. What made things worse for Ronda was that the children were being unruly, and they didn't want to go either. Normally, Ronda would just go about getting them ready and take them anyway, figuring she could control them if the need arose. But on this particular morning she simply gave up. Ronda knew she had to get out by herself.

Instead of heading straight for church, Ronda took a detour—she felt she was going to burst into tears and she did not want her friends to see her cry. She went past First Assembly and drove to Dick Kleberg Park at the south end of town, parking the car under the shade of a tree. There she cried, and wrote a two-page letter for her diary, addressed to her fellow churchgoers. She felt like a nobody, with no control over her own life, and she prayed that someone would see through her defenses and reach out to her. For her own part, she could open her mouth and exchange pleasantries, but she was unable to spill her pain out of the shame of failure and the need to project normalcy.

I'm all confused. Even if you did reach out to me now, I'm not even sure that I could reach back. Don't you see? All we want is for someone to care whether we make it or not. At this point it seems that the "nobodies" rank at the bottom of the list. Quote me your scriptures all day long, send me your words of reprimand in the guise

of wisdom and love. But now I'm not even sure I could
reach back. It might hurt, and Mrs. Nobody can stand
the hurt no longer.

Ronda later went to church alone; when she returned home,
Eddie asked how it went.

"I wrote a letter," she said.

"You did what?" Eddie responded. Ronda went to her purse
and handed Eddie the letter. Eddie quietly read it and handed it
back. He seemed choked up after seeing his wife's emotions
poured out in black and white, but he said nothing. Soon after,
he left the house and drove off without saying a word.

Not all of the women of Kingsville had let down their guard. With
the rape of Kyung Ellis, many who had sighed with relief in
September had the point nailed home that the capture of that
one rapist did not mean the end of the wave of rapes in their
small town. And while nearly all of the rape victims who had
come to light in the past year had been relatively young women,
the town learned over Thanksgiving that no woman could consider herself immune to attack.

On Thanksgiving Day, a young man knocked on the door of
an eighty-three-year-old woman's house on East Huisache Avenue, telling her he was from the telephone company. When the
elderly lady opened the door to him, he rushed inside and grabbed
her. He forced her into her bedroom and ordered her to take off
her pants. The lady refused. Instead, she reached down under her
bed and grabbed the handle of a small ax that she had started
keeping nearby because of the spate of assaults. The man was
too startled to move for a second as the woman began to swing
the ax at him. He then quickly reversed himself and bolted out
the door.

A psychology professor at Texas A&I volunteered to look at
the unsolved cases and come up with a profile of the man they
were seeking. Captain Gomez thought it was a cockamamie idea,
but when the profile was completed, the detectives found a help-
ful suggestion. The psychologist told them they should be looking

for an ex-convict, basing his assumption on the descriptions of the assaults. All of them involved anal sex. It was highly likely the attacker had picked up that propensity in prison, he told the police.

Meanwhile, Treviño's pursuit of the source for the green tape finally paid off. After eliminating all of the retail outlets in town, Treviño discovered that the tape was available at the Naval Air Station, where it was used in the repair of jet-fighter bodies. Treviño visited the Naval Investigative Service on the base and discussed the rapes with Officer Burt Cavazos, who agreed to help track the rapist any way he could.

Shortly after reopening the rape investigations, Treviño took a call from a security guard at an apartment complex near the naval station. One of the earlier rapes had occurred at this complex. The guard told the police that he had seen a man acting suspiciously in the parking lot, looking into car windows. When confronted, the man said he was waiting for someone, then quickly went to his car and drove away. The guard said the man was Anglo, of medium height and thin build, with short brown hair and a mustache. The guard noted that the man left in a blue Plymouth Valiant with a white roof and a lousy muffler. In the dim light of the car's rear bumper, the guard saw the license plate number: HUE-907.

Treviño appreciated the information. Often, such bits and pieces lead nowhere. But sometimes they yield an important piece of information, or reveal a missing part of a pattern. Treviño took the guard's report, sat down at a motor vehicle computer terminal, and typed in the plate number. It came back as "no such plate" in Texas. Treviño thought maybe the guard got a number or letter wrong, and he filed the report away.

Ronda did not give much thought to all of the talk around town about the rapes. She had never felt in much personal danger despite the headlines in the paper and the anxious mood of the people. After the Nuñez shooting, she had felt some relief that the streets would be a little safer. But overall, Ronda felt very secure in her own person. None of the rapes had occurred in the northwest part of town, where she lived. Every once in a while, however, the Kingsville rapes became a topic for discussion among Ronda's friends in Bible study or the navy wives. Then one day in early December, after a phone call from a friend, Ronda approached Eddie in the living room to discuss it.

"You know who called today?" she asked him.

"Who, honey?" Eddie answered.

"Kathy Carter. She's married to that guy you know who works at the base with you."

"Oh, yeah. What's she want?"

"Her husband's going on graveyard shift next week, and she wanted to know if we'd mind if she slept over at our house," Ronda told him.

"How come?"

"She's really nervous with this rapist going around town, breaking into houses where women are alone," Ronda said. "She's afraid to stay alone in her house and would just feel safer if she could spend a few nights with us. Is that okay with you?"

"Sure," Eddie answered. "If it'll make her feel better."

"Thanks, Eddie. I'll call her back and let her know." Ronda smiled. "I really wouldn't think she'd have to worry about it."

"Probably not," Eddie agreed.

"I mean, she's overweight and all. I can't imagine a rapist picking her out. If a man is going to rape someone, wouldn't he pick out the prettiest woman he could find?" Ronda asked.

Eddie looked at her blankly. "I really wouldn't know, honey-bun," he said.

Ronda grinned. Of course Eddie wouldn't know, she thought. Later it hit her that there was nothing to grin about. Eddie appeared to have no interest in sex at all, she thought to herself, let alone be so obsessed with it that he would understand what drives a rapist. Ronda called Kathy back and told her she and Eddie would love to have her stay over if it would put her mind at ease. They did not talk any more about the rapes and burglaries. After Kathy's husband went on nights, Ronda made up the sofa for her, and Kathy slept blissfully secure there before imposing on other friends for the duration.

Bobby Ellis, on the other hand, thought a lot about rape since Halloween night. The rape of his wife had made him a much more vigilant man, even though it was after the fact and nothing he could do now would make things the same as they were before Kyung was raped. In his anger and frustration over what had happened he took to noticing things he might not have before. Such was the case on Sunday, December 6, when he and Kyung were out in the parking area. Bobby noticed a man walking aimlessly around the apartment building. That made him suspicous. And when Bobby saw the man glance at Kyung before getting into a silver car and driving away, he was convinced the man was a potential suspect in the rape.

The next morning, Bobby Ellis called Detective Treviño to report it.

Nine days later, Ellis was at work at the Naval Air Station when he saw what he thought was the same silver car on the base. He watched it for a while, and eventually saw the man who got into it. He called Treviño again with the tip. Treviño realized the odds were long that the husband of a rape victim could manage to finger the culprit on the basis of spotting an aimless stranger. But the detective also knew that the green tape used by the rapist came from the naval base. Treviño followed up right away. Workers at the base had to register their cars in order to obtain parking passes. Burt Cavazos of naval security checked the registrations and found that the silver car belonged to Edward Eugene Wyatt, a corrosion control worker on the jet aircraft used at the base for fighter-pilot training.

What's more, Cavazos told Treviño, Wyatt had a second car registered at the base. It was a white-over-blue Plymouth Valiant, Virginia license plate HUE-907. That rang a bell with Treviño, the suspicious plate he had tried to run through Texas motor vehicle records, the possible prowler who had been reported by the security guard at the apartment complex near the base. That was Wyatt, too. Treviño obtained Eddie's photograph from navy security and opened a file on him. At this point, Wyatt was one of many possibilities in the investigation. It would take a lot more solid evidence to link him to any of the rapes.

*   *   *

Several couples had already arrived at the spacious home of James and Barbara Crowell by the time Eddie and Ronda got there. The Crowells had met Eddie at church, the few times he accompanied Ronda, and they liked him. They wished that he would come more often. Barbara opened the door and welcomed them in. Several of the men came up to Eddie and, when Ronda introduced them, they embraced him and bid him welcome.

It was Wednesday evening, nine days to Christmas, and instead of the usual home fellowship sharing, the Crowells hosted a holiday dinner for the people in their small group. By the time everyone gathered, there were eight couples. As was typical at functions such as this, the men talked among themselves in one room while the women did the same in another.

Among the women, one brought up the resumption of Kingsville's rapes. Ronda mentioned her friend Kathy Carter's nervousness and need to stay with the Wyatts while her husband worked the graveyard shift. The women talked for a bit about the sexual assaults. None of them knew any of the women who had been raped during the last year, and that made it much easier to feel secure. During the conversation, Ronda saw Eddie standing in the group of men in the kitchen. They were talking animatedly about something. Ronda smiled to see Eddie join in the conversation, appearing to be enjoying himself. It looked so natural for him.

After the fellowship dinner, Ronda had a renewed desire to get to the bottom of the problems she and Eddie were having, fix them up, and get on with their marriage. She was tired of the unrelenting drain on her self-esteem that followed his persistent rejection of her. She was weary of feeling inadequate, and she wanted to identify once and for all what it was she should do to make things right again. She began to pray earnestly for God to bring everything to a head so she and Eddie could battle it and get on with their lives. Ronda telephoned her good friend in Norfolk, Joanie Sargent, and told her how perplexed she had been to see things going sour, while not knowing what was causing it.

"I've been praying that whatever is going on here will be brought to light," Ronda told Joanie. "I've grown so weary of dealing with it, I just want it to come out in the open."

"Well, you'd better be sure about that," Joanie warned her in a playful manner. "Sometimes you get what you pray for."

All Allison Shaw had to do was get up and push two buttons, RECORD and PLAY, then she could flop back into bed and doze off. Her mom could not stand to miss "The Young and the Restless" while she was off at work. Allison relaxed in bed half asleep while she occasionally glanced over at her digital alarm clock. Although it was Monday, the seventeen-year-old senior at King High School was at home because it was the first day of Christmas break. And she was sleeping late because she had stayed up until 2:30 the night before with her boyfriend.

Allison lived in a small, bluish-gray frame house her parents owned on South Sixteenth Street. They had added a small room onto the right rear of the house, jutting into the backyard. The addition had an exterior door on its north side that opened onto the side yard. There were a number of trees and bushes in the backyard that shielded the house from the gravel alley behind it. Allison's bedroom was in the southeast corner of the house, opposite the addition. It had windows on both walls, close to the corner of the room. Directly under the backyard window was a small planter that could serve as a step stool. The bottom half of the windows had louvered slats made of frosted glass. Small yellow curtains covered the top half of the windows.

Allison had her room painted sky blue. There was a Princess-style phone on top of her bookcase headboard, next to her makeup mirror. All sorts of hairstyling apparatus was spread out on her dresser. On a small table in the corner under the windows, where her clock radio rested, she had set up a small display of wine bottles that were mementoes of special occasions. Snapshots of her and her friends were arranged around the room.

Allison flipped her long blond hair to the side as she turned to look at the clock. It was 10:58, almost time to turn on the videocassette recorder. She had fallen asleep in her T-shirt, a pair of maroon panties, and blue socks. Allison knew she was alone in the house, so it startled her fully awake when she heard a sudden noise from beyond the kitchen. At first she thought it might be the cat getting in, or perhaps her dog, Killer, a wiry mutt with black fur, knocking into something. But she quickly discerned the sound of footsteps moving through the house. Allison was terrified, and she pulled her bedclothes up over herself, hiding everything but the top of her head.

With a sudden rush, a masked intruder bolted into her room and leaped directly onto the bed. Allison glimpsed his ski mask and knife, and began to scream. The man warned her to stop as he ripped the covers off her partially clad body. The masked man squatted on her back and began to wrap a length of brown masking tape around her head.

Suddenly, the sound of scampering came toward the room, and Allison's mutt, Killer, jumped up onto the bed. The dog began to bark furiously and to scratch at the attacker's back as he struggled to blindfold the teenager. The dog's small teeth made little headway through the man's jacket, but as the dog kept up its high-pitched yelping, the man became increasingly agitated. Finally, he grabbed his buck knife and jabbed savagely at Killer. As the knife sank into the dog's chest, the animal let out a shriek. The intruder plunged it a third time into the dog's abdomen, and blood spurted out of the dog's torso as it went limp. The attacker swatted at the carcass so that it rolled onto the floor. Allison heard her dog take its last breaths. The violence of these moments left her terrified. The man resumed wrapping the inch-wide tape around and around her head, until it encircled her and covered her eyes. But in his haste and distraction, he had left gaps between the pieces of tape. Allison realized that she could see.

"Roll over," the man ordered. She turned onto her back, and the man stared at her T-shirt and lace panties. He took off his ski mask, secure in the belief that she could no longer see, and Allison looked at his face from behind the darkness of her blindfold. He had a mustache and short, dark hair, and a small scar near his left eye. His face was angry.

"You can have the money," Allison said fearfully. "Just take the money. Take the video recorder, just please leave me alone."

"You have money in here?" the intruder demanded.

"No, my parents have money," she answered.

"Where is it?"

"In their room."

The man grabbed Allison by the arm and led her into the master bedroom. He looked futilely for money, and soon gave up. He took Allison back to her room and shoved her onto the bed. She then suggested several other places he could look.

"It better be here," he warned her a few times, but he still could find no money. He kept coming back to Allison's room to check on her between rummaging through drawers and closets. It soon became apparent that she did not know anything about her parents' money, and was just stalling for time.

"My father will be home for lunch soon," she said, hoping the attacker would turn tail and flee.

"You stay put while I try to find the money," he ordered her. "If you cooperate with me, everything will be all right. Don't try to get away, and don't move." Allison, weak with fright, obeyed when he left the room. She made no attempt to reach for her Princess phone, afraid he would come in and fly into a rage. Allison was completely unaware that the man had left the house to bring his car up the alley to her back door.

Down where the gravel alley emptied onto Caesar Avenue, Luis Godines was spending his morning cleaning out his garage. His two-car garage in the backyard had a small driveway covered with a fiberglass canopy that met the alley at a wooden privacy fence. Godines planned to finish up by lunchtime, then take a shower before heading to work as a swing shift fireman at the Exxon natural gas plant on the King Ranch. Shortly after 11:00 A.M. he heard a noisy car slowing down and shifting gears just short of his garage apron. He stopped and walked out toward the alley, where he saw a blue sedan with a white roof backing its way into the alley from Caesar. Godines did not recognize the car as belonging to any of his neighbors, but that would not be unusual since the alley was the equivalent of four blocks long and there were many houses on the block. While the car went backward past him and proceeded up the alley, Godines looked at the driver square in the face, and saw an Anglo man with a mustache and short, wavy brown hair. Then he went back to cleaning his garage.

Allison had been motionless on her bed for about ten minutes when the intruder came back into her room.

"You can't see me, can you?" he asked her.

"No, I can't see anything," Allison told him. She did not look directly at him at first. She did not want to catch his gaze and tip him off.

"You better not. If you was to see me, I'd have to hurt you," he told her as he yanked her arms behind her back and bound her wrists together with more masking tape. He wrapped her ankles in the same manner. Then he took off his jacket, spread it over her, and lifted her from the bed. He carried her through the house to the open back door and placed her on the floor of the backseat of his car. Cranking the car's engine to a rough start, the intruder-turned-kidnapper put it in gear and started down the alley toward Caesar Avenue.

It had been only ten minutes since he saw the blue car. When Luis Godines heard the same engine sound, he again dropped what he was doing in his garage and took a look. When the blue car reached the corner, Godines saw the driver look quickly in both directions, then make a left onto Caesar, heading east for the U.S. 77 bypass.

At that very moment, just two blocks away, a group of a half dozen women who worked at the Angle Medical Center were taking a break for their office Christmas party. One of the women was a cousin of Allison Shaw's. They ate snacks and sipped their drinks while talking about their plans for the holidays.

When they exchanged gifts, someone handed Ronda a small, lightweight package that had her name on it. Ronda tore open the wrapping. The box inside had a small piece of tape on it to keep it shut. Ronda ran her finger between the top and bottom of the box to pry open the tape. When she lifted the lid, she saw a lavender nightie—a very sexy sheer lavender nightie. Ronda let out an embarrassed smile, and lifted the nightie out of the box. The other women giggled.

Looking at it, Ronda's thoughts went straight back to that wonderful little apartment in Dallas with her new husband. How he might have ravaged her then if she had walked into their bedroom wearing this item, and how wonderful it would make her feel to be embraced so warmly and lovingly again! If the women of the office thought this little number would do the trick, Ronda thought, let's test that theory tonight. She put the nightie back in the box and prepared to go home for a quick lunch. She was expecting a package of gifts to arrive from her parents, and she had asked Eddie to be alert for it.

About an hour later, Allison Shaw's fourteen-year-old sister, Jenny, showed up at home and called out for her sister. Allison should have been home, Jenny knew, because she was supposed to go to her part-time job at 3:00 P.M. When there was no answer, she walked back to Allison's bedroom, where she saw the dead body of Killer on the floor. Horrified, Jenny ran to the phone and called her father, Charles Shaw, who worked over at the *Kingsville Record.*

Charles Shaw rushed home and surveyed the scene. The dog's stab wounds had bloated up and there was not much blood immediately visible. He noticed that the carcass was next to a frayed set of electrical wires and initially thought the dog might have been electrocuted while chewing on them. Shaw did not want Allison to come back and find her dog dead like that, so he carried it out to the backyard and buried it alongside the fence.

But when he got back to straighten up the room, he spotted the blood at the foot of the bed. Suddenly, he realized the implications of what he had found, and he hurried to the phone to call the police.

CHAPTER 8

JUSTICE IN A SMALL TEXAS TOWN

Kind of a sad thing happened today. Vera, Dr. Foster's nurse, has a cousin named Allison. Someone broke into her house, killed her dog, kidnapped her, and raped her several times throughout the day. I feel so sorry for her. I told Eddie about it when I got home. He didn't act real concerned—just mumbled something like, "Oh, really?" That's par for the course.
—from Ronda's diary

Killer was dug up from the backyard grave. Hector Treviño brushed some dirt from the matted fur and looked at the lifeless body of the Shaw family dog. He rolled the carcass over on its side and saw the two gaping holes in the left chest, bloated red muscle protruding through them like the bulging tube of a slashed tire. A third stab wound was farther down in the lower right abdomen. Remarkably, there was very little blood, almost as though the muscle had inflated like a bladder and plugged the holes in the skin to act as a dam.

Up to that point the police were not sure about what had happened in Allison Shaw's bedroom, but now they knew there had not simply been an accident. The dog had been killed and Allison was missing. Investigators looked over the frame on the outside door of the washroom addition and saw evidence that the lock had been forced open. Treviño and the other officers combed through the house with Charles Shaw, looking for clues. They checked with nearby doctors' offices and at Kleberg Memorial Hospital to see if the missing teen had shown up with an

162

injury. They fanned out to talk with neighbors to ask whether any of them had seen Allison. They called her boyfriend and her school chums to find out if she might have gone visiting.

The police were certain that the disappearance of Allison Shaw was more than a simple missing person incident. But without a witness, all they had was the carcass of the dog as mute evidence of the danger Allison might be facing.

Luis Godines finished up with his garage cleaning and, after lunch, took a stroll west down Caesar Avenue. Looking north when he reached the corner of Sixteenth Street, he noticed a lot of activity far up the block, so he began walking that way. Soon he could see several uniformed police officers and others who were in plainclothes. There were police cars parked along the curb near Johnston Avenue. Luis did not know very many of the neighbors this far up in the very long block. One came walking toward him, and Luis asked the man if he knew what the commotion was. The man shrugged and continued walking. Luis watched the activity from a perch on the sidewalk, then turned around and walked back home. He had to get ready to go to work.

At the very moment the police arrived at the Shaw house to begin their missing person investigation, Allison was securely bound and in the trunk of her abductor's car, headed back to Kingsville. Her kidnap ordeal was more than two hours old and no end was in sight.

In the darkness of the trunk, Allison felt every bump and turn. At one point, she was sure he had driven her back into Kingsville because traffic was moving slowly and the car stopped more often. Once, the car pulled up next to a police car, and Allison could heard the police radio crackling. She was about six feet away from possibly ending her torment, and she debated whether or not to scream out at the top of her lungs. But she was not sure the policeman would hear her in time, and it might anger her kidnapper. So Allison kept quiet.

At one point, the noisy car made a left turn, and Allison bumped into a tool box. Then she felt the jarring crunch of the axles going over a set of railroad tracks. She was keeping mental notes on everything, even though she was not sure whether she would ever get to tell anyone.

Within minutes of crossing the railroad tracks, the car stopped, swung into reverse, backed over a curb, and came to a stop. The trunk opened, and the light flooded into the gaps in Allison's blindfold. She had worked it up with her hands, which were now bound in front of her instead of in back, so she could see better, and she prayed that her abductor would not discover her secret. The man threw his jacket over her and lifted her out of the trunk. Quickly, he went inside a house, and placed Allison down on the kitchen floor. She rolled over onto her stomach.

"If I cut your hands free, am I going to have any trouble?" he asked her.

"No," Allison answered. The man used his knife to slice loose the tape that bound her wrists, then he removed the tape from around her ankles. She suspected that this was his house, and she started to catalogue details of what she saw through the slit in the tape around her eyes. The man went into another room for a few minutes. When he returned, Allison heard him strike a match, and soon she smelled the sweet aroma of marijuana.

"How about a joint? Would you like to smoke some dope?" the man asked her, sounding strangely polite. Allison agreed and took several drags.

"Would you like to have some sex?" he asked her, apparently more at ease now that he was in familiar surroundings. Allison was confused by his asking for sex. It was as though he was role-playing. She really had no choice in the matter. Through the blindfold she could see he was already anticipating her cooperation—he was removing all of his clothing. She turned away quickly after seeing his wiry body and his hairy thighs, then thought that she should not do that. A move like that could tip him off that she could see. He ordered her to remove her clothes, and she complied by stripping off her T-shirt, panties, and socks. She was entirely naked except for the brown band of masking tape around her blond head. The kidnapper directed Allison to the living room and ordered her to lay down.

She could see that she was now in a boxy, dark-paneled room. On the front wall was a double window, and centered in front

of it was a scrawny Christmas tree, about four feet tall and ar-
tificial. In the corner to the left was an end table, and on it was
a lamp with a ruffled shade. As she turned around and faced the
other direction, she saw a spartan sofa against the side wall, and
past it a small, green vinyl chair. On the wall behind the chair,
Allison saw a framed photograph. It looked like a woman and a
small child, posing against the backdrop of a forest. On the near
side of the room, Allison could make out a digital clock with red
numbers.

Over the next three hours, the man raped Allison again and
again. He kept his voice low and threatening as he worked himself
up to several orgasms. He forced her to repeat that he was good
and that she was enjoying it. Allison did not physically fight him.
The terror and brutality of her ordeal left her limp.

At one point, Allison tilted her head back, and the man jumped
up.

"Did you see me?" he demanded.

"No, I didn't," Allison answered, nervous that he might have
seen her eyes in the darkness under the tape.

"If you was to see me, I would have to hurt you," he said.

"If you don't believe me," Allison pleaded, "just blindfold me
again. I'm telling you I didn't see you. I don't want to see you."

The man went to another room and quickly returned with a
roll of green tape. Going back to Allison, he picked up one of her
socks and pressed it against her eyes, over the brown masking
tape. Then he used the green tape to secure the blue sock over
her first blindfold. He wrapped the tape tightly several times
around her head. When he was finished, Allison found she could
still see by looking downward through a space left open over the
curve of her nose.

He resumed raping her, and Allison thought she heard the
sound of a cassette tape recorder being loaded and turned on.

"Say I'm good," the man whispered to Allison, who assumed
that the sounds of her rape were being recorded.

"Oh, you're good," Allison responded in a frightened voice.

"Tell me you want me to fuck your ass," he ordered in a very
low, breathy voice. Apparently, he wanted the recorder to pick
up only Allison's words.

"I want you to fuck my ass," Allison replied. "Because you're good. Oh, oh, you are good."

The attacker immediately moved Allison around and began to enter her from behind. It was the most painful of the assaults, and she cried in agony and protest. He warned her to be quiet, and called her a whore and a bitch as he rapidly reached a climax. He left the room for a minute, leaving Allison to wonder what was next.

"Why did you stop?" Allison asked when she heard him walk back in the room.

"Because I'm gonna get a picture of this," he responded snidely. The man moved around, and about fifteen seconds later, Allison saw a flash and heard the whirring sound of an instant camera. Afterward, the man raped her again, this time vaginally.

Close to 4:30 in the afternoon, the rapist cleaned himself and got dressed. He wrapped Allison's wrists together again with tape before covering her with his jacket and carrying her back to the trunk of the car. He drove around for a short time before he stopped and let her out in a men's room in Dick Kleberg Park, on the south end of Kingsville. It was near the spot where Ronda had written her despairing letter from her diary. The man tossed a pair of pants at her before leaving. Allison, who had been in mortal fear the entire afternoon, no longer had to think about being killed. Now she could concentrate on remembering as many details as she could. She knew one thing.

She would never forget that face.

The police dispatcher notified George Gomez as soon as she got the call from Allison Shaw, who had shown up in someone's front yard across the street from Dick Kleberg Park. The police captain yelled for Treviño and Hayes to hurry down to the scene, and told the dispatcher to keep the teenager on the telephone line.

"I was working in the front yard when she ran up my driveway and said she'd been raped," homeowner Bob Bertics told Treviño when he and Hayes arrived at 5:07 P.M. Bertics led them inside and toward the kitchen, where Allison stood holding the phone.

The dispatcher had kept her on the line until the two detectives reached her. Allison seemed to be in shock. She stared at the man and woman in the kitchen doorway. Judy Hayes was in uniform, while Hector Treviño was in plainclothes. Allison eyed the two officers from head to toe, as though she could not believe that she was finally safe. Hayes heard the dispatcher's voice coming out of the receiver next to Allison's ear, saying, "It's all right now, Allison, you can hang up the phone now." Hayes took the receiver from her and placed it on its hook.

Allison told them she had been kidnapped and raped by an Anglo male, and that she had stared right into his face over a period of several hours. That made her the first victim to have a solid chance of identifying her attacker. She led the two detectives to the rest room where she had been set free only half an hour earlier. Treviño's eyes widened when he looked down to the floor. There was the tape Allison said her attacker used to wrap the blue sock around her eyes. He zoomed in on the color. It was green, the same type that had been used on Kyung Ellis, the tape he could find available only at the Naval Air Station.

Treviño and Hayes hurried Allison to Kleberg Memorial Hospital for a battery of tests. During the short drive up Brahma Boulevard, Allison told how she had been locked in the trunk of the man's car, but saw clearly that it was a blue car with a white roof. Treviño stayed at the hospital only long enough to make sure that doctors were caring for Allison. He left her with Judy Hayes and Captain Gomez, who met them there. Treviño broadcast a description of the suspect's car to all patrol units.

He clipped the microphone back into its mount on the radio, looked straight ahead, and put the car in gear. Within ten minutes, Treviño was parked on Mesquite Avenue, down the street from Eddie Wyatt's house. He saw the blue Plymouth Valiant with the white roof. Satisfied that Eddie still owned the car, Treviño decided to bring Allison out to Mesquite Avenue first thing in the morning to look over the Valiant. If she could identify it as the car in which she had been kidnapped, Treviño knew he could make quick work of the case.

*   *   *

When Ronda came home from work that evening, after picking up the children from day care, she found Paul and Diana wound up and wanting to walk down the block to the playground at Brookshire Park. She asked Eddie to walk along. He seemed very preoccupied and Ronda thought it might help him relax. Paul and Diana ran ahead while Eddie and Ronda followed behind. At the playground, Ronda helped the kids on the equipment while Eddie sat on a nearby picnic bench.

Ronda chuckled to herself over Joanie Sargent's warning that God might answer her prayer about Eddie. Since that prayer, Ronda had felt a soothing wave of calm wash over her. Maybe it was Christmas coming in four days, but things seemed lighter around the house. Previously, the tension had almost been too much for her. Ronda needed to cut through it and get to the bottom of Eddie's problems. Whatever was wrong, Ronda believed, there would be relief in finally discovering it and dealing with it.

That evening, Ronda made a quick dinner for the family, and they watched a little bit of television while sitting around the Christmas tree. After the kids were asleep, Eddie seemed more tired than usual, and he went to bed early. Ronda took the Christmas present the women at the office had given her, the lavender negligee, and went into the bathroom to undress and put it on. She was anxious to try one more time to seduce her husband despite her earlier resolve to avoid his continued rejection.

Eddie was half asleep when Ronda entered the bedroom.

"Eddie?" she asked from the foot of the bed. "What do you think?"

Eddie opened his eyes and propped himself up on his elbows. He looked at his wife, and ran his eyes up and down to take the full appeal of the skimpy and suggestive nightie. Ronda turned to show it off. She smiled at her husband, anticipating that he would reciprocate her advances.

"Well, what do you think?" Ronda repeated. "The women down at the clinic gave it to me today at the Christmas party."

"It's very nice, honeybun," Eddie said. He paused, and then settled back down onto his pillow. "I'm really tired from working that weekend shift," he said, then rolled over and went to sleep. Ronda cried herself to sleep that night.

In the morning, after their regular Tuesday morning women's Bible study at the church, Barbara Crowell noticed something was wrong with Ronda Wyatt. Before Ronda rushed off to work, Barbara hurried over and reached out for her arm. Ronda looked flat and unemotional, a rare mix for the young woman whom Barbara knew as normally bright and full of joy.

"Let's go to lunch," Barbara suggested.

"Oh, I don't know," Ronda said. She fumbled for some excuse, but Barbara was a take-charge person, and before Ronda realized it, the two of them were walking into a restaurant on South Fourteenth Street. After they ordered, Barbara immediately set about discovering what was bothering her friend.

"I really don't know, that's what's killing me," Ronda said. "Something is wrong in my home, between me and Eddie, and I just have no idea what it is." For the first time since she had been to Kingsville, Ronda opened up to a friend. She told Barbara about Eddie's depression since his father died, and how their marital relations had dwindled to almost nothing. Barbara promised Ronda that she could always count on her being there if Ronda needed her. For Ronda, it felt good to unload some of her inner pain, and to leave the protection of her shell for just that one time.

"I want everyone to feel a personal stake in this case," Captain Gomez told Judy Hayes. So Gomez brought Allison Shaw to the squad room to tell of her ordeal in front of all seven detectives, and answer every question they had. The detectives could read the affidavit based on Hayes's lengthy and detailed interviews with the victim, but Gomez knew that if they saw Allison, and heard it from her own lips, they would feel an urgent sense of rage at the terrible crime. He wanted them to think of Allison as if she were their daughter, their sister, their wife, their close friend. Gomez wanted his people to close this case before the rapist struck again.

Allison told them of her terror as a man wearing a dark ski mask with a light design on front rushed through the door to her room and jumped on her. He was carrying a large knife. She spoke of her dog's pathetic attempt to protect her, and the man's brutal stabs in response.

"He held Killer up to my face and told me that's what would happen to me if I didn't cooperate," Allison told them. "Then he finished wrapping my head with masking tape and told me to turn over. That's when I realized I could still see. I saw him take off his ski mask. I saw his face as plain as I can see all yours right now."

Allison described the rapist as an Anglo male, five-foot-six to five-foot-eight, and in his twenties. He had a slim, wiry build, and short, dark-colored hair. There was a burn scar or discoloration of some sort next to his left eye.

"He carried me out to his car and covered me with his jacket on the back floorboard, then he drove me somewhere out into the country. I don't know where it was, but I think it was south. He stopped once and got out, and did something next to the car. He left it running. I could hear people nearby, but I was afraid he'd hurt me if I screamed. Then he got back in, made a U-turn, and drove about ten minutes more. The second time he stopped, he opened the back door and got in with me."

What Allison described next was the first of five episodes of rape by her abductor that she would detail in her session with the detectives. She told them that he cut loose the tape around her wrists, and ordered her to get up on the seat. With that, he yanked off her maroon panties and her socks. She heard the sound of his zipper coming down, and then he pressed down on top of her and forced himself inside her. After he abused her that way, he got back in the front seat, drove to another spot, stopped the car, and got in the back again with her. There, he forced her to perform oral sex on him and raped her a second time, she told the squad.

"After he was finished with that I got my panties back on. He tied my hands and feet again with the masking tape and he put me in the trunk of his car. He kept saying he wouldn't hurt me if I kept cooperating with him," Allison said. The man stopped at a gas station—she could hear the gasoline pouring down the neck of the tank next to her in the trunk—and her sense was that they were at the Bradlee station down Highway 77 near Ricardo. The detectives made a note to check with the attendants who were on duty Monday around noon to find out if they had seen a blue car, and if they had, whether it had a loud muffler.

At the rapist's house, she told them, she could see a little better because in the trunk she had been able to slide her blindfold up slightly and enlarge the opening near the tip of her nose. The man carried her inside through the kitchen, and placed her on the kitchen floor. She described the house from the pattern of the kitchen linoleum to the small Christmas tree in the living room. Her attacker took instant photographs of her, she said, and perhaps even turned on a tape recorder.

Over the next three hours at the house, he raped her again and again, vaginally, orally, and anally, she told them, before finally packing her away in the trunk of his car and releasing her in Dick Kleberg Park. On the way, she told them, she could hear the man gunning the engine and feel him doing doughnuts with the car.

Captain Gomez had a stack of ten Polaroid photographs of men matching the general description of her attacker. Allison examined all of them, and found one that resembled the rapist, although she was sure it was not the same man. She told Gomez it closely resembled the man she was trying to describe.

Hector Treviño took Allison in his detective's car and started out toward Mesquite Avenue. All night he had been thinking of Eddie Wyatt, since he reconfirmed that the navy man still had the blue car with the white top. It was only one of several blue-and-white cars he wanted to show the teenager, but it was first on his list.

"I'm not saying the car you were in will be among the ones I'm going to show you. We don't know that. I just want you to take a look at them and see if you recognize any," he told her as they headed north up Sixth Street from the police station. They crossed the railroad tracks on the way, but it did not trigger any recognition in Allison. Treviño felt keen anticipation when he rounded the corner of Third and Mesquite. He pulled slowly to the curb a door or two down from Eddie's house. The blue Valiant was still parked there.

"The one in front," Treviño directed her. "Does that look like it?"

Allison focused hard on the Plymouth. She examined the lines of the trunk, and the side panels where she had been put into the backseat. She studied it for a long time before answering.

"No, that's not it," she finally told the disappointed detective. "I don't think that's the one."

"Are you sure now?" he prodded her.

"Yeah, that's not the car. I'm positive it's not."

Treviño put the detective's car in gear and started out, passing Eddie's car slowly so that Allison could take another look.

"I'm positive," she repeated as they left the block. Treviño took her to several other places where he knew blue cars were parked, but Allison could not identify any of them either. Finally, feeling as if he had struck out with the bases loaded, he took her home and joined the detectives who were canvassing the Shaw neighborhood.

By late afternoon, they located several people who had noticed something the day before, but there was little solid information. Two housewives on Doddridge Avenue heard a loud car cruising the area Monday morning. The next-door neighbor saw a blue car driving down Sixteenth, but after the kidnapping. A man on the corner of Sixteenth and Caesar saw what he thought was a blue Nova backing into the alley that morning. A couple on Sixteenth Street saw a blue car with a white roof in the alley. A woman on Sixteenth Street looked out through her backyard and also saw the blue car, and she noticed an Anglo male with short brown hair driving it, but she did not get a good enough look at the face to describe him.

By the time an investigator got to Luis Godines's house, it was after 3:00, and he had already reported to work for his night shift at the Exxon plant on the King Ranch. No one answered the door.

Nevertheless, word of the latest rape was spreading quickly

around the small town. At Angle Medical Center, Allison's cousin tearfully told her colleagues about the crime of the day before. That evening, Ronda was making dinner in the kitchen and Eddie was in the living room watching television, appearing tired and not looking forward to going to work late that night.

"I heard about something terrible at work today," Ronda told her husband.

"What was that, honeybun?" Eddie asked.

"You know Vera, the nurse down at the office? She's got a teenaged cousin in town, and somebody broke into the house yesterday, and kidnapped her and raped her several times. It was just awful"

Eddie appeared unmoved.

"Killed her dog, too," Ronda continued. "Stabbed the girl's dog to death right in front of her. She's only seventeen. It's all so horrible."

"Oh, really?" Eddie answered. Then he turned back to the television.

How typical a reaction from her husband, Ronda figured. Lately, nothing gets a reaction out of Eddie, not even this awful news about Kingsville's latest rape.

One of the workers on the evening shift at the natural gas plant was chatting with a group of men at about 7:00 P.M., when Luis Godines passed by them.

"Hey, Luis, you live over by Sixteenth and Caesar, don't you?" the worker called to Godines.

"Yeah, why?" Luis asked.

"Did you hear about the kidnap and rape over in your neighborhood?"

Godines suddenly became interested.

"Some guy kidnapped a teenager out of her house there on Sixteenth, and raped her for six hours," the co-worker said. "Let her go out by the ball fields. Carried her around in the trunk of his car."

Luis's eyebrows arched at the last statement. Could the blue car he saw have had that poor girl in its trunk when it went by his garage? Could he have seen the rapist? He looked around for the closest telephone.

Hector Treviño and Judy Hayes walked into the detective bureau shortly before 8:00 P.M. and were told that an Exxon worker named Godines had called in with information related to the Shaw case. Treviño immediately called the King Ranch plant. Godines told him that he had seen a blue car with a white top backing into the alley sometime around 11:00 A.M., and leaving fifteen minutes later. He thought it was a Chevrolet Nova. Treviño realized that would be precisely the time that Allison confirmed she was being taken away in a blue car. Treviño arranged to meet Godines after work.

A half-hour before midnight, Treviño picked up Godines at his house and brought him down to the station. Godines looked over the selection of photos that Allison had seen and pointed to the same one that Allison had selected, saying it resembled the man he had seen but was not him.

"I got a clear look at the guy," Godines said, "but I can't remember everything."

"Would you be willing to be put under hypnosis?" Gomez asked the witness. "We might be able to bring out a lot more details that are escaping you." Godines readily agreed. Then Treviño took Godines on a late-night tour of Kingsville for an hour to look at blue and white cars whose locations had been compiled by the entire department over the last day. They drove down Mesquite Avenue to examine Eddie Wyatt's Valiant, but the witness could not positively identify the car. When they returned to the station, Gomez told them he had made an appointment for 3:00 P.M. the next day with a hypnotist from the Texas Department of Public Safety in Corpus Christi.

Treviño got little sleep that night. He had thought that the odds were in his favor after Bobby Ellis spotted Eddie Wyatt around the scene of his wife's rape, and after the private security guard reported Wyatt's car at the location of another. When Allison was kidnapped in a blue and white car, Treviño thought that was simply too coincidental. But after Allison and now Godines failed to identify Eddie Wyatt's car, his spirits sank. He had to find out where he had taken a wrong turn.

The next morning's semi-weekly edition of the *Kingsville Record* carried the story of Allison's rape and abduction prominently across the top of page one with the headline, "Police seek help in apprehension of rapist." Above and to the left was a smaller-print kicker headline, "Pet dog stabbed to death as warning to victim." In the article, Gomez described the man the police were seeking:

"Anglo male, 5 foot 6 inches to 5 foot 8 inches tall and in his 20s. He has a slim build, short hair and a burn scar or discolored area on his left cheek near his eye."

It was a fair description of Eddie Wyatt. Because the Wyatts did not subscribe to the paper, Ronda never read it.

Shortly after 9:00 A.M. Wednesday, Treviño picked up Godines and drove him over to the Naval Air Station to look at more blue cars. None was familiar to the witness. They hit the parking lot of an apartment complex on South Sixth Street, where another possible suspect's car was parked, but again, Godines shrugged. After a late lunch, they went up to Corpus Christi with Gomez for the session with the hypnotist.

Once Texas Ranger Jim Peters put Godines under hypnosis, Godines began to recall things much more vividly. He remembered exactly what he was doing when he first head the rumbling of the car's bad muffler. He remembered looking up and walking out his short driveway to the alley. And he could remember the face. He described the driver with great detail. The police had not expected to hear such a vivid description. Unfortunately, the staff artist had taken time off for the holidays and would not be available for five more days. So Gomez arranged for another session on the Monday after Christmas, this time with the police sketch artist.

It took quite a bit of work, but Eddie finally got both of his children's new bicycles assembled after the little ones had gone to sleep Christmas Eve. Ronda smiled and took a picture of her husband barefoot, in blue jeans and sweatshirt, surrounded by instruction sheets, an assortment of tools, and pieces from the two bikes. On the front door, she taped up cards from friends, and below those, handmade cards drawn and colored by Paul and Diana.

"I hope the kids like these after all this work," Eddie said with a sigh as he struggled to tighten one of the nuts on the hub of a wheel. He wiped his brow with his forearm. Eddie and Ronda had saved to buy the bikes this Christmas, and Eddie was pleased. He was a better father to his children than his dad had been to him. And despite agreeing with Ronda that they would not exchange gifts with each other because money was so tight, Eddie had gone out and bought Ronda something anyway.

"I'm going to make us some chugalugs," Ronda said, putting the camera down on the table. That was their special Christmas drink, hot chocolate made with a mixture of cocoa, sugar, salt, and vanilla, topped with melted marshmallow. She set to work over the kitchen range while Eddie attached the training wheels to the bikes. It felt good for the two of them to be together.

Ever since her lunchtime confession to Barbara Crowell, Ronda felt better. She was still praying for God to reveal what was happening to her marriage, but that purging of pent-up emotions made her feel as if she were no longer alone. Ronda resolved to enjoy the Christmas holiday. Everything was now in God's hands, and he would make all things clear when the time was right.

In the morning, the children squealed with glee when they saw their new bikes, and begged their dad to go outside and teach them immediately to ride. With Christmas music on their stereo, Ronda and Eddie opened the packages that Paul and Erna had mailed, most of them containing clothing. After that, Eddie grabbed a small package from beneath the tree and handed it to Ronda.

"Eddie!" Ronda said. "We agreed we weren't going to get each other anything!"

"That's all right, honeybun, just open it. It's just a little something I picked up at the store," he said.

The gift was not wrapped. It was still inside its small, brown paper shopping bag, the opening secured with green tape, that tape Eddie had been bringing home from the Naval Air Station to use around the house. Ronda ripped the bag open; inside was a wristwatch. Ronda was very touched and thanked Eddie for the gift.

Ronda made a nice Christmas dinner that evening, and the next day, Saturday, they played all day with the children and their bikes. Ronda had a smile on her face all day, and toward evening, while Eddie watched television, she sat down at the kitchen table with her journal and in it she thanked God for helping her through the bad days.

That evening, Ronda went to bed alone. Eddie seemed distant again, and when she retired, he went into the bathroom and stayed in there for a long time, until after she went to sleep. Later, she stirred at some noise in the living room, the sound of a woman screaming. She realized Eddie was sitting up late and was watching some late night movie rather than coming to share their bed.

Ranger Peters put Luis Godines into a hypnotic trance once more on Monday afternoon. Trooper Alvin Hale, back from his holiday break, was an experienced sketch artist who was used to working from a witness's verbal descriptions. Captain Gomez and Detective Treviño were in the room, and they watched as the face and figure took more definite shape on Hale's pad.

The Exxon worker, answering Jim Peters's questions, was able to pull forth details about the man he had seen in the alley. The shape of the suspect's thin face came first. Then the short, wavy hair with thin sideburns coming down even with the bottom of his ears. Godines described the thin lips, short mustache, and ruddy complexion as he had seen them. The eyes were beady. While Hale put his finishing touches on the sketch, Hector Treviño leaned over the artist's shoulder.

"Hey!" the burly detective let out a yell of recognition. "That's Eddie Wyatt!" The drawing looked amazingly like the mug shot of Wyatt that Treviño had seen at naval security. Gomez walked around to share a look at the sketch.

"Who's this Wyatt fellow?" he asked.

"I've had him in mind for a couple weeks now," Treviño explained to his commander. "I took Allison by his house the day after she was raped; she didn't recognize his car. It matched her description, but she said she was sure it wasn't the one, so I put him out of my mind."

Treviño related how he had first come across Wyatt, about the security guard who saw the license plate of a suspicious character, and how the number failed to turn up in the Texas motor vehicles computer; how Bobby Ellis, Kyung's husband, spotted a man in a silver car he thought was snooping around his wife, then a week later saw the same man getting into that car at the Naval Air Station; and how it fell into place when that man was identified by Naval Security as Eddie Wyatt, who also owned a blue and white Plymouth Valiant with Virginia license plates of the same number as the one reported by the security guard.

And to top it off, Treviño knew that Wyatt had access to the green tape in the course of his job.

"When we get back to town, I want to bring this guy in for questioning," Treviño said. "It may not be the guy, but it keeps nagging at me."

After driving back from Corpus Christi and taking Luis Godines home, Treviño stopped at the station to pick up Detective Keith Durham and head out to Mesquite Avenue. Eddie was home alone when he heard the knock on his door shortly after 3:30.

"I'd like to have a talk with you about some cases that we have pending," Treviño said to Eddie.

"Sure, you want to come in?" Eddie responded. He was cool and apparently not nervous.

"No, actually, we'd like for you to come down to our office," Treviño said.

"Well, okay, but can you give me about twenty minutes? I'll drive down, if that's all right with you guys?" Eddie replied. Treviño and Durham looked at each other, then Treviño told Eddie that would be fine. Eddie asked where the police station was, and they told him. Then they went back to the station, with Treviño still reeling with doubt about Wyatt. The man was behaving like he had nothing to hide. Even so, Treviño radioed for an officer to sit on Mesquite Avenue, just in case Wyatt decided to go north instead of south.

Eddie dutifully came down to the station, easing his noisy Plymouth Valiant into one of the dozen curbside diagonal parking spaces on Sixth Street in front of police headquarters and the detective division. Treviño éscorted Eddie through the squad room and into a small office in the corner of the building. The room was brightly lit by a south window. Gomez waited in his captain's office across the center hallway from the squad room. Texas Ranger Kasey King, who had been involved since September, was on hand along with most of the detectives, including Judy Hayes.

Treviño read Eddie his Miranda rights, and Eddie said he understood them, and that he would be happy to talk with them because he had nothing to hide. He was only too willing to help. Treviño opened the interrogation with a few simple questions about Eddie's background, then told him that his car matched the description of the one used by the suspect in a kidnap-rape that had occurred a week earlier. Treviño asked Eddie if the police could search his car. Eddie readily agreed, somewhat to Treviño's dismay. Either Wyatt was not the rapist, Treviño figured, or he had so thoroughly cleaned the car that he was confident nothing would be found. Eddie signed a consent to search form and handed Treviño the keys. Then Treviño asked Judy Hayes and Sergeant Cruz, the evidence technician, to go out and take a look inside the blue Valiant.

Treviño went back to the interrogation room with Eddie and photographed him for the files. He tried to talk with Eddie about the crime, but Eddie changed the subject away from Allison Shaw. He wanted to talk about Jesus.

"I'm a Christian," Eddie told him. "I turned to Jesus many years ago. I wouldn't have anything to do with this rape you're talking about. Call Brother Fields, or call Alvin Hall, he used to be my pastor up in Norfolk."

Judy Hayes went to the Valiant's backseat while Cruz went to the trunk. In the late afternoon light, Hayes strained her eyes while she got down on her hands and knees. It looked like the carpeting had been freshly vacuumed, with the brush strokes still visible across the floor's nap. Hayes shrugged that off and continued to search. She noticed a hair on the floor, behind the driver's seat, right where Allison said she had placed her head. With a sudden sense of excitement, Hayes pinched the hair between her thumb and index finger. Pulling it up, she found that the hair was long, and it was blond. She backed out of the rear seat and stood up. Quickly, she turned to the back of the car to show Cruz what she had found. Instead, she saw Cruz standing and looking right at her, with a smile on his face.

Hayes looked at Cruz's right hand. He was holding a spool of green duct tape, similar to the tape that had been used on Allison. In the trunk, which also looked like it had been cleaned recently, he found a tool box right where Allison had described one, and he spotted what might be dog hairs.

Hayes and Cruz went inside to show Captain Gomez what they had found. Treviño joined them, saw the new evidence, and was convinced that Eddie Wyatt was their man. Gomez ordered that Eddie's car be subjected to a proper and thorough search. Treviño went back into the interrogation room, where Eddie patiently waited for permission to go home.

"I hate to tell you this," the detective said to Eddie. "But it's not looking too good for you."

"What do you mean?" Eddie asked.

"We found some blond hair in your backseat..."

"My little girl is blond," Eddie replied.

"...and some tape just like the tape that was used to bind the rape victim," Treviño finished.

"I'm sorry, I don't know what you're talking about," Eddie said. "I don't have anything to do with this rape."

"I recommend that if you did something, let's just get this thing cleared up right here," Treviño pressed him.

"There must be some mistake. You don't understand. I'm a Christian man."

Treviño could see Eddie start to pull back. With each question, Treviño believed his suspect was closing up more and more. Treviño wanted him to sign a second consent to search form, this one covering his house. Eddie at first agreed, and began to sign it. But after he wrote "E," he stopped the pen for a second, then put it back down.

"No, I'm not going to let you just search through my house," Eddie said.

Gomez then came in the room. In the manner that a gruff father might use in talking to a wayward son, Gomez tried to extract some information from Eddie. Hayes was listening at the doorway of the squad room.

The captain said it was time for Eddie to get this terrible burden off his chest, that he knew Eddie wanted to talk about it. Gomez accused Eddie of holding back confessions to at least two of the unsolved rapes. Eddie denied any involvement in the previous week's crime, as well as any knowledge of the Ellis rape on Halloween night. They did not have enough to hold Wyatt at the station, and Gomez knew it. Eddie knew it, too.

"Well, I guess I'm going to go home, if y'all are through with me," Eddie said when it got to be near 5:00 P.M. "Can I have my car back?"

"We're not done looking through it yet," Gomez said. "I'll call your wife and maybe she can come get you." Eddie winced.

With the children trailing her, Ronda unlocked the front door and walked inside her house. She looked around and saw some of the same things cluttering the living room that had been there at lunchtime when she asked Eddie to pick them up. Now he was gone, and the mess was still there. Ronda was a little miffed at that. She sent Paul and Diana outside to play while she proceeded to pick up the mess. When the telephone rang, she reached for it while her mind was going over the evening's dinner menu.

"Hello?"

"Mrs. Wyatt? This is Captain George Gomez of the Kingsville Police Department."

"What can I do for you?" Ronda asked, startled.

"We have your husband down here at the station, Mrs. Wyatt. We're asking him some questions about this kidnap and rape case we have from last week. Have you heard about that?"

"Yes, that was the cousin of a woman I work with," Ronda answered. "Why on earth would you be talking to my husband about that?"

Gomez told her about the similarity between the kidnapper's car and the Valiant that Eddie drove. What a terrible thing to do, Ronda thought, to take a man down for questioning just because he has a blue car. Why were they picking on Eddie, just when he could least afford another problem? It all had to be a mistake. The thought of her asexual husband being a rapist was just too preposterous for her to entertain.

Gomez asked Ronda whether she could come down and get Eddie, since they were still examining the car. The detectives would like to talk with her as well. Ronda said she could not do that, since there was no one to watch the children.

"We'll bring him home for you then, ma'am," Gomez said quickly. He was anxious to get a look inside 418 West Mesquite, to see if it matched the description Allison had given of the house to which she had been taken for repeated raping.

Ronda quickly dialed Pastor Fields. Dolores answered. Ronda sounded flustered as she asked Dolores whether she and James could come over right away. "I need you," Ronda told her friend. "The police are coming over with Eddie. They think he had something to do with that rape last week." Dolores was floored. Eddie suspected of rape? The Eddie Wyatt she knew was too nice, too quiet, too polite to be a criminal. Her husband, who had counseled him throughout the summer, was aware of a deep depression and of a conflict over his relationship with the Lord. How could such a withdrawn young man commit rape? He thought it impossible.

The Fieldses got to the Wyatts' house almost as quickly as the police, and Dolores, after leading her husband up the step and through the front door, stayed close to Ronda while Captain Gomez busily asked questions. Ranger Kasey King and Detective Hector Treviño came along. Paul and Diana remained outside playing, oblivious to the crisis going on in their living room. While everyone was present, Eddie retold in front of Ronda the story he had given the police. He said that the previous Monday morning, he had gone shopping at Winn's department store for some

Christmas gifts, and then came home after lunch to take a nap because he had to work that night.

Why couldn't the police believe that, Ronda wondered? That was what their life was like, dull and predictable. So lackluster that even having normal, marital sex would be a special event. Ronda wished that there was some way to indicate Eddie's disinterest in sex without opening up that embarrassing and most personal aspect of her life.

Gomez's tone made it clear he did not believe Eddie's story.

"Where does this back door lead to?" the captain asked, wandering around the small living room and kitchen area before coming to the utility room door.

"Out to the laundry room, then the backyard," Ronda answered.

"Do you own a Polaroid camera?" he then asked.

"Why, yes," Ronda said. Eddie was silent, letting his wife answer the questions for a change.

"Can I see it?" Gomez asked.

Ronda went into the bedroom and located their instant camera, and gave it to the captain. Gomez noted that it had a stripe across its white casing. Ronda was beginning to feel bothered by the intrusion of these strangers.

Treviño and King were silent while they visually scoured the two rooms. Treviño bent over and rubbed his hand along the carpet. King walked over to look at the studio portrait of the children against a Christmas tree background. They looked at the stereo, and the portable tape recorder. Treviño stood in the kitchen, looking down at the gold and brown tile.

Ronda did not fuss until Gomez asked whether the police could snip a sample of their carpet for analysis. At that, she said no. The three officers finally were ready to leave. Within minutes of their departure, James and Dolores Fields left, too.

"Eddie?" Ronda asked, her question apparent in its absence.

"Like I said, honeybun, I went shopping that day, that's when I bought your watch for Christmas. Then I came home and took a nap in the afternoon."

They talked the rest of the evening about how the police could make such a mistake and disrupt the lives of two struggling people. Ronda wondered whether this was going to be another injustice, like the time Eddie had to spend a weekend in the Norfolk jail all because he took a shortcut across some guy's yard. Things were hard enough on military families, having to move from place to place and sinking no roots. Why didn't the towns ever make them feel welcome?

After getting the children to bed, Ronda decided she, too, would retire early. The day had been an ordeal. Eddie joined her in bed. The day had been long and difficult for him.

"Honey, don't you think we should pray?" Ronda asked as Eddie got between the sheets.

"Yeah, sure. Why don't you, though? I'm tired," he said.

"No, I think you should," Ronda answered.

Eddie then recited a brief prayer asking the Lord to help them though this ordeal. He quickly closed his eyes and went to sleep.

Poor Eddie, Ronda thought. He's exhausted by all this. But his behavior reinforced her conviction that her husband was innocent. No guilty man could be so nonchalant as to shrug off this police questioning that was upsetting Ronda's stomach so much. No man could sleep so peacefully if he had really done the dreadful things that her coworker Vera told her were done to her cousin Allison.

Now the police had the photograph of Eddie Wyatt that Hector Treviño had shot. Royce Johnston, the assistant district attorney for Kleberg County, wanted Allison brought down to look at another photo lineup. That night, after returning from the Wyatts', Gomez put the picture among fifteen other Polaroid mug shots for Allison to view. He placed Eddie's picture eighth in the stack. Allison was scheduled to go to Corpus Christi the next morning to be put under hypnosis with the state sketch artist. Gomez was nervous that if Allison failed to pick Wyatt's picture from among the others, all of the photographs would clog her memory and taint her session with the hypnotist. Nevertheless, about 7:00 P.M., with Gomez pacing the hallway, Judy Hayes phoned Charles Shaw and asked him to bring Allison down to the station to look at another set of photographs.

Allison arrived with her parents and her boyfriend. Gomez took her into the captain's office and sat her next to his desk.

"I want you to just look through this stack and tell me whether the man who attacked you is in there," Gomez told her, handing her the photos. He was careful not to say that the man they suspected was in the stack, even though it was understood that they had someone in mind. Allison looked over the top photograph and quickly decided that it was not the man. She took the photo and transferred it to the bottom of the stack. She went through the first seven photos that way, studying them a bit before decidedly passing on to the next.

When Allison removed the seventh photo and looked at the one below it, she stared straight into the face of the man who attacked her. Immediately, she threw the entire stack of photos to the floor and began to cry.

"That's him! That's the one!" Allison kept saying. Gomez and Hayes got down on the floor to gather the pictures.

"Which one?" Gomez asked.

"Him," Allison said, pointing right at the mug shot of Eddie. Gomez picked up Eddie's mug shot, and had Allison initial it and note the time, 7:47. Royce Johnston had seen enough to satisfy his legal thresholds. He told Gomez to have his detectives draw up an arrest warrant for Wyatt.

Ten minutes later, Eddie called and asked for Treviño, who had just started typing the affidavit for Eddie's arrest.

"You guys done with my car yet? I'm gonna need it tomorrow," Eddie asked the detective.

"No, not yet. We're almost done. I'll let you know," Treviño said.

Only twenty minutes after she and Eddie had gone to bed, Ronda heard cars pulling up to the curb outside her house. Soon there was knocking on the door.

"Police! Open up! We have a warrant for your husband's arrest!"

Ronda could not believe her ears. She had been so sure that everything was going to work out, yet each passing hour this evening threw things into more and more confusion. She was speechless as she watched the police grab Eddie, who had thrown on a pair of jeans, a pullover shirt, and a plaid jacket. Gomez read Eddie his rights once more, then the DA's investigator Adan Muñoz and Ranger King handcuffed him and led him to a waiting car. Gomez stayed behind. He could see that Ronda was very upset, but he still had to ask several more questions.

"We need to search the house, Mrs. Wyatt," Gomez said after she declined to give answers to other questions. "Would you give us permission to do that?"

Ronda did not know what to say. Suddenly it occurred to her that anything she did from here on could influence Eddie's fate.

"I don't know what to do," she pleaded as she thumbed through the small Kingsville phone directory. She looked for an attorney's listing, and began to call at random, until someone gave her free advice: Don't tell the police anything until her husband was represented by a lawyer. Ironically, the attorney Ronda had reached was the Shaw family attorney.

"I'm sorry, Captain Gomez, but I don't want you to search my house, and I won't answer any more questions," Ronda told Gomez after she hung up the phone. The police captain obligingly left, but told her they would return in the morning with a search warrant, giving them the legal right to go through the house. Ronda immediately tried to call Pastor Fields but he and his wife had gone out to dinner. Ronda then dialed her parents' number in Colorado. It was one of the most difficult calls she ever had to make.

Ronda broke into tears almost as soon as she started telling her mother the story of coming home to the call from the police. She ended it with the terrible scene that had just occurred, with Eddie being dragged out of the house in handcuffs to face the charge of rape.

"Oh, Mom, but he didn't do it," she cried. "It's all a terrible mistake, but no one will listen to him!"

"Ronda," Erna paused for a second. "Are you sure that he didn't do it?" Erna had seen her daughter stand by Eddie before. When he was charged aboard the *Kennedy* with drug possession, Ronda was right there believing in her husband. When the trespassing charge was leveled in Norfolk, Erna listened to Ronda express the belief that it was another injustice through which their faith would be tested. Ronda always wanted to believe the best in Eddie.

And once again, Ronda would hear of no doubts. The very facts of this latest rape confirmed for Ronda that her husband could not have done it.

"The man killed the girl's dog when he kidnapped her, Mom," Ronda said. "Eddie could never have done that. Eddie wouldn't harm a fly. Mom, it's just not in him," Erna offered to come down to Texas to be with her, but Ronda said that would not be necessary. "This is all a big mistake, and they'll find out soon enough, Mom," she said. "Eddie's so passive and nonviolent. I just dread us having to go through this until they find out they're wrong."

The police took Eddie to the same room where he had been questioned only five hours earlier, and confronted him with the fact that the rape victim had positively identified him as the attacker. Eddie gave deliberate, and short, answers. Most often, he gave no answer at all. Finally, he said that he wanted a lawyer, effectively ending the interrogation.

About 10:30 P.M., Luis Godines called in from the Exxon plant to ask how things had progressed since his session with the sketch artist that afternoon. Treviño told him they had some more photos they wanted him to inspect, so Godines drove to police headquarters after his shift. He was shown the same stack of sixteen mug shots that Allison had seen. Without hesitation, he also picked Eddie Wyatt's picture.

While arrangements were being made to transfer him to the county jail, Eddie was left in the small corner room, and Gomez directed Judy Hayes to stand guard. Detective Hayes had spent the last sixteen months mopping up after crimes like the one Eddie was going to be charged with. She had faced the unpleasant and formidable task of trying to pry the most private details of the crime of rape out of nearly twenty women while at the same time trying to provide a soothing blanket of comfort and security around them. She remained on friendly terms with some of the women who had been raped, and observed firsthand the impact of that crime on their lives. They all changed, in different ways to be sure, but they would never be the same women they had been. Some handled it with bravado, some withdrew into denial, but Hayes knew the effects would be permanent. Shelly Polk, the newcomer to Kingsville who had been so terrorized by threats that she blacked out the crime for hours, had already moved back to the Midwest with her husband.

For over a year, Judy Hayes had endured the gut-wrenching tension that came from knowing that yet another woman would be brutalized and violated if they did not solve these cases soon. She did not buy any of Wyatt's protestations about being a born-again Christian incapable of committing such a terrible crime. She could only feel for Allison Shaw, whose brave participation in her own investigation—hitting the streets to look at cars, facing the entire detective squad at one time to talk in detail about the crime, and finally selecting Wyatt's mug shot unequivocally out of a stack of sixteen photos—was the luckiest of breaks. Hayes had no doubts at all that she was guarding the right man.

She and Eddie spoke politely during the fifteen minutes they were left alone. They did not talk about the crimes at all. But as Hayes looked into Wyatt's eyes, she saw one of the coldest gazes she had ever encountered. Hayes thought that even while they were chitchatting, Wyatt was looking disdainfully at her, disposing of her physically and emotionally. She kept her hand ready to go for her gun in case the suspect made the slightest aggressive move. She would not have flinched if Wyatt rose from his chair. She would shot him in a flash.

Hayes felt that Wyatt must have sensed her fire. He was on extra-good behavior, not so much as twitching a muscle until Treviño and Lieutenant Amando Vidal returned to take him over to the country jail. Soon, Eddie found himself on the top floor jail of the Kleberg County Courthouse, being held in lieu of $90,000 bail set by local Justice of the Peace Gary Bigger.

Pastor Fields called Ronda as soon as he got her message, which she had left for him at the restaurant. She asked him to go with her to the jail to find out what was happening. Dolores volunteered to stay at the house with the children.

Although she was driving, Ronda could not concentrate on the road. She looked at some of the people still out on the streets late at night. It seemed so odd to her that they appeared to be going about their normal business, totally oblivious to her crisis. How could the rest of the world not see her pain? How could it keep going on when she desperately needed it to stop and notice that she was drowning?

Ronda led Pastor Fields down the north stairs to the courthouse basement office of the Kleberg County Sheriff. They both asked to see Eddie Wyatt and were told to wait. Ronda heard the deputies talk about the charges leveled against her husband—burglary with intent to commit rape and sodomy. Captain Gomez arrived and wanted to talk with Ronda.

"We have a cut-and-dried case against your husband, Mrs. Wyatt," he told her privately. "I think you ought to do whatever you can to get him to confess so it'll go easier on him."

"What do you mean a cut-and-dried case?" Ronda demanded. "He's innocent. I know he could not have done this. Why are you doing this to us?"

"Mrs. Wyatt, the victim has positively identified him. If he confesses, the courts may be more lenient with him."

Inside, Ronda was screaming *You Liar!* at the police captain. She was the one who had lived with Eddie for nearly seven years. She knew him better than anybody. She wanted to scream at someone to stop this nightmare. Finally, a deputy came downstairs and told her she could have a few minutes with her husband. She went up to the top floor visiting area.

They embraced briefly, then Ronda asked him for some explanation.

"I didn't do it, honeybun," Eddie told her. "It's a terrible mistake. I couldn't do something like that, but they don't believe me."

"I believe you, Eddie," Ronda said. "I'll stand by you through this."

Then Eddie looked at her and hesitated before speaking again.

"Honey, I need you to do something for me. Get rid of my gun. I'm not supposed to have it because of my record. It's behind the bed. Throw it away!"

Ronda's mind began to spin. The man she loved, to whom

she had given her life and for whom she promised to do anything, was asking her to do something she knew was illegal. She was torn between her heart and her mind. The thought came to her that she had to think of her children and what would be right for them. When their visit was over, an officer led Ronda away from Eddie.

"Remember, if you get rid of any evidence, we will file charges against you," said the deputy, who had not heard Eddie's request. On the way out of the courthouse door, Ronda turned to her pastor.

"What is sodomy?" she asked Fields. "That's what they said was one of the charges against Eddie." Ronda had heard the term before but was unsure what it actually meant.

"Deviant sexual practices," her pastor replied. "Usually it refers to anal intercourse."

Ronda cringed instinctively at the thought. She remembered how Eddie wanted to try anal sex with her, but she had refused. The last occasion that he had even mentioned it, and they ended up having coital intercourse instead, was the night she became pregnant with Diana when he was in Denver on leave from basic training, more than three years earlier. He had dropped all mention of anal sex since then. Actually, for a long time since, Eddie showed no interest in sex at all. The idea that he could be guilty of having committed these violent sexual acts against this teen-aged girl was entirely incompatible with Ronda's image of her husband.

Dolores Fields drove her husband home, packed some clothes, and prepared to return to spend the night with Ronda. While they were gone, Ronda thought about Eddie's request to get rid of his gun. She groped around behind their water bed's headboard until she felt it, and pulled it out with its zippered carrying case. She knew she could not dispose of it in good conscience, but out of loyalty felt she had to make some kind of effort to comply with Eddie's wish. She decided to place it up in the attic crawl space. But when she tried to put it inside the gun case, she found it did not fit. The gun's barrel was longer by a couple of inches, and the zipper would not go around it. It could not have been the same gun he had before, and Ronda wondered where it had come from. She stood on a chair and reached up into the crawl space, dropping it right next to the opening's frame. Ronda had never been up in the crawl space, which had no flooring.

Ronda tried to reach Eddie's oldest brother in Galveston to let him know what had happened, but had to settle for leaving a message on his business answering machine. Dolores Fields returned with some belongings to spend the night. They prayed together and got to bed about 1:30. As Ronda was dozing off, the telephone jolted her awake. It's probably Eddie's brother, she thought as she rushed to answer it. When she said hello, an unfamiliar male voice came out of the receiver.

"I hope that bastard goes to prison." Click.

Ronda stared at the phone for a second, then started to cry. Dolores came out to comfort her. Suddenly, she felt very unsafe in her own home. Before they returned to bed, Ronda told Dolores that she had to stand by Eddie until this misunderstanding could be cleared up.

"But nothing I've ever been through has prepared me for the pain I'm feeling right now," she confided tearfully.

Early in the morning, Eddie's oldest brother returned Ronda's call and she filled him in on the arrest. He said he would try to do what he could to arrange for a lawyer. Ronda then decided she would take Paul and Diana to the sitter as though nothing had happened. She wanted them out of the house when the police came to search. Soon, Paul came into her bedroom and saw that Dolores Fields was there.

"Mommy, where's my daddy?" the five-year-old asked.

"Daddy has left for the day, Paul. He's already downtown," Ronda answered truthfully.

"But Mommy, I thought I heard you say on the phone that Daddy was in jail?" Paul replied. Ronda swallowed hard. Her son must have heard the conversation she had with his uncle. She lifted Paul onto her lap and held him tightly. She knew she had to be honest because she sensed that in the days ahead, he would need to trust her a lot.

"Honey, Daddy is in jail," she said.

"Why?" Paul asked.

"Because the police think that Daddy did some things that he shouldn't have done," Ronda replied in as soothing a voice as she could manage.

"Did he?" Paul wanted to know, as if his mom should know the answer.

"I don't know, Paul," she said, surprised at her own response.

Paul went into his room to get dressed, and Diana soon awoke, too. After a while, the telephone rang, and Paul rushed to get it.

"Mommy, it's for you," Paul called to her. Ronda came and took the phone.

"Mrs. Wyatt?" the male caller asked.

"Yes?" she replied.

"How does it feel to be married to a rapist?" the man said, then he hung up.

How should I know? Ronda wanted to scream at the departed voice. *How could I know?*

CHAPTER 9

THE FAMILY LAID NAKED

This hurts like nothing else has ever hurt. We are being broken into very small pieces. Our lives are being laid bare before the eyes of strangers. It doesn't really matter that they gossip, or are so very curious. Or that they judge and are so critical as though they have never done wrong. Someday they too will be crushed. Maybe then they will understand.

—from Ronda's diary

A task force of Kingsville Police, sheriff's officers, Texas Rangers, and the DA's investigator pulled up to Ronda's house at twenty minutes after noon on Tuesday, armed with a search warrant sworn out by Hector Treviño and signed by District Judge Vernon Harville.

"Grab that trash and stick it in the trunk," Treviño said to Detective Keith Durham when he saw the family's overloaded curbside bin waiting for collection. "We'll go through it back at the station later." The crew then walked up the driveway to the front door. No one was at home. A neighbor said Ronda had left a little earlier with the children.

They found an unlocked window and sent Judy Hayes through to open the front door. Marching into Ronda's living room, Treviño put a copy of the search warrant on the coffee table, then directed the searchers to various parts of the house. Adan Muñoz, the DA's investigator, and Bob Dornack from the sheriff's department made video and still photographs of the house while the others began rummaging through the bedroom, hall closet, and kitchen. Within ten minutes, they found some of what they had come for.

Treviño discovered two rolls of tape in the top drawer of

Eddie's bedroom dresser. One was green, just like the tape used on Allison Shaw, Kyung Ellis, and Shelly Polk. It was also similar to the tape used on two earlier victims, Cheryl Palmer and Kim Sullivan. The other roll was Borden's Mystik tape, light brown in color, just like the tape that was used on Allison's initial ineffective blindfold. Treviño saw what looked like blood inside the brown tape carton.

Five minutes later, Treviño found a second roll of brown tape in a paper bag on the floor next to the dresser.

It took a half hour for Judy Hayes to come across a roll of brown masking tape in the hall closet. Ten minutes later, Treviño found a dark blue ski mask with a multicolor design across the front in the bottom dresser drawer.

After Ronda had left the house that morning she dropped off the children at the sitter's, then she and Dolores went shopping at the HEB Grocery market. Ronda took Dolores home and picked up James Fields, who had agreed to spend some time with her during the afternoon. Now, as she turned the corner from Armstrong Street onto Mesquite Avenue, two blocks from home, she saw the commotion in front of her house.

Texas Ranger Kasey King was posted in her yard with a rifle.

"They're searching the house. What do I do?" Ronda asked her pastor.

"Just park the car. You'll be all right."

Ronda turned slowly into her driveway and stopped short of the carport. She told King who she was and identified Pastor Fields. King said Ronda could go inside, but the blind minister could not go any farther as long as the search was being conducted. Ronda entered her front door and saw four men and a woman looking over every corner of the house. Even though she understood why they were doing this, she felt an overpowering sense of violation. George Gomez picked up the copy of the search warrant from the coffee table and handed it to Ronda. She staggered to the sofa to read it while those around her continued to search, seemingly oblivious to her pain. She looked up once, and caught Judy Hayes looking at her. Ronda thought she saw the policewoman smile at her. It was the only measure of comfort she would feel through the afternoon's ordeal.

The search warrant affidavit spelled out why the police thought Eddie had raped Allison. As Ronda read it, she felt her stomach churning. The document outlined repeated acts of rape and sodomy in the backseat of the family car and inside her house, in the very room in which Ronda was seated at that moment, on the carpet not three feet away from her. Ronda realized that when the officers had looked all over her house the previous night, they were looking for items Allison had mentioned. They saw the children's portrait on the short wall, the brown and gold kitchen tile, the green chair, the stereo table. And the affidavit stated that Allison was able to positively identify her husband's photograph because, during the course of the six-hour crime, she was able to see his face clearly.

This has to be wrong, Ronda kept saying to herself. She pored over the two-page document, looking in vain for the loophole that would stop this charade, the loose strand she could grasp and use to unravel these allegations that threatened to tear her family and home apart forever. Just then, Ronda heard a commotion in the front yard, and the sound of voices coming toward the door.

"Now when you get inside, you don't have to say anything," a male voice said. "Just nod, okay?"

Ronda looked up and saw a man in a suit with his right hand grasping the arm of a teenaged girl. How pretty she was, with her long blond hair and her downcast eyes. Then it hit Ronda who this young girl was. She was the victim. Royce Johnston, the assistant DA for Kleberg County, escorted Allison Shaw into the house. Instantly, Ronda's eyes narrowed with anger for the girl who was at the very center of her family's disaster. How dare she come into this house, Ronda thought! She wanted to scream at her to stop telling lies about her husband. Instead, she watched as the girl with the golden hair stepped gingerly into Ronda's living room and inspected the rug, the stereo, the digital clock on it. She nodded yes each time. Johnston led the girl into the kitchen, and Allison looked down at the tile flooring and nodded yes. Then the teenager began to sob loudly. Ronda watched one of the officers take that snip from the carpet she had denied them the night before.

"Take her down to the station,'" Captain Gomez told Judy Hayes, referring to Allison, "and get a statement from her on her ID of the house."

Ronda was stunned. This could not be real, she thought. *Eddie didn't do it!* An officer came over and showed Treviño another roll of green tape that had been found in a kitchen drawer. Ronda knew that tape. Everybody takes supplies from work, Eddie had told her. How could that be evidence of Eddie's guilt in a rape when every man on the naval base must have taken some?

Someone then directed Ronda to get off the sofa so it could be photographed. Made to feel like an intruder in her own home, Ronda turned and saw the children's bedroom. She felt drawn to it in her crisis, and went in to sit on her son's bed. She loved that little room. It was bright and sunny and filled with happy memories for her. Thoughts of the children came to her as she looked out the window, and then she broke down. Her tears came slowly at first, but soon they fell in torrents, and she began sobbing.

Captain Gomez saw her in the bedroom and walked in. Standing over her, he said a few things and then insinuated that her fundamentalist faith may have had some influence on Eddie's actions. Maybe he couldn't live up to her standards, he suggested.

"You're the only one who knows what went on behind your bedroom door," Gomez said. "You probably made demands on him that he couldn't meet."

Ronda was stunned that this policeman was making conclusions about her private life that way. It finished off what little dignity she had managed to cling to during the last few hours. Ronda felt humiliated, as if she were being stripped naked in front of a roomful of strangers. All of her neighbors were being questioned. And now Captain Gomez was talking to her as though she should have the answers to the entire mystery about her husband. She resented his bringing up her sex life as though it were something for public consumption. He even insinuated that she might have been involved. The thought sickened her to the point of gagging.

"If you're hiding evidence," Gomez finally warned her, "we'll file charges on you, too."

About ten minutes to three, Treviño finished filling in the search warrant inventory to give Ronda a list of the property that was being seized. It did not include Eddie's gun, which apparently had fallen into a niche in the crawl space when Ronda placed it there, and was overlooked when the search party went up into it. Treviño handed the inventory to Ronda, and was the last officer to walk out the front door. Ronda followed them, reading what was being taken from her house. Mostly it was rolls of tape. There was also some clothing, a ski mask, and their Polaroid camera. Pastor Fields was still there. As they walked by Ronda's silver Dodge Aspen, she was feeling intensely bitter.

"Don't you want to search my car, too?" Ronda, her voice weary with resignation, asked the captain.

"No," Gomez replied. Then he looked back at Ronda. He knew it was beyond her ability right now to appreciate the fact that they had to do what they had done, that they had to come in the middle of the night to rip her husband from their bed and charge him with this hideous crime.

"Are you going to be all right?" Gomez asked Ronda, as if he could solve her problems, the ones he himself brought to her door.

"Just leave, please," Ronda said. "I'll be fine."

Back at the station, the evidence was logged and the trash bags from the Wyatts' curbside bin were secured. The trash would be sorted the next day. Later that afternoon, Treviño took Eddie out of the Kleberg jail and over to the base, to witness the search of his two lockers at the corrosion control shop. Police found nothing in them that was incriminating.

Pulling a rubber glove onto his right hand, Detective Keith Durham began on Wednesday morning to sort through the clear plastic bags filled with trash that police had seized from the Wyatts' curbside bin the day before. Piece by piece, out in the police parking lot, Durham pulled out the family's weekly trash, examined it for any relevance to the case, then set it aside in the sopping mixture of food remains, paper products, and other goop.

Gradually the bags emptied, until Durham reached in and grabbed an old Borden's Egg Nog carton. He shook it slightly, and heard something rattling inside.

Durham peeled back the top of the waxed paper carton, and saw a wadded-up heap of recording tape that had been yanked recklessly out of a white cassette. Sergeant Cruz, on hand to photograph the search, began to snap pictures.

Carefully, Durham lifted the tape out of the carton. It was smeared with eggnog residue. There was a small sticker on it with green printing. It said "Matt. 5:16." Part of it was scorched, probably with a match or lighter, but the rest of the label quoted the Gospel verse: "Let your light so shine before men, that they may see your good works, and glorify your Father which is in heaven." When Durham inspected the bottom of the cassette, where the tape ran over the rollers, he saw that someone had tried to burn the tape as well. The plastic casing was melted and scorched in places. Cruz, the evidence technician, took the tape and cassette into the police station, where Treviño was sitting with Captain Gomez.

"The tape?" Treviño lit up with anticipation. Treviño knew that if this was the tape recording Allison suspected had been made of her, Wyatt was nailed cold. "Where did you find it?"

"In an eggnog carton," Cruz said.

"Blech. I hate eggnog," Gomez piped in.

The police gingerly undid the rat's nest of recording tape and dabbed the excess eggnog off it. They decided to let it dry by draping it all around the captain's office, like a clothesline. They suspended it from the coatrack, stereo system, file cabinets, and other points until the office looked infested by huge spiders that spun brown webs. Early in the afternoon, when the tape had dried, Treviño took the lengthy strand to an electronics store in town and had it rewound onto a new cassette.

"Keep your fingers crossed," Gomez told his crew as he popped the cassette into a player. They all sat down quietly and strained to listen as the tape hissed for about fifteen seconds. Then some rumbling noise could be heard. Finally, there were voices on the tape, one male, the other female, both faint and muddled:

"Say I'm good," the male voice said in a very faint whisper.

"Oh, you're good," a frightened female voice came back on command.

"Tell me you want me to fuck your ass," the male said in a low, breathy tone.

"I want you to fuck my ass, because you're good. Oh, oh, you are good."

After several seconds, grunts of pain and protest were heard.

"Ugh, uhn. Oh! You're good," the female voice said. "Oh! Uh-uh!"

"C'mon!"

"Ooh! You're good," she repeated with a tone of distress. "Oh, uhn."

"C'mon, bitch! Come on!" The male was becoming more agitated.

"Oh! Don't move," came a cry of pain.

"C'mon!" the male said low and threatening.

"Oh, don't ..." the female cried louder.

"Shut up!" he said harshly. "C'mon. C'mon. Come on, you whore. You bitch."

"Argh! Oh! I came a bunch of times! C'mon, you gotta ..."

"Come on, c'mon, whore!"

"Are you talking to me?" the female cried out.

"Damn right I'm talking to you," came the threatening reply.

"I told you I came already!" she answered in a loud sob.

"Come again," was the order.

"I did, and I'm gonna come again. I'm coming now," she groaned in pain.

Gomez snapped off the machine while the detectives gasped in horror. There was no doubt that the male voice was Eddie Wyatt and the female voice belonged to young Allison Shaw. It was unassailable evidence. The hardened detectives had read Allison's affidavits, they had heard the teen's descriptions first-hand. But the powerful impact of hearing the actual assault sickened them and filled them with rage, both at once.

Gomez finished playing the tape. It went on for twenty-five minutes, filled with long pauses during which only background hissing could be heard. The man told the woman he was going to take a picture, and soon the sound of an instant camera spitting out a photo was heard. They heard several other assaults, and finally, they heard the man tell the girl he would take her home soon if she took him on again.

Suddenly, the background hissing ended, and out came the clear and booming voice of a preacher, blaring into Gomez's office before he had a chance to adjust the volume.

"...now the tables have been completely turned. Before, they're saying I'm so smart and you're down here in kindergarten believing the Bible. Now the situation is they don't even understand the main message of the book that they have rejected. Now the question is, do they want you to share the answer with them, what that message is, or do they want to remain in their ignorance?"

It was a guest speaker at a Bible class that Ronda had recorded back at Ocean View Assembly of God in Norfolk. Gomez shut off the tape player

The arrest made the papers Wednesday morning, even up in Corpus Christi, where the daily *Caller-Times* had a story headlined, "Abduction, rape suspect nabbed," and a subhead beneath it reading, "Navy man charged in Kingsville case." The story printed Ronda's address. It quoted a naval spokesman on the fact that Wyatt "is married and has two children." Ronda read it with anguish. It was so unbelievable that the entire day seemed unreal, nightmarish.

Later in the afternoon, Allison was brought down to the police station to listen to the tape recording. She verified that it was indeed a recording of part of the rape. Meanwhile, Ronda showed up at the sheriff's counter with Eddie's oldest brother, sister-in-law, and younger sister, who had hurried down from Galveston on Wednesday to see him. Jailers decided they would allow one visitor at a time, so Ronda stayed behind while the brother went upstairs.

Ronda noticed the other people in the waiting room staring at her. She felt like an object of scorn. As she sat on a hard chair, a short, paunchy fellow dressed all in white, with a matching

cowboy hat and a big cigar poked into his small mouth, came
into the waiting room. He was having a conversation with a few
deputies, and Ronda overheard one deputy ask him, "What do
you think they ought to do with that Wyatt fellow?"

"I think they ought to take him out and shoot him, that's what
I think they ought to do," pronounced the cigar-chomping fellow
to appreciative laughter. A shiver of fright went through Ronda.
Then she heard the men whisper and glance in her direction.

After Eddie's brother came down, and deputy told Ronda they
were taking Eddie to the police station for a lineup. Allison's
neighbors and the attendant at the filling station were going to
see if they recognized him. The deputy said she could have a
minute with Eddie in an area next to the waiting room. Eddie
and Ronda embraced when he was ushered in, and just as quickly
the visit was over. The deputy pulled on Eddie, and he clung to
Ronda like a frightened child. It tore Ronda's heart when he was
pried loose. Ronda feared that might be the last time she would
embrace her husband.

After Eddie was taken out, and deputy approached Ronda.

"Mrs. Wyatt, I want to apologize for what happened a little
while ago out there," he told her.

Struggling to control her emotions, Ronda looked at the man.

"They can afford to laugh about things that don't touch their
lives," she said.

Ronda saw Eddie's family off, heading back to Galveston,
then went home to call her mother. She wanted her parents to
come and take Paul and Diana back to Colorado. The anonymous
phone calls had continued, and she did not feel safe now that
her address had been in papers up and down the Coastal Bend.
She was particularly fearful of the children's safety, and what the
schoolchildren might say to Paul when kindergarten started up
again in a week.

Erna said she and Dad would start right out for Texas.

When Eddie arrived for the lineup, he asked for his court-
appointed lawyer. But the attorney who had been appointed refused to come. Public revulsion over the crime had persuaded
him to stay away from the defense table for this case. Eddie was
entitled to defense, but it would not be easy to find a Kingsville

attorney willing to risk the goodwill of the town by defending a
newcomer who had raped a local high school senior. Gomez
contacted Judge W. C. McDaniel, who immediately ordered another attorney to represent the suspect at the lineup. The attorney
arrived at 5:15 P.M., and advised Eddie to sign the form agreeing
to appear in the lineup.

Soon, Eddie was joined by five volunteers from the Naval Air
Station who would stand with him in front of the witnesses. Eddie
was fourth in line. The three guys to his right were all lighter but
the same height as he. The two on his left were much younger
but had the same build.

First to view the lineup from behind a one-way glass was a
neighbor of the Shaws. He did not recognize any of the six. Next
was the couple from down the street who had seen a blue car in
the alley. The husband viewed the lineup but he did not see
anyone who looked familiar. His wife recognized Eddie from
somewhere, but she was not sure where. Finally, police brought
in the young man who was the attendant at the Bradlee station
in Ricardo, where Allison thought her kidnapper had stopped for
gasoline. He remembered a blue and white car, but he recognized
no one in the lineup. Eddie was back in the Kleberg jail by 7:00
P.M., the lineup having provided no additional evidence against
him.

Ronda spent New Year's Eve with her parents, and away from
Eddie. It was like the first New Year's Eve after she and Eddie
met, when he remained in Dallas and she went to prepare for the
wedding. And just as with that first time, she was beset with
uncertainties about her future. There was no money coming in
because the navy had cut off Eddie's pay until after his trial.
Would Eddie be proven innocent and come home to her and the
children? And what if he wasn't proven innocent? Ronda felt her
first pangs of doubt about her husband.

Most immediate, however, was the danger in Kingsville for
her and her children. On New Year's Eve, with people out drinking
and the Wyatts' address known to all who loved and cared about
Allison Shaw, Ronda was frightened that someone might come

by and try to harm her or the children. Paul and Erna had towed their camper to Kingsville, and the five of them rang in the new year sleeping in the camper parked on the street, outside a friend's house on the other end of town.

During the two days Ronda's parents stayed with her, they helped her begin to pack some of her belongings. Ronda knew she had to move because she had no rent money and her parents were going to take a few boxes back to Colorado with them. Before Erna folded Eddie's good suit, she ran her hands through the pockets to make sure they were empty. She felt something in one of the outside pockets of the jacket, reached in, and pulled out a ring. Erna's eyes narrowed on it. She could not recall Ronda ever having such a pretty ring. It had diamond in the center and was circled by a collection of smaller diamond chips.

"Ronda, where did you get this ring?" she asked. Ronda examined it and was puzzled.

"That's not mine," she replied. "I've never seen it before. Eddie's always doing painting work for other people in exchange for things. That must be how he got it. That's how he got me my sewing machine." Erna Hunter finished packing, and put the ring in the box with the suit.

On January 2, the Hunters left with their grandchildren. Ronda had to fight back her tears, as she herself was not free to leave with them. The police had not ruled out the possibility that she was somehow involved in Eddie's activities, if only having knowledge of them. Apparently, Ronda learned, police commonly discover that a rapist's wife or girlfriend actually participates in the crime. The very thought made Ronda sick to her stomach.

The next day she went to Sunday services at First Assembly, where she felt welcomed in spite of what had happened. Pastor Fields and Dolores came up to her after the service and offered to let her stay at their house on Wanda Street. They had a spare bedroom in the front corner of the house, and it would not be the first time they put up someone in need of refuge. Ronda accepted.

That night, cocooned in the brightly decorated spare bedroom at the Fields residence, Ronda felt safe for the first time since the arrest, and she thought about how the folks at church expressed their support for her. It made her wonder how blind she might have been to them just a month earlier, when she wrote her "Mrs. Nobody" letter to a congregation she thought did not care. On January 3, 1982, she wrote in her diary:

> *Today, Lord, today I went back to church, to the people who not less than three weeks ago seemed so uncaring, and they loved me and prayed for me. I wonder why there is not hate and bitterness in my heart. Perhaps that will come in time. For now, it hurts.*
>
> *Jesus, I place this whole situation in your hands. Have your way in our lives. And if you will, heal our home, and our marriage. We need you now as we have never needed you before.*

On Monday morning, Ronda called Angle Medical Center. With the navy cutting off Eddie's pay, she needed to go back to work. But there was Vera, Allison's cousin, to consider. What would she think of working next to the wife of the man charged with raping her cousin? Ronda's boss said he would talk to Vera. The next thing Ronda knew, Vera called her back.

"How could you ever think I would not want you to come back to work," she told Ronda. "You are my friend." Both women cried. Ronda was grateful for Vera's courage, and went back to work Tuesday for a half day. At lunch, a friend told her that there had been some death threats against Eddie if he should be set free. Ronda feared more than ever for her own safety, and began to realize that she would no longer be able to live in Kingsville even if Eddie was exonerated and released with a full apology. Her friend said the rumor mill also had it that "Wyatt's wife had left town." Good, Ronda replied, let them think that. It would be true soon enough.

As the evidence in the case began to accumulate, Detective Hector Treviño prepared to send it all to the Department of Public Safety crime laboratory in Austin for analysis. He had hair and fiber samples gathered from Eddie Wyatt's car and house, the ragged pieces of tape used to bind and blindfold Allison Shaw to compare with the ends of the rolls seized during the search of the house. He had skin and hair samples from the dead dog to compare with hairs found in the car. He had Allison's panties and shirt to examine for semen, and her bed sheets and blankets to verify the presence of dog blood. The package included a six-inch knife police seized from the trunk of Eddie's car—he maintained it was a fishing knife. The largest piece of evidence was the Valiant's backseat, which Treviño ripped out to take to the lab.

On Wednesday afternoon, Treviño visited Eddie at the jail and asked him to give blood and saliva samples for analysis. Eddie had already voluntarily given Treviño hair samples combed from his head and pubic area, but he balked at giving the fluids. Treviño walked out, telling Eddie he would file for a court order.

When Ronda and James Fields arrived at the jail soon afterward for a visit, the pastor went up first. Fields had sensed that the young man was hiding some very painful things behind his depression, but Eddie had never revealed anything to him. Finally, on the afternoon of January 6, Eddie was ready to talk.

Ronda was in the basement waiting area when the pastor, being led by a deputy, returned from his visit with Eddie. Taking Ronda by the hand, Fields wanted to speak with her before she went upstairs.

"Ronda, you need to open your heart to forgiveness for Eddie," Fields said.

"What do you mean?" she asked him.

"Eddie is guilty. He just told me."

As Ronda went upstairs, her mind was reeling. Her worst nightmare had suddenly become real, obliterating all of the rationalizations she had made since the night of the arrest. The closest one to Eddie was the last to see it. After praying for him to come back in her life to make everything right again, she felt cruelly betrayed.

She walked into the small, drab visiting area and saw Eddie seated in one of the booths. His eyes were puffy and red. Ronda's tears started to flow uncontrollably. There could be no more denial for her. She had to prepare herself to deal with whatever Eddie was going to tell her.

His words coming between sobs, Eddie told his wife that he had kidnapped Allison and raped her, even taking her to the house after Ronda went back to work from lunch.

"Why?" she sobbed. "I just can't understand this, why? I would have given anything for your attention. I wanted you so much and you turned me away. Oh, why did you have to force yourself on a stranger? Eddie, I love you and I wanted you so bad." Tears of anguish streamed down her cheeks.

"I don't know," Eddie answered while crying. "I was just always afraid of what was going on inside of me. I could never talk about it. It just took me over completely." Eddie told Ronda that he had sent her a letter that she should receive the next day. He wanted her to stay by him through the coming ordeal. Ronda's time was soon up. She returned to the Fields residence and collapsed in exhaustion in the guest room.

That evening, Ronda went to the weekly fellowship meeting at the Crowells, hoping to find some understanding. The group was larger than usual, with several people there whom Ronda did not know. During the singing and the Bible study, Ronda's thoughts were elsewhere. She thought about how Eddie had raped that poor girl in Ronda's own living room, "repeatedly" as the papers reported, over almost seven hours. She remembered how that very night she had tried to arouse him with her sexy negligee. Toward the end of the session, a prayer call went out, and a couple from the visiting group spoke up with their request.

"Let's all pray for this sailor who raped that teenage girl in town," the woman said sincerely.

"Oh, yes," her husband added in a tone that made Ronda cower in shame. "I feel sure he was demon possessed!"

The entire room fell into total silence. Ronda was panic-stricken, not knowing what to do. She fought the urge to yell at the man to shut up, that he had no right to judge her marriage that way, until Barbara Crowell stepped in to clear the air.

"This here is the man's wife," she announced to the strangers. An embarrassing stillness enveloped the room.

"I'm sorry," the man mumbled. Everyone knelt to pray. Ronda wanted to run for the door. Then the woman next to her leaned close and looked her right in the eye.

"Honey," she said softly. "Do you have Jesus in your heart?"

Now her very faith was being questioned, Ronda thought, and it was too much for her to take. She had not done wrong! She had tried for the past two years to get help for her husband, and had been told she was making a mountain out of a molehill. And now the world had the nerve to question her faith, the very foundation of her being. It was all she could stand.

"Yes, I have Jesus in my heart," Ronda answered stiffly, then got up to leave. Her friend Barbara rushed to her and held her tight. Ronda sobbed from the depths of her soul. Never before had she felt hurt like this. When the tears subsided, Barbara took Ronda's face in her hands and pulled it close to hers so that she could whisper to her.

"Honey, you hold your head up high," Barbara said. "You have nothing to be ashamed of." Those healing words helped get Ronda back to James and Dolores's house that night. On the way, she watched a car in her rearview mirror and was sure she was being followed. She was terrified until the car behind her turned. That night, she asked her diary:

I am so afraid, how long will the night hold terror for me?

The morning sun streamed through three windows into the corner bedroom of the Fieldses' house and chased away the fears of the previous night. But Ronda had a new set of uncertainties to face. For nine days, she had clung resolutely to the conviction that Eddie was innocent. Now she had to start thinking of her life in an entirely different way. She felt very unsure of the future, but more devastating still, she realized that the past she had shared with her loving husband was not what she had thought. All of her happy experiences as a wife and mother were suddenly cast in the light of this sudden revelation. Had it all been a sham? Her entire identity as wife, mother, and Christian woman was now open to question and reevaluation.

Even so, she could not in one instant go from loving him so much to not loving him at all. The love in her heart could not just be carved out with a scalpel and discarded. She had to sort out her emotions first, and that would take time. She had lived with Eddie for nearly seven years. How could she not know this man? What should she have seen that would have tipped her off to the tremendous pent-up hostility and frustration that resulted in his kidnapping and rape of Allison Shaw? Even more frightening, Ronda began to ask herself, what else did she not know about her husband?

Ronda's doctor put her on medication for her agitated state but Ronda tried to use it sparingly. She handed the pills to Dolores Fields, who agreed to stick them away and only give them to Ronda if she asked. Ronda saw where Dolores put them, however, high in a wall cabinet in the bathroom.

Late Thursday morning, the mailman brought the letter Eddie had promised. With trepidation, Ronda opened it. She began to read an extraordinary outpouring of Eddie's sentiments and guilt. Her husband rambled on about a great struggle he had fought between evil impulses left over from his youth and his will to be good. How could this war have gone on in her marriage without her knowing it, Ronda wondered as she read. She did not know whether her husband was full of sincere contrition or false piety. Was he taking responsibility, or trying to blame God and Satan? Eddie wrote:

> It hurts so bad to know I've hurt you, the one closest to my heart. I love you very much. . . . I tried so very hard to work things out. It only seemed to make things worse. I've never been able to surrender my sex life completely to God. That's the only area I never felt God had control of. I used to plead with our Lord to please take control for I feared above all things that this would happen.

Ronda could only feel anger. If Eddie feared losing control, then why did he not take advantage of her persistent efforts to help him? He had deceived her. Yet, in his letter, Eddie wrote that Ronda had been the perfect wife for him:

God gave me the best when he gave you to me. I used to dream of us together and I thought surely now God has answered my prayer. But as my thoughts became twisted over the years, I wrestled and struggled and fought to resist those thoughts surely Satan must have planted in my mind. My pride refused to accept help for I thought surely God would not allow such a thing to happen for I knew my heart had God's love there, and in due time he would allow me to surrender this rebel area of my life to him.

Remember how I used to fast and pray so regularly? It was for this very reason. Never, never, never have I ever fought and wrestled against anything so strong and stubborn. It has tormented me my whole life. Yet even when God saved me in prison, I thought, "The battle is over." But when the drive prevailed, I would masturbate, then I was ashamed and felt guilt. It all seemed so ugly and I waged war against it. I seemed to be on top of everything but this. But as I fought it, it returned again and again, and again. I could never understand why God allowed it to rage on in my life.

The shame of it all prevents me from talking to anyone about it, especially someone who has never experienced such a thing for how could they understand? Since I've been here now, I've cried, begged, pleaded, fasted and prayed with all my heart to God. Must I die with this thing raging in my soul? I had never gone as far as to actually commit such a crime. You must believe this. For now I'm being completely honest and showing you the whole truth of me. I only hope you can bear it all, for no longer will I hide it. It must come out or I feel I will lose my mind and soul.

Though it was against my will that it happened this time, it all happened so fast. It was as though I had no say. I was not in control. I seemed helpless to resist. I do need help—yes, I now know. My Lord will lead. He will guide me to the help I need. If it be prison for the rest of my life, if my two precious little ones must grow up fatherless as I did, if we must never kiss again, I will accept whatever my Lord puts in my path though I may never understand in this life.

Eddie was scared and Ronda knew it. Yet she no longer knew if she could trust his declarations of faith. How could she understand this "drive" of which he wrote? He had hidden the most tormented aspect of his life from her so successfully beneath his veil of depression that Ronda realized she did not know Eddie at all. Did he really trust in the Lord now, or was he simply saying that to hold onto her and the children? The letter made Ronda feel very uneasy. Throughout all his words, and what had been revealed to her thus far, she could not suppress the feeling that much more had gone on in her marriage than Eddie was telling. The police seemed to think Allison Shaw was not Eddie's first victim, and Ronda wondered whether Eddie was being completely honest.

Two days later, Ronda received a second letter from Eddie, written when he returned to his cell after his jailhouse confession to her. He was much more desperate to persuade her of his love. Confronted with the consequences of what he had done, he wanted to hold on to the woman who had stood by him in the past. He was frightened and alone. Ronda, his devoted wife, was his only hope.

Dear Ronda,

Hi, honeybun. It was so good to see you today. Honey, will you forgive me? I need you more than you know. You have every right to leave me, but oh God! I could never go on without you. Can you find the strength in God to be strong for me? I know I am asking a lot, but you are all I have in this life that I love. I know I could never find anyone to love me as you have. I've fallen so far these last few years, and I know now how it must have hurt even then, but I never dreamed you might one day leave me because of it. Now the very thought hurts

*me because through it I've learned how very much I do
love you and need you.*

*I know words may not mean much now, but if you
could only see my heart now, you would know. It's so
full of love for you. Please don't turn it away. Write me
back and tell me you will try me, test me and see. I'm
not the same. If only someone would believe me. I would
die if you left. I could never forgive myself if you ever
left me. I never wanted to hurt you. You are my love, my
life, my whole world. Stay by me, watch me prove it to
you once again.*

I love you,

Eddie

These were words Ronda would have given anything to hear
before this happened. She had prayed to hear Eddie say them
again, when there was still time for hope, and yet now they
sounded so hollow. Although she had told him that she would
stand by him no matter what, she had no idea then what Eddie's
problem was. She knew he had been smoking pot and that he
was depressed because of his father's death. If this had been
all, she could help him find the right counseling and stay by
his side. But sexual assault was simply beyond the realm of
Ronda's imagination. How could she support him in the face of
this most gruesome betrayal? Was he free to do anything beyond all reason, to reject her so emphatically, and then come
back and expect her support? Ronda was tormented by the huge
gap between her discoveries about Eddie and his pleas for
understanding.

On Friday, January 8, Eddie was indicted by the grand jury
on one count of burglary with intent to commit rape, which, under
a quirk of Texas law, at the time carried a longer sentence upon
conviction than a straightforward charge of rape. In addition,
because of the burglary convictions he had on his record from
his teen years, he was also charged with being a habitual criminal.
That additional line in the indictment meant that if convicted,
Eddie could be sentenced to life in prison.

*   *   *

That weekend, Eddie's family drove down again from Galveston to visit him in the Kleberg jail. After Ronda came home from church, she and her sister-in-law sat down to talk. She asked Ronda if she recalled the occasion during the previous July when Eddie left to visit Galveston. Ronda nodded that she did. How could she ever forget that week, she thought, when everything went wrong and Eddie was not around to fix them.

Her sister-in-law told Ronda that she had to clear the air about something.

It seemed, she told her, that Eddie had a long-standing, un-fulfilled passion he carried around since his teen years. And when he returned to Galveston that summer week, he indulged it. Eddie looked up Patty Battaglia, an old girlfriend. Eddie had loved her deeply when they were both teenagers, and he had hoped to marry her, but his second confinement in reform school when he was fifteen ended those dreams, Ronda's sister-in-law told her.

Ronda's face was immobilized with a look of astonishment. The shock of discovering another humiliating betrayal by her husband was numbing. That week in July while Ronda was sitting in Kingsville, needing Eddie more than ever, he was up in Gal-veston having sex with an old girlfriend? Ronda had never even heard of Patty Battaglia. Eddie was never very specific about some aspects of his childhood. But how could he have clung to this ancient, consuming passion without her ever picking up a clue? Ronda was crushed by her sister-in-law's revelation. The weight of each discovery about her husband seemed like torture.

While Ronda tried to come to grips with this unwelcome news, she was hit by another revelation. Dave Houser, Eddie's navy friend, came by her house to borrow something the morning after Eddie's family left for home. Dave told Ronda how sorry he was about what had happened. Then he looked down at the floor for an awkward silence.

"There's a lot of stuff you don't know about, Ronda," Houser told her.

"What do you mean? What else is there?" she asked him.

"You remember that bust on the *Kennedy* the first time we shipped out on the Med cruise?" Dave asked her.

"Yes, Eddie was so upset about that."

"Well, he was guilty. We were smoking hashish."

It should not have surprised her at this point, but it did. What a fool she had been to believe in Eddie and stand by him when he insisted that he was an innocent bystander when the military police rushed into his bunk area. It made her wonder about his arrest for trespassing in Norfolk.

"I should also tell you that on our second cruise, on the *Forrestal*, Eddie took up with a woman in Athens and had an affair with her," Dave continued.

Would this never end, Ronda asked herself? She now knew that she had never really known this man at all. What other monstrous things must he have done? She was now beyond incredulity, yet Dave would tell her no more.

"There's other stuff me and Peggy know about, but I don't think we can tell you," Dave said. "Not yet."

"You might as well," Ronda answered, the numbness preventing her from crying. "Nothing more you can tell me could hurt any more."

"I'm sorry, Ronda," Dave said. "I just don't think we can tell you right now." Dave froze and would not explain what else he knew.

"Why was he doing all this?" Ronda cried. "I loved him so much. I would have given anything to make him happy. Why couldn't he come to me?"

"I don't think you really could have helped, Ronda. See, the problem was, he told me one time when we were fishing down on the bay, that he was getting tired of you and the kids. He said he just needed to get away. He was tired of all of you." That was the last time Ronda ever spoke with Dave or Peggy, so she never heard the rest of what they knew.

Judge Walter Dunham set Eddie's trial for February 15, just over a month away. That would be the day after Eddie and Ronda's seventh wedding anniversary. His arraignment was scheduled for February 5 in district court. But Eddie still had no lawyer. The members of the bar in Kingsville were not anxious to associate themselves with the defense of someone who, there seemed to be little doubt, had committed one of the most horrible crimes the little city had ever seen. Dunham had to skim his list of attorneys to find one who would represent Wyatt without concern for the repercussions.

Ronda, hit hard in the past week, felt the worst pain for Dave's revelation that Eddie was getting "tired" of her and the children. All she wanted to do was to curl up in her room at Pastor Fields's house and stay there until something came along to make things right again. She began to take the antidepressants that had been prescribed for her. One bright spot was that Navy Relief offered to pay her way home to Denver and Captain Gomez told her she was free to leave.

That night, January 12, 1982, Ronda expressed her ambivalence in her diary.

> *I need to go home. Mother said that Paul is getting withdrawn, and cries easily. I know that soon I have to say goodbye to Eddie. My children need me. I am torn in two.*
>
> *Sometimes I wonder what would have happened if I had come in the house while Eddie was raping Allison, what he would have done to me. He must have waited and watched until he was sure I had gone back to work after lunch.*
>
> *This has been one of the most difficult days. I feel like screaming it out. I even want Eddie to hold me, and he can't. For some reason, I feel like I have to give the appearance of being in control; I don't want anyone to see me cry. I feel exhausted even after a full night of rest.*

Ronda returned to the home fellowship at James and Barbara Crowell's house the next evening. It was not done without fear— she was still full of shame and guilt after the remarks made by the visitors at the last session. Fortunately, the evening was much more pleasant, with only the original group of a dozen regular participants. When Ronda found it impossible to talk about what she was feeling, the regulars had no trouble understanding her quiet. Even among friends, she could not share her feelings of devastation. Ronda was finding that, with each day, she was feeling worse, not better. As they sat in a circle, a young Texas A&I student named Mike told about a dream he had had recently in which he was bitten by a vicious dog. As painful as that initial injury was, he later found that the long healing process hurt even more.

Mike looked toward Ronda as he finished recounting his dream.

"I just couldn't see it at the time," Mike said. "It hurt so much, I just couldn't see that it would eventually get better."

Ronda's worn face broke into an expression of relief for the first time in days. She was grateful to him for telling her it was okay to feel the insecurity, the fear, the rage, the entire spate of conflicting emotions that beset her. There was no pressure to start feeling better so soon after being wounded the way she was. Mike and the others in her fellowship were giving her the space she needed, and they were going to accept her no matter what her feelings were.

For the first time since her husband was pulled out of the house in handcuffs three days after Christmas, Ronda went back to her room at Pastor Fields's house and was able to write in her diary: "I feel loved."

Ronda decided late that week that it was time to return to Colorado. Her children needed her. She quit her job and booked a late Monday afternoon flight to Denver. She planned to spend the weekend cleaning up the house. The women from First Assembly came over to Mesquite Avenue to help Ronda finish her packing. They moved through the small four-room bungalow gathering clothing, housewares, and other items, and placed them in boxes to be stored until Ronda could return for them.

Ronda overheard one of the women comment that so many of the items were little more than junk, she did not understand why Ronda was bothering to pack them. Ronda stopped to look around her rumpled house, and realized there was little in the house of any real value. She and Eddie had little to show for nearly seven years of marriage. Most of their belongings were junk, just worn-out junk. Living there from day to day in ignorant bliss, it had not occurred to Ronda. Her entire life had unraveled in the span of two weeks, and now there was nothing left, at least not in Kingsville. There was only Eddie in the top-floor jail down at the courthouse, and she did not know him anymore.

On Sunday, Ronda paid a last visit to the Kleberg County Jail to visit her husband. She left several personal items for him, including a book on inner healing and forgiving oneself. They had no money to hire the attorney Eddie wanted to retain, she told him. He would have to put his fate in the hands of court-appointed counsel, and the trial was scheduled for only four weeks away. They were both crying as they looked at each other through the visiting room glass. Ronda had a feeling that this would be the last time she would see him. She thought back to the day they embraced briefly outside the waiting area of the jail two weeks earlier, when she was still convinced of her husband's innocence. Ronda told Eddie she was leaving Kingsville.

"I realize now how much I love you," Eddie pleaded. "Won't you stay with me? I know I have to pay for what I've done, but I can't lose everything, not the children. I love them more than I knew."

"Eddie, I have my plane ticket for tomorrow. I have to leave. I just can't stay here," Ronda told him. His pleas had begun to seem remote. How did it go wrong, she wondered? She thought of the first few years of their relationship and how she had looked up to him so much. The memories made the pain much more searing. She wanted to turn back time, armed with the truth, but she knew that could not be done. On January 17, 1982, as she prepared to spend her final night with the Fieldses, Ronda made another entry in her diary before slipping it into her carry-on bag:

> *This is by far the most difficult day of my life.*
> *I hurt so bad that it makes me wonder if my life will*
> *ever be whole again. I told my Eddie goodbye today, and*

*feel in my heart of hearts it will be the last time I will
ever see him again. God, why? Why did you have to
destroy my home and take away my husband, and my
children's father? Why couldn't you have done it another
way? I need him, God, don't you understand?? I need
him!! And I will never have him again.*

It hurts so bad. God, how it hurts so bad.

Dolores and James bade Ronda farewell the next afternoon,
and told her she was welcomed to stay at their house when she
returned later to retrieve her items in storage. High above Texas,
once her airliner reached cruising altitude, Ronda looked out the
window and watched the faint glimmer of lights on the dark and
flat earth below. Always, when she had imagined how her life
would be, she had pictured it with a happy ending. She was
determined to start over again and try to form some solid and
stable foundation for her future.

She was leaving Texas defeated, betrayed, and humiliated,
her life stolen from her bit by bit by some insidious evil in her
own family. By the time the essence of her marriage had been
sucked entirely out of its shell, she was not even aware of it. She
was still admiring the shell, not knowing it was already empty.
She had been the fixer, her sights set on the happier days she
knew had to lie ahead once she found the root of Eddie's withdrawal and depression. But she was the last one to know that it
could not be fixed.

She knew the children would not understand what was happening, not for years at least. Ronda pulled her journal out of the
bag and wrote a letter to her children that she would not show
them for several more years, but which she resolved would help
them in the future:

Dearest Paul and Diana,

*It's 7:15 p.m., on January 18, 1982. I'm enroute to be
with you, my loves. Our lives have taken a rather unexpected turn and will never be quite the same again.
Someday you will ask me questions about these days,*

and maybe this note will help. You must know how very dearly your father loved you, and that what happened was not your fault at all. Daddy had some big problems that he couldn't handle, and he was afraid to get help for them. He thought people wouldn't love him anymore if he told them that he needed help, so he let those little things become big things, and those big things took control in his life.

Your daddy told me a few weeks ago how very much he was enjoying you. He has a special book that he keeps with pictures just of you two because he's so proud of his children. You will be hurt and angry about what is happening. You are too little to understand, and even if you never do, remember daddy as the man he was. He cried yesterday when I told him goodbye. It may be that the only way for daddy to get help is for him to go to prison. He has finally made his peace with God, but he still has to be punished for what he did.

We'll go on and face life without daddy if we must. God will help us to do our best. You mustn't hate your father, if you only understood you would feel only sorrow in your hearts. This is how I feel, my babes. I am excited and anxious to be in your arms and to hold you in mine. Chin up, my loves. We'll make it, and make it victoriously!

Mommy

CHAPTER 10

STRANGER IN HER BED

Frustration.
Frustration is knowing that I loved him—and cannot have him.
I care—and cannot tell him.
It has to be over—and it was only beginning.
I need him—and he will never be there again.
I want to tell him so much—and can tell him nothing.

—from Ronda's diary

Back home in her parents' house, Ronda grappled with the inevitability of the breakup of her family. Since the day she spotted Eddie praying at Dallas Teen Challenge, courageously facing down his past in his testimonies at church services, she had believed in him. She had known about his problems as a teenager in Galveston, but none of that ever mattered to her. That person was someone entirely different from the Eddie she knew.

So what did she owe him? Should she stand at his side, see him through the agony of the trial, wait faithfully for whatever length of time he might go to prison, then rebuild their marriage upon his release? Or had the trauma of discovering this treachery in her marriage shattered it beyond all repair? Her deliberations would not be easy. Within a week of her return to Colorado, Ronda received another letter from Eddie that tried to reach out and hold onto her:

Thank you for the books you left, especially the one on inner healing. I don't know how something so ugly came out of my heart. I must have been further from God than I realized. I don't really understand it all by any means, but I do believe this inner healing could very well be the root of it all. Remember how I told you how the memories of my daddy leaving me when I was little used to bother me, and I'd just shove it back inside of me and forget it all?

There are a lot of other things inside that need to be healed, memories I thought I had forgotten that hurt and are now taking its toll on my life.

That made Ronda recall occasions when Eddie told her there were things in his past that he could not talk about, even with her, because they were too painful. She wondered what could have been so terrible that he could never utter the words.

Ronda went to the Jefferson County welfare department to apply for assistance. After her forms arrived in the mail, she found that to complete them she had to drive to the courthouse in Golden to obtain a copy of her marriage certificate. A grim feeling came over her when the clerk handed her the microfilm copy and Ronda saw the signatures. She knew she could not put off a decision about the future of her marriage much longer.

The following morning, Ronda went to the social services office in Lakewood for an interview. Even though she knew it was necessary, it felt degrading for her to apply for welfare, especially in the town where she grew up and went to school. She was not comfortable living off her parents' charity, and so she vowed to become self-sufficient as soon as she could.

Because she had come to recognize her tendency to submerge her own personality in order to become the person others wanted her to be, Ronda found it easy to blame herself for what had happened. She was plagued with questions about what she could have or should have done to intervene in Eddie's problems. The self-doubt grew into a series of questions, and before they could overwhelm her, Ronda decided that she had to have some answers. On February 4, she sat at the kitchen table and wrote out her questions to Eddie. She believed she was entitled to some straight answers. Why, she wrote, had he done this? Who was this Allison Shaw girl? Did he know her before the attack? Why did Eddie resist Ronda when she tried to seek help for him? Why didn't he seek help for himself when he realized he was losing control?

And most importantly, why couldn't she, as his wife, have given Eddie the love and the satisfaction they both craved from the marriage?

Satisfied she had written down the most painful of her questions, Ronda sealed the envelope and mailed it to Eddie at the Kleberg County Jail a thousand miles away.

Ron Barroso heard about the Kingsville rapes even before he read in the Corpus Christi paper about the arrest of a navy man. During his infrequent visits to Kleberg County over the last year on various legal matters, his Kingsville colleagues mentioned the rapes. The young lawyer knew that the town was unnerved by them.

Barroso had been in private practice less than two years, concentrating on criminal defense. But his training came from the other side of the aisle, as an assistant district attorney in Nueces County, Texas, from 1977 to 1980, part of a team that included the district attorney and seven assistants. The tall, dark-haired lawyer then left the DA's office and opened his own practice in downtown Corpus Christi near the Nueces County courthouse. From time to time, he took court appointments for defendants who could not afford their own attorneys. The judges used a core group of attorneys in the Corpus Christi district as an ad hoc public defender's office since Nueces County didn't have an official one. That was how Barroso came to defend Eddie Wyatt.

Judge Walter Dunham had telephoned Barroso and asked if he would take an appointment to the rape case in Kingsville. The members of the Kleberg bar shunned the Wyatt matter like a prudent dog would avoid a skunk. If the case worked out with Wyatt getting off lightly, the disdain the defense attorney would earn among the populace might take years to wear off. Kingsville attorneys could not afford to scare away a small pool of paying clients by being an advocate for the defendant in this highly publicized crime.

Dunham described Wyatt's case as interesting, and a big case for a small town like Kingsville, particularly with the possibility of more than just the single rape. Barroso liked the challenge. It did not take him long before deciding that he would accept the appointment.

Barroso drove down U.S. 77 to the Kleberg County Jail on January 25 and visited with assistant DA Royce Johnston and the office investigator Adan Muñoz. There he learned that the Corpus Christi district attorney, Bill Mobley, had assigned one of his top assistants, Ken Botary, to prosecute the case. Barroso had worked with Botary during the few years he was a prosecutor. The selection showed that Mobley was giving the case a high priority. Barroso picked up the indictment that had been issued more than two weeks earlier by the county grand jury, a copy of the arrest warrant affidavit, and the consent form Eddie signed allowing his car to be searched. The first court appearance, on February 1, was only a week away, when he had to defend against Botary's motion forcing Eddie to give blood and saliva samples for the lab in Austin. He knew there was little he could do to quash the motion. The state crime lab needed the samples to compare with the items the police had sent up for analysis, and the courts had long ago settled the Fifth Amendment conflict between a suspect surrendering his bodily fluids versus his right to be free from self-incrimination.

He read everything through once before heading up to the Kleberg County Jail to meet his new client.

Barroso had defended many criminal clients since leaving the prosecutor's office. He had worked rape cases as well as capital murder trials. His clients were angry men, aggressive and misanthropic felons with chips on their shoulders. When Barroso asked to see the prisoner Eddie Wyatt, he expected a pent-up, agitated sex offender. Instead, he found Eddie Wyatt to be a highly depressed young man. Eddie was quiet but polite when he greeted his attorney. He seemed withdrawn and defeated.

Barroso rarely asked a client if he was guilty—that was not the point. What mattered was whether the state could prove he was guilty. Calmly and deliberately, Eddie proceeded to outline for Barroso his life of quiet desperation. He painted the double life of someone who claimed he wanted urgently to be a good and caring Christian man, could not live with himself or be around others when he fell far short, and gradually succumbed to the demons he felt inside of himself. Finally, he told Barroso that he had raped Allison. He said it so softly that Barroso had to strain to hear.

Eddie told Barroso that after Ronda left the house with the children on the morning of the rape, he became extremely restless.

"I'd worked graveyard, and got home about eight," Eddie told his lawyer. "Ronda left about fifteen minutes later, so I went out to the Stop N Shop at Third and Corral and bought myself a six pack. I drank that up, then went and got another. About ten o'clock, I got feeling real unsettled, you know, so I went out for a drive. I stopped at Winn's and bought some Christmas gifts, then I drove around the neighborhood there until I spotted this house."

Eddie thought he saw the front door left open, so he parked on a side street to go back and take a look. From this point on, Eddie's version of events began to diverge sharply from Allison Shaw's reports to police. He professed to some difficulty recalling details that he said were still hazy in his mind.

"I was meaning to steal something," Eddie continued. "I didn't know if anyone was home." Once he got in and looked around, he told Barroso, a small dog came into the room and began to attack him.

"I grabbed that dog and killed it with my pocket knife, and that's when I heard someone in the bedroom. I found this teenage girl in her bed. She just had a T-shirt and panties on. I told her to lay still and be quiet while I tied her up with masking tape."

Eddie told Barroso he went to his car and parked in the alley behind the girl's house, then went back and saw she had not moved. He wrapped her arms and legs in tape, and when she said her dad was coming home soon, he made the impulsive decision to kidnap her.

"She didn't scream or cry or anything," he told Barroso. "I carried her to the car, laid her in the backseat, and drove out the alley." He recalled taking her to a park, where he stopped momentarily. He said the girl heard voices and asked him what he would do if anyone spotted them. He then put her in the trunk and drove her to his house.

"I didn't force her," Eddie maintained. "I asked her if we could have intercourse, and she said yes. I know she was scared, but if she had've said no, I might not have done it." It was a self-serving recollection that did not match what Barroso had just read in the police reports.

"The police found some rolls of tape in their search of your house, Eddie. Were those the ones you used?" Barroso asked him.

"No," the prisoner answered. "It was the same kind of tape, but the actual rolls, I threw away."

"The police found a tape recording they say is you raping the girl. Is that true?"

"Yeah, I made a tape recording when we was screwing. I don't know why. She was saying to do it more, that it was good, and I thought, 'I gotta get this on tape.' I tried to destroy the tape and threw it in my trash, but they found it."

"The police also said you took some Polaroid pictures of the victim. Did you?" Barroso asked.

"Yeah, again it was just something that popped into my head to do," Eddie said. "I couldn't stand to look at them, so I burned them at my house, then I threw the ashes in the dumpster down at the corner store."

"The police think that you did some of the other rapes here in town."

"I didn't have anything to do with them other rapes," Eddie interrupted. "They put me in a lineup, and there was no IDs."

After a two-hour visit, as Barroso prepared to leave, Eddie started to talk about Ronda.

"My wife and I have, uh, had some, you know, some sex problems," Eddie hesitated. "I feel like what it was, was when I got sent out to sea for six and eight months. I know that's when my problems started."

After the session ended, Barroso pointed his sports car back up U.S. 77 for Corpus Christi. His new client, he thought, was a much more complicated and guarded man than he had imagined.

Rolling the interview over and over in his mind, Barroso had the feeling that Eddie Wyatt's problems started long before his naval cruises.

Captain Gomez wanted to put Eddie Wyatt away for ninety-nine years. After all, Geraldo Nuñez got fifty years and a bullet near his spine, and he was only accused of *trying* to rape Marleen Grimes. Gomez had Treviño, Hayes, and the other detectives sift through the unsolved rape cases with the evidence from the Shaw case as their sieve.

The Kyung Ellis rape figured to be one they might be able to charge against Eddie. It had many of the earmarks present in Allison's case, from the tape to the sound of the rapist's voice. The man had even started to kidnap Kyung from the apartment house, although he changed his mind and took her back to her own bedroom. The Ellis rape occurred after the captures of Nuñez and Billy Joe Garner, so it had to be a third man or, God forbid, a fourth. And it was Kyung's husband who had led them to Eddie Wyatt, through either his persistence or his paranoia, depending upon one's point of view.

There was another striking similarity in some of the unsolved cases, and it also pointed to Wyatt. Six of the victims, including Allison, were raped anally. If Wyatt raped Allison Shaw, he had to be considered a principal suspect in five other cases, starting with Sue Wilson back in June in her house on Wanda Street, up through the Kyung Ellis rape. And in the middle, there was that horrifying ten-day period from August 24 to September 4 when three women were raped with an escalating degree of ferocity.

But the plain fact was that until Allison Shaw peered through the slits in her blindfold, none of the victims in the unsolved cases, including Kyung Ellis, had seen the face of her assailant. The victims who remained in Kingsville were shown Eddie's photograph along with others, but no identification could be made. Circumstantial evidence was all the police had, for the time being.

On Monday afternoon, Barroso drove down from Corpus Christi for Eddie's hearing on the fluid samples, but Dunham was in no mood for a protracted argument. After half an hour, he approved the motion, and Treviño made arrangements to take Eddie to Kleberg Memorial Hospital the next morning so the fluids could be taken.

On Thursday, Barroso visited the DA's office in the Nueces County Courthouse to meet with prosecutor Ken Botary. There he learned how the Kingsville police were trying to link Eddie to some of the unsolved rapes. In the meantime, Botary told the defense attorney, he was going to file a motion in court the next day to dismiss the original indictment. The Kleberg grand jury was going to issue a new indictment, Botary told him, adding two more counts. In addition to burglary with intent to rape, Eddie would be charged with burglary with intent to kidnap, and with intent to assault. And the grand jury was going to keep the final provision, the habitual criminal count that could earn Eddie a life sentence.

Because of the way Texas criminal law had been written, Botary and his boss, Bill Mobley, sought to charge Eddie with the felony crime of burglary with intent to commit rape, instead of with rape itself. This was done to ensure a longer minimum sentence upon conviction. At the time, rape was a second-class felony carrying a minimum of two years in prison. With Eddie Wyatt's prior criminal record, the law allowed the minimum sentence to be enhanced to five years, equivalent to a first-class felony.

Burglary with intent to rape, however, was already a first-class felony. With enhancement because of his record, Eddie would face a minimum prison sentence of fifteen years instead of five. The maximum sentence was ninety-nine years to life. So by charging the burglary instead of the rape, Botary raised the sentencing floor and turned up the heat on Barroso and his client.

In light of this development, Dunham canceled the arraignment that had been set for the next day and moved the trial date from February 15 to March 15. That would give Barroso more time to prepare a defense. But it would also give the Kingsville police more time to develop the evidence they needed to link Eddie to the other rapes.

*   *   *

On Valentine's Day, her wedding anniversary, Ronda found herself thinking as much about her children's state of mind as about the state of her marriage. She had dreamed about her wedding day from the time she was a little girl, and that day had lived up to the dreams. But now, haunting memories of the marriage tore at her, and she realized that the children were being torn as well.

Paul had been quiet through dinner that evening, and sometime after Ronda and her mother finished cleaning up the kitchen, the boy approached his mother with a question.

"Mom, when Daddy gets out of jail, will he come to live with us in Colorado, too?" he asked.

"No, honey, I don't think so," Ronda replied gently. "We're just going to have to go ahead and live our own lives."

At that, the six-year-old came to tears and began to sob in frustration about "that girl," who in his mind was somehow responsible for taking his daddy away from him. Ronda knew that she had to handle this situation carefully, or her young son would be carrying a heavy burden.

"Paul, Daddy had some problems," she told him, taking him into her arms. "He did some things he shouldn't have done. That girl didn't do anything. Even daddies have to be disciplined when they do wrong. It doesn't mean that he doesn't love you. He just did something wrong."

"What did he do?" Paul asked.

"Daddy took some things out of her house that he shouldn't have taken," Ronda explained. Paul's frustration eventually eased, but it was emotionally taxing on Ronda. That night, before she went to bed, she wrote in her diary to mark the bittersweet remembrance of the day she married:

Our seventh and last anniversary. I know it will be. If only we could have seen ahead and could have bypassed the problems that have destroyed our marriage.

Ronda began to look at past events with greater suspicion, wondering whether her impressions at the time were accurate or whether she had been deceived. She recalled the brief time when they lived near Denver's Washington Park, and she showed

Eddie the item in the paper about the rape that had occurred nearby. Was there a more sinister reason that his reaction was so disinterested, she thought? No, Ronda decided, she had to guard against letting her imagination run away with all reason. But she was especially apprehensive of Eddie's response to the letter she had written ten days earlier. She wondered what answers, if any, he would provide to her painful questions.

Then, as Ronda sorted through the next morning's mail, she came across an envelope from Eddie. It was thicker than his other letters, and she realized it must have been his lengthy answers. Nervously, she opened it. Inside were two separate notes, each folded over several times. One was a two-page poem. Eddie used to write touching poetry to her before they were married, but now he wrote of the pain he had brought to his family.

The other was a three-page letter, each page filled on both sides. Ronda steeled herself against feeling any more pain, but, instead, as she read it, she was surprised to find herself becoming angry:

Dear Ronda,

I received your letter dated Feb. 4. I don't really know where to begin to answer it, and I wonder if anything I say will really satisfy you. I have prayed and asked the Lord to help me give you the best answer I know that will help, for you do deserve to know. I did say I would be honest with you, and I intend to be, but there are some things I still do not honestly know. The questions you have asked me are the same ones I have asked God.

Before I do, I want you to know and realize a few things. First that I love you and I always have. I married you because I looked to God and asked Him for the right woman for me, for I knew then somehow it would take a very special woman to help me stay by the Lord's side. You have not failed me in this. . . . You never knew how desperately I wanted help or how much I needed it. If you had, I know you would have done more to get it for me.

Ronda paused to turn the page. She had pushed, argued, and cajoled, and even went behind his back to set up "coincidental" meetings with friends and pastors for Eddie, all of it meant to draw him out and give him counsel. She urged him to go to a professional counselor, and she warned him that things were only going to get worse if he did not. And each time she tried to get through to him, he told her he could handle it, and that no one else would understand. It seemed to Ronda that her husband was saying, in essence, that he forgave her for not seeing how deep his problems were, when in fact he had tried his best to hide them from her. She felt her face going flush with hostility as she read on:

You have asked me to explain why I did this as if I were God. You talk as if I knew her and had planned it, but it was not like you're thinking. You didn't know I had tried to kill myself the night before. The feelings of total failure I had, of hate and rejection of God. Though you could never see it made me wonder. Honey, I had a nervous breakdown and nearly lost my mind, and you just went on as if nothing had happened. I injected myself with ½ gram of cocaine the night before, which should have killed me. I thought it had, but I came back. Did you find the syringe in my chess case? I would have lashed out at you but I never blamed you for anything.

I broke into that house because that is what I have always done under Satan's influence as a teenager. I broke into more houses as a kid than you could count. That's what I went to reform schools for. That's what I went to prison for. Yet I never raped before in my life. She was just there. Satan put in my mind step by step what to do. Don't you see it was not really me? I could not see what I was doing, not to myself or to you and the kids.

I don't know what else to say except you know me better than anyone and through this we're really getting to know each other. If you leave me there will never be anyone else, I know. If you feel you just cannot trust me

*anymore and you no longer can love me then I will not
ask you to stay.*

All through Ronda's marriage, she had gone along where
Eddie led. But with this letter, she felt manipulated, and it made
her angry. He was trying to throw responsibility onto forces outside himself. He was trying to avoid facing up to what he had
done by hinting that Ronda could have done more. He was telling
her that he had a nervous breakdown and had tried to kill himself
while she remained ignorant of his plight. Is that really what he
was doing the night after Christmas when he stayed so long in
the bathroom, attempting suicide with a syringe and cocaine, and
she did not know it? That evening, February 15, 1982, her mind
firmed up by what Eddie wrote, she turned to her diary:

> *Eddie seems to have no concept at all of what he has put
> us through these past few months. He seems to feel that
> we should blindly accept what he has done, and should
> remain loyal and committed to him. I fight a real struggle
> with that. It hasn't been but about five months since I
> told him that no matter what came our way I was com-
> mitted to him as my husband, and would stay by his
> side. And now this has happened and I cannot keep that
> commitment.*
>
> *Eddie knew what he was doing in order to carry out
> the events of that day. He may not be "possessed," but
> he is deceived. His heart departed from me a long time
> ago. He made the choice to do what he did. When will he
> accept the responsibility for his action? I am angry and
> hurt. His letter really threw me into a tailspin.*
>
> *I have made my decision to proceed with a divorce.
> The time has come for me to be released from this ordeal.
> The change will come in my mind and in my attitude.
> My only choice now is to start over.*

The next day, Ronda was sorting though Eddie's things that
she planned to send to his oldest brother in Galveston. Her mother
gave her a hand and began to fold Eddie's good suit jacket.

"What do you want me to do with the ring I found?" Erna asked her daughter.

"What ring?" Ronda asked.

"Down in Kingsville, I found that diamond ring in this suit coat pocket, remember?" she said. "What do you want to do with it?"

Ronda felt a wave of anxiety come over her when she recalled the incident. It was back when she still thought her husband was innocent and she believed that he came by the ring honestly. Now she suspected Eddie of pocketing the ring, and she decided to turn it over to the Lakewood police.

The local police accepted the ring and told Ronda they would contact Kingsville police about it. If it had not been reported stolen, Ronda could have it back, they told her.

On the same Monday morning that Ronda received her letter from Eddie, Ron Barroso filed a dozen motions with the court. Most of his requests were routine and customary. He asked the state for a list of its witnesses, their statements, and any criminal records they might have. He demanded the production of any exculpatory or mitigating evidence the police may have found. He motioned the court to set punishment in the event of a conviction rather than the jury, a common move in this part of Texas by defense attorneys who knew that juries usually gave tougher sentences than judges.

But Barroso pinned his hopes for helping his client on two other motions. The first sought to suppress Allison Shaw's identification of Eddie Wyatt.

Barroso was going to attack it on three fronts. He would try to show that Eddie had inadequate legal counsel from the time of his initial interview and arrest right through to the lineup. Eddie may not have understood his right to have a lawyer present during questioning, Barroso believed. True, Eddie signed a consent form to allow the search of his car, but that was not the issue. It was during the interview that Detective Treviño took a photograph of Eddie, the one that Allison identified later in the evening as that of the man who raped her. It was only a small opening at best, but Barroso would attempt to show that Eddie's Sixth and Fourteenth Amendment rights were violated by that process of identification.

Another way of attacking Allison's strong identification testimony was for Barroso to zero in on police conduct after they obtained Eddie's photograph. His attack would focus on whether the detectives, who already believed Eddie to be guilty, in any way steered Allison toward that particular mug shot. When George Gomez called her father to bring her down to the station, did he suggest that police had the rapist? And when he handed Allison the stack of sixteen mug shots, rather than simply asking her whether anyone looked familiar, did he ask her to pick out her attacker, thereby indicating that the man had to be in the stack and pressuring Allison to pick someone?

And Barroso's final opening to cast doubt on Allison's identification centered on her strongest point, the fact that she could see him clearly over the entire six hours. Barroso saw that in all of her statements to police, Allison never once mentioned Eddie's tattoos. If she could see him as plain as Botary indicated to him, then she had to have seen the tattoos Eddie carried on each upper arm, Barroso felt. He wanted a hearing before Dunham on whether the identification was tainted and should be ruled inadmissible. During the hearing, he intended to call Allison Shaw to the stand and take her through the events of December 21, trying to find a toehold to shake her identification of Eddie Wyatt.

The second motion in which Barroso placed his hope was a request for a psychiatric examination for Eddie. When Barroso first met Eddie, he was struck by how depressed and withdrawn Eddie seemed. He was concerned that Eddie might not be able to go straight to trial because of his mental state. Dunham approved this motion shortly after the filing, and ordered Eddie to be evaluated by Dr. Joel Kutnick of Corpus Christi. The session was scheduled for March 1.

Prosecutor Ken Botary also kept busy during the time the defense gained by the trial postponement. He was working with the Kingsville police, who needed to prove, to their own satisfaction, that Eddie Wyatt was indeed the last serial rapist in town.

There had been no more sexual assaults reported in Kingsville since the rape of Allison Shaw four days before Christmas. The intervening two months was the longest the town had gone without a rape since the string of assaults that began in September 1980.

Initially, police hoped to add the Ellis rape to the charges against Eddie. Ellis thought Eddie's voice sounded like her attacker's. The method of assault was nearly identical to that used on Allison Shaw, right until the moment the man changed his mind about kidnapping Kyung. There were also other elements in the Shaw rape that were present in the other unsolved cases. They were all accompanied by home burglaries. All involved use of a deadly weapon. And all but one of the victims had been bound with tape, either silver or the green duct repair tape that Hector Treviño could find only at the Naval Air Station.

And there was one more invariable element, the assailant raped his victims anally as well.

There was, however, one major difference between the Shaw case and the others. All of the other victims were attacked at night. Allison was kidnapped during broad daylight and held for six hours. This was a significant deviation from the pattern, even after it was noted that Wyatt's work schedule had changed from the day to night shift. Without a solid identification from the other victims, it would be difficult for Botary to build a serial rape case against Wyatt based on the circumstantial evidence.

Botary had another concern. Although Allison Shaw had been brave and cooperative in the prosecution of her rapist, everyone wanted to spare her the ordeal of reliving the nightmare from the witness stand. But the hearing on Allison's identification of Eddie Wyatt, scheduled for March 5, required her to face Eddie in the courtroom and testify. Botary would try to hogtie Barroso's questioning and keep it narrow, preventing him from wandering off the point of her identification of Eddie. Not only might it spare her the emotional stress of reliving the actual sexual assaults, but it would lessen the chances of her saying something that could be taken as contradictory to any of her earlier statements, thus damaging her credibility.

Ultimately, the prosecution hoped that a trial would not be necessary. If Dunham ruled Allison's identification of Eddie admissible, Botary could use it as leverage to obtain a plea of guilty and bypass the agonizing prospect of the teenager taking the stand to tell the full story.

Ronda prepared to return to Kingsville at the end of February to get her things out of storage. The children appeared apprehensive when she told them she was going, and Ronda wondered how they would react when it hit them fully that their father was not going to be coming home at all. She had done some legwork about the procedure for getting a divorce. She had to live in Colorado for at least ninety days before she could file. With this information in hand, Ronda was at a crossroads since Eddie was imploring her to stand by him through his ordeal.

Meanwhile, her son was in a new school, and it was apparent that he was having a difficult time. Ronda got a call from the principal asking her to come in for a talk. Paul's kindergarten teacher said the boy was refusing to do things with the other children, and rebelled when corrected in class. After he got into a shoving match in line, the teacher, who knew what was happening in Paul's family, decided it was time to call in Ronda and have Paul see the school's child counselor.

Witnessing the effects of the family turmoil on her son, Ronda became angrier at Eddie. Paul was the same age Eddie had been when his father abandoned the family, and she did not want her son to suffer the same repressed rage that had driven Eddie's life. She felt that she had to separate cleanly from Eddie, and give her children and herself a respite from the pain and despair. Arriving at the school early for her appointment on February 18, 1982, she drove to a nearby park to wait. Her emotions were flowing high, and she found it coincidental that she had detoured into a park to cry, just as she had the time she sought refuge in Dick Kleberg Park instead of going to church. Ronda began to write her goodbye letter to Eddie. He would not get to see it, however, as she sealed it in her journal:

Dear Eddie,

I know full well this letter will never be sent. There will be no more coming your way. After much struggle, I have decided to file for a divorce. Obviously, you have no idea of the terrible pain you have caused in our lives. I am not away from God, Eddie. How could you suggest that because I want out of this marriage I am out of the will of God? God hasn't told me that the days ahead are to be my happiest, that I'm to wait for you. I don't want to try anymore. I have given up. You don't know the tears [I have shed] and prayers I have prayed for you. Do you take me to be a stupid ignoramus???? How could I have lived with you and not known your pain? How dare you lay the blame on me. You made your choices. I told you over a year ago that if you kept on going the way you were, that in a year our home would be as your parents home was. You wouldn't listen. Remember? You said, and I quote, "I can handle it." Well, you handled it well, didn't you?

Today I think I hate you. I never thought that could be so. I am tired of trying, of being hurt. Now all I want is to pick up the pieces and try to put them back together again. I only pray that God will send a loving man to help me do that; it will never be you again. You had your chance, and you blew it. No more, Eddie, no more.

Ronda

At Ron Barroso's request, Ronda wrote him a five-page, single-spaced letter outlining what she knew of Eddie and their marriage. She called up memories of things long forgotten. She recalled their happy times together, when Eddie seemed to have discarded the effects of his troubled youth. Ronda recounted Eddie's severe head injury and the employment problems that followed it until he joined the navy.

And as difficult as it was, Ronda detailed some of the sexual problems she and Eddie had been having for the past few years. Ronda still could not understand Eddie's need to go out and rape when she was waiting at home, unfulfilled and anxious for his love. The last time they attempted to have intercourse, she admitted to Barroso, was the previous July. She initiated it, and Eddie quickly tired and gave up. He seemed totally uninterested in, and even a bit fearful of, a sexual encounter with her. He even displayed an aversion to kissing. Ronda was still struggling to understand it herself and was at a loss to offer anything to Barroso but the facts of the matter themselves. She was just beginning to understand that Eddie's acts of rape had nothing at all to do with a need for sex.

Ronda went back to Kingsville that weekend with her brother Randy, his wife, and a nephew. James and Dolores Fields hugged her when she arrived at their house on Wanda Street, and Ronda felt herself start to cry upon entering the bedroom where she had found shelter during the days after Eddie's arrest. She could never forget the love and kindness she had found in that house.

That Saturday, some of Ronda's friends from First Assembly of God came over to the storage yard out at the west end of King Avenue to help Ronda pack her trailer. She made on-the-spot decisions to leave a few things behind, and when the job was done, she felt ashamed that after seven years of marriage, nearly everything she had could be loaded into the back of a one-axle trailer. It was as though she had been sent back to the starting line to begin over, except she had these few remnants of her shattered life to remind her of what she had lost.

On the way out of town, Ronda drove down King Avenue toward U.S. 77 bypass, and went within a half block of the courthouse square. As she passed, she turned left and looked toward the top-floor jail. She knew Eddie was up there, but in the day and a half she spent in town she had not tried to visit him. Instead, she said a silent goodby to her husband as she drove the family Dodge past the jail. There were no tears. It hurt too much to cry.

Ronda's return to Colorado was accompanied by some anxiety. So much was up in the air. There was no clue as to how long Eddie would have to spend in prison. There was the possibility that Ronda would have to return to Kingsville and air the most intimate details of her married life to a packed courtroom. No one could yet tell her what other sordid surprises might be revealed about Eddie's life. And most important, she had no sense of who Ronda Wyatt really was anymore. For years, she had an image of herself that was fortified through her marriage, her mothering, her church activities, her music, and her craft work.

But the inferno of the last two months had completely consumed the person she thought she was. Now she had to admit to herself that she had been so terribly wrong about so much that had happened. After she got back to Lakewood, she realized that the healing process was not one straight progression from injury to full recuperation. Instead, she was beginning to feel that it was more like bobbing in a life jacket on high seas. No sooner would she have a day of feeling better than the next day would bring an inexplicable retreat. Her long-held ideal of being a wife and mother would nevermore apply to her, and that was one of the most difficult things to try to accept. She wrote in her journal shortly after her return home with her things:

> I'm sitting here at the kitchen table. I should be joyful looking at the beautiful blue sky, seeing the first signs of spring on the trees and in the grass. Truly it's a beautiful day. But it's not so pretty on the inside. For the first time this morning I couldn't find a reason to get out of my bed. I am so battle-weary, and wish that I could run far away from it all. Maybe a nice little cabin, in a pretty, peaceful little meadow. Just somewhere my heart could heal.
>
> Some days it seems as though things are getting better, and then a turn in the road and it is dark again. I wrote Eddie yesterday and told him that I am filing for divorce. Lord, my heart still loves him, and I think that it wishes there could be another chance. But my head tells me that the wounds are too deep, the trust and hope has been destroyed. I know that it is time to break those ties. And I am so confused. I wish I could put into words how my heart feels inside today.
>
> Please prepare Eddie's heart for that letter, so that it

won't be so hard for him. Somehow, once again give him
peace and strength to face his tomorrows. Don't leave
him alone.

Allison Shaw walked with confidence into the courtroom while
Eddie Wyatt sat impassively at the defense table. It was a striking
reversal from the situation a little more than two months earlier,
when Eddie randomly selected her as his victim. Now, his fate
was riding on Allison. Considering the ordeal she had endured,
the seventeen-year-old had not only survived the harrowing
crime, but she had come out of it with a firm resolve to convict
her attacker.

The afternoon session on March 5, a Friday, got under way
at 1:30 in the Kleberg County Courthouse. It was a good while
before Allison was called to the stand. The arraignment went
first, and Barroso was successful in getting the trial put off for
two months. Dr. Kutnick had examined Eddie Wyatt only four
days earlier, and his report would not be ready until the end of
March at the earliest. Eddie was still showing signs of severe
depression whenever Barroso met with him, and had not been
of much help to his lawyer. He sat quietly, almost motionless at
the defense table, dressed in a tan pullover shirt and a pair of
slacks that Ronda had delivered to the jail before she sent all
their things to Colorado.

After the preliminaries were handled by Judge Dunham, Botary called Allison to the witness stand. He quickly took her
through a few questions about herself, and how she came to be
lounging in bed on the morning of December 21, relaxing on
Christmas break. Then Botary got right to the next events, when
she was startled by the sound of noise from her kitchen. Allison
described her terror when a masked intruder pounced on her
bed and began to wrap tape around her head to blindfold her,
then as he stabbed Killer to death. But because of the attack by
her dog, the rapist had not been careful with the blindfold, Allison
told the court. For the first time, Eddie heard from his victim's
own lips about how she could see him as plain as day. He had

asked her over and over, saying he would hurt her if she could see him, and she had denied it.

"Were any kind of garments placed over your eyes or hands or legs?" Botary asked her.

"He put tape over my eyes and hands," Allison responded quickly.

"Describe the type of tape that was used," the prosecutor said.

"It was a white plastic, kind of brown and white," she replied.

"Did it have adhesive on the back of it?"

"Yes."

"And was it placed all the way, wrapped around your head or partially taped over your eyes?" he asked her.

"Wrapped around."

"Were you able to see through that tape?" Botary asked.

"Yes," Allison answered.

"While the individual or intruder was taping your eyes ..." Botary began, but Judge Dunham interrupted him.

"You say you could see through the tape?" the judge asked Allison directly.

"Yes," she turned to him to reply.

"All right," Dunham said, turning the witness back over to Botary.

"Were you able to see him through the tape?" Botary asked Allison, to clarify what she meant.

"Yes, sir," she said.

"How well could you see through it?" Botary inquired.

"Just like it was not there, just spaces at a time," Allison responded firmly. "I could see clear."

"Did you make any indication at all to this intruder at the time that you could see?"

"He did not think that I could see," Allison replied.

"How do you know that?" Botary prompted her.

"Because he told me he did not want to hurt me, and he hoped that I did not see him, because he would have to hurt me if I could see him," she answered.

Allison went on describing how she tried to avoid looking

right at the man as he carried her to his car and later as he raped
her. She could not stand to look at him, even though she knew
she had to remember. But also, she did not want to give him the
slightest reason to think she could actually see him. Allison then
described what happened after the man drove her out to the
countryside, but Botary was careful to elicit answers that per-
tained only to her ability to identify Eddie Wyatt, euphemistically
guiding her around the actual assaults.

"How far did y'all travel?" Botary asked.

"About ten minutes," Allison replied.

"All right, and then, did the intruder ever come back to the
back of the car to where you were at?"

"He stopped one time, and did something, and then we left,
and then he came to the back of the car," Allison said.

"And at that point in time, did he have a sexual relationship
with you?" Botary asked.

"When he came back there," she said.

"Were you able to see him at that point in time?"

"Yes."

"At the time that he stopped the car and forced sexual advances on you, did he remove the mask on his face?" Botary
asked.

"Yes," Allison answered. "He took it off as soon as he taped
my eyes."

"Were you able to see him at that time?"

"Yes."

"What other place did you travel to?" he asked her.

"He went somewhere else out in the country, and then he
abused me again, and he said he was going to have to put me in
the trunk."

"At the second time that you stopped that he, in your language,
abused you, were you able to see him on that occasion?"

"Yes."

"And how long were you in a position to see him at that
time?" Botary asked.

"For about fifteen or twenty minutes," Allison said.

"Okay. Before you were placed in the trunk, were any of your
garments removed? I am talking about the tape."

"Yeah, he took the tape off my hands and my legs."

"All right, and placed you in the trunk?"

"Then he put, well, he abused me, and then he put me in the trunk," Allison recalled. "He taped my hands in front."

"While you were in the trunk, did you do anything with the tape that you had across your eyes." Botary asked her.

"I moved it with my finger," Allison replied.

"How did you move it?"

"I slid it out of the way so I could see better," she said.

"Were you able to pull it off entirely?"

"No, I did not want it to be noticeable," she said.

Botary took her up to the time the rapist carried her into a house. Asking her questions about when she arrived, and establishing that the tape blindfold remained in place, Botary asked her:

"Were you in a position where you had face-to-face contact with the intruder?"

"Yes," Allison replied.

"How long were you there with him at that time?" he continued.

"About three or four hours," she answered.

"Okay. You were able to see him at that time?"

"I looked at him eye-to-eye," Allison answered.

Then Botary asked her about the evening a week later when Captain Gomez called her down to the police station to look at some mug shots of Anglo men. The prosecutor was careful to have Allison make it clear that she was not steered in any way to Eddie Wyatt's photo. Captain Gomez, Allison testified, did not ask her to pick out anyone at all when he handed her the stack of photos. He did not even indicate whether police had anyone in mind, or had a suspect in custody, she testified. She told the court that after she picked out Eddie's photo from about eight down in the stack, she did not even need to look at the others.

"If you saw this individual that assaulted you today, do you think you would be able to recognize him?" Botary finally asked her.

"Yes," Allison answered. Botary wanted to drive home the point that Allison's identification of Eddie Wyatt as the man who raped her was the result of her crystal clear memory of the event and not the power of police suggestion.

"Would you recognize him because you recall what he looked like on the day of the assault, December 21, 1981, or would you recognize him because you identified a photograph?" Botary asked.

"I recognize him because I remember him," Allison answered.

"All right, would you look around the courtroom and tell me whether or not you recognize anybody?" Botary requested of her.

"Yes," Allison answered after a quick scan of the uncrowded room.

"Do you see the person that assaulted you on the twenty-first day of December, 1981?"

"Yes."

"Is he in the courtroom?" Botary asked.

"Yes," Allison replied.

"Would you point him out, please?"

"He is sitting right there," Allison said, pointing straight at Eddie.

"Is he the man in the tan pullover-type shirt?" the prosecutor asked her.

"Yes."

"Had you ever seen that man before the twenty-first day of December 1981?" Botary asked.

"No," Allison replied.

"Have you ever seen him since?" he went on.

"No," she answered.

"Pass the witness," Botary said, looking over to Ron Barroso as the defender rose to begin his cross-examination.

Barroso had visited with Botary the day before and obtained the names of potential witnesses. The only other eyewitness who could place Eddie at the scene of the kidnapping, and only after hypnosis, was Luis Godines, the Exxon fireman who saw Eddie Wyatt back his blue Valiant into Shaw's alley and shortly after drive out. Several other neighbors saw a blue car with a loud muffler, but they had not spotted the man driving it. Still, based on Allison's testimony alone, the case was not a good one from the defense standpoint. Barroso would try to shake Allison's certainty if he could, and in the meantime he would question her as much as he could about details. If she said something that contradicted any earlier statements she had given, Barroso might get a slim opening through which he could deal Eddie a stronger hand of cards in negotiating with the district attorney. He knew, however, Botary would not let him go far with that.

Barroso had Allison start over, when she was waiting in bed to get up and videotape a soap opera for her mother. He pushed her for details, at one point asking her if she heard drawers opening and closing, at another point seeking a clarification on exactly what noise her floor produced, a rattle or a squeak. Botary's first objection came when Barroso pressed her for details on what words the attacker used in conversation as he carried Allison to his car.

"Your honor, I don't think that is part of the identification," Botary objected to Dunham. "I think it is getting a little broad."

"Sustained," Dunham agreed.

Barroso then questioned Allison about the ride out into the country south of Kingsville, where the car stopped once briefly before the kidnapper got back in, made a U-turn, and went somewhere else. It was at the second stop that Allison testified she was first sexually assaulted, on the backseat of the car. Allison was consistent in remembering details of this and a second sexual assault in the car, before going to the house. Eddie had confessed to Barroso that he raped Allison at his house, but he steadfastly maintained that he had not touched her in the car. He claimed he was marking time until he could be sure that Ronda had left the house following her lunch break.

Barroso was venturing into areas where Botary would try to cut him off. As he questioned Allison about the stop in the country, Barroso asked whether she noticed any marks on his arms when he took off his shirt. Allison said she had not.

"No tattoos?" Barroso asked specifically.

"No, not that I noticed," Allison answered.

"How close was he when you saw him?" he inquired.

"Right up close," she said.

"You were not having difficulty seeing, were you?" he asked.

"No."

"You said at this point in time he unzipped his pants."

"Uh-huh."

"And he did not have intercourse with you there, did he?" Barroso asked.

"Yes," Allison corrected him.

"How long were you stopped there?"

"About twenty minutes, I guess," Allison said. "I don't know."

Then Barroso started to glean for details.

"The second time here when you say that you were there for about twenty minutes, and he made you submit to intercourse, did you—he got you on top of the seat?" he asked.

"Yes."

"Did he remove your clothes at that point in time?"

"Yes," Allison said. "Just my underwear."

"Just your underwear? Did you still just have on your T-shirt and underwear and socks?" Barroso asked.

"Yes, and my socks came off," she answered. "I guess they came out on the ground somewhere."

"What happened after that?" Barroso continued.

"Excuse me," Botary got up and interrupted before Allison could answer. "I think we are going far afield. I let it go on for about three questions. I think he should go on to another area."

"Sustained," Dunham said without flinching. Barroso regrouped and went to another question.

"What I am talking about, Miss Shaw, after you left, did he tape your eyes again?" Barroso asked.

"He never untaped them," she replied, correcting him so a wrong impression would not be left unchallenged.

"Did the tape come loose at all?"

"Well, in the trunk, it kind of slidded loose," she explained.

"After you left this second area, was this the point in time he placed you in the trunk?" Barroso asked, confused by the details of what she was saying were three stops and two assaults.

"No, we went to another place and he abused me again, and then he put me in the trunk," Allison replied.

"What do you mean when you say he abused you?" he asked.

"Forced me to have sex with him," Allison replied.

"Okay. Was part of this oral sex?" Barroso inquired.

"Yes," Allison answered before Botary, suddenly sitting up straight, could interrupt.

"Your honor," the prosecutor called to Judge Dunham. "Again, I object to that. That is outside the scope of this hearing."

"Sustained," Dunham ruled.

Later in the questioning, when he got to the point when Allison was taken to the house, Barroso tried to find out why Allison saw no tattoos on her attacker's body. If she had seen him naked, then she should have seen them. They were hard to miss, the one of the snake on his left arm, and the name of his old girlfriend Julie on his right.

"Did he ever completely disrobe?" Barroso asked.

"Yes," Allison replied.

"Did you ever describe any other markings on his body?"

"No," she said. "I did not look at him. I did not care what he looked like."

"You just looked at his face?" Barroso wondered. "Do I understand what you are trying to tell the court that you were embarrassed to look at him?"

"Yes," Allison said.

"You still got a look at him without his clothes on, didn't you?" he pressed her.

"Yes," Allison answered.

"You never noticed any scars?"

"I did not see him up close all the way," she tried to explain. "He was standing across the room."

"He was standing across the room when you saw him?"

"When I saw him taking his clothes off," she replied.

"Did he ever get close to you when he performed these sexual acts that you are talking about?" Barroso asked.

"Yes."

"Did he have his clothes off?"

"Yes."

"Well, did you see him up close, then?"

"I did not look at him then," Allison said.

"You did not look at him then as he was walking toward you?" he asked her.

"I had no desire to look at him," she answered.

"Did you close your eyes?"

"I looked off around the room," Allison said.

Barroso established that Allison had glanced at his torso and could not recall having seen any tattoos. But it was weak. Although the man was naked for at least three hours, she said she tried not to look at his body, and she was believable. Still, when Barroso finished and it came time for Botary to follow up, the veteran prosecutor moved to shore up any doubts about the identification, even with her admission that she had not seen the obvious tattoos.

It was nearly 7:00 P.M. when the hearing wrapped up, with Luis Godines still waiting to testify. But Dunham recessed the hearing until Monday morning. It was dark by the time Barroso was able to start back up Highway 77 to Corpus Christi. He knew he had not been able to chip away enough at the identification, and it was highly unlikely that Judge Dunham would rule it inadmissible as evidence.

Sure enough, when the hearing resumed and was completed the following Wednesday, Dunham immediately ruled the identifications of Wyatt by both Allison Shaw and Luis Godines as admissible. Eddie Wyatt would be going to prison for sure, and he was not holding a good hand for bargaining.

When the subpoenas went out in anticipation of the May trial, police and prosecutors believed they not only had built a strong case against Eddie Wyatt on the charge in question, the rape of Allison Shaw, but that they also had a decent circumstantial case to make on some other open cases. While Eddie was not charged with those other crimes, at least not yet, police knew they would put a scare into him when he looked at the list of witnesses.

Heading the list was the homeowner on Escondido Drive,

who was the first person to see Allison Shaw after her release in Dick Kleberg Park. After that was Allison, her father, sister, and a neighbor. Then came Luis Godines.

After that, there was a battery of police and expert witnesses, starting with one of the naval security officers who had assisted in the investigation once it was determined the tape being used on the rape victims could only have come from the Naval Air Station. Kingsville detectives and evidence technicians, along with a laboratory expert from the Texas Department of Safety's criminal lab in Austin, were also being called as witnesses.

But possibly the most portentous names on the list were those of five women. The specific names were entirely unfamiliar to Eddie, yet he knew who they were. George Gomez had warned him they were going to try to pin other crimes on him and put him away for ninety-nine years. In return, Eddie had told the police nothing. He had refused to talk from the moment Hector Treviño and Gomez took him home just before his arrest. Gomez thought Eddie Wyatt was one of the stone-coldest perpetrators who had ever crossed his path. In the meantime, while Eddie had confessed to Ronda, Pastor Fields, Ron Barroso, and some family members that he had raped Allison Shaw, he denied any involvement with the others. Falling back on his instincts about the police when he was a juvenile, Eddie just shrugged and figured cops will be cops, and that they were using him to clear their books of some unsolved crimes.

The women's names were listed in chronological order, from the most recent rape to the earliest. First was Kyung Ellis. Then came Shelly Polk, wife of the fast-food manager; Cheryl Palmer, the college student in the alley apartment; and Kim Sullivan, one of the three victims from Pastor Fields's neighborhood. The last woman named on the list was Sue Wilson, awakened in her house the previous June by a man who raped her.

But there was one last name on the list that took Eddie by surprise: Captain Robert Sawyer of the Norfolk, Virginia, Police Department.

Ken Botary told Ron Barroso that follow-up contacts from Kingsville with the Norfolk Police Department had turned up two sexual assaults in that city and one in nearby Virginia Beach that fit into the pattern police in Texas believed was used by Eddie Wyatt. Police in Virginia were investigating it.

Eddie told his lawyer he had nothing to do with any rapes in Virginia.

Then, word came in from the Galveston Police Department. Sargeant Ray Rubio, the officer who had arrested Eddie in the 1970 burglary for which he was sent to prison as an adult, was investigating two sexual assaults, one of which took place near Eddie's childhood home. The rapes occurred during the same week the previous summer that Eddie went up alone to Galveston to fulfill his lifelong fantasy of having sex with his childhood sweetheart.

In the meantime, the lab results came back from Austin, mostly with negative results. As a matter of routine, the lab confirmed that the bloodstains on Allison's bedding came from her dog. It confirmed the finding of semen on her shirt, panties, and socks, and on the backseat that had been yanked out of Eddie's blue Valiant and sent to the lab. There was no sperm present, consistent with a man who had undergone a vasectomy. The brown and the green tape that had been used to bind and blindfold Allison was the same type as the rolls of tape found in the search of the Wyatt residence. However, the technicians were unable to match up the torn ends from Allison's bindings with the loose ends of the rolls police found, so they could not confirm that the rolls of tape from Eddie's house were the actual ones used on Allison.

The most significant finding was that hairs matching those of the dead dog Killer were recovered from the carpet sweepings police took from Eddie's Valiant, and from a roll of tape found in Eddie's house. The lab could not confirm that any human hairs recovered from the trunk, backseat, or house belonged to Allison. Eddie still insisted to Barroso that he had not raped Allison on the backseat, and he was at a loss as to how the lab could have found a "massive quantity" of acid phosphatase, a constituent of semen, on the seat center.

*   *   *

Dr. Kutnick's psychiatric evaluation of Eddie came back about this time, and it provided no mitigation for the defense either.

Eddie was in handcuffs when Kutnick interviewed him just a few days before the arraignment, so his hands always moved in unison when he gestured. He struck the psychiatrist as alert, logical, and rational. But when Kutnick asked Eddie whether he thought he had mental problems, Eddie bent over and began to cry.

"Something is taking over my mind," he sobbed. "It started about a year ago, when I was out to sea. It's like something inside me, another person telling me all sorts of things. It's like a force. Sometimes it makes fun of me. Sometimes out at sea, when I got close to the ship's rail, I felt like the force was trying to push me over into the water."

Kutnick took notes and prodded Eddie with follow-up questions. He wanted Eddie to describe the voice. Was it a disembodied sound from the outside?

"No, doctor," Eddie replied. "It's something that talks to me inside my own head. Like I say, I don't know if it's my own thinking or not, but it forces me to think about sex, especially anal sex. I feel like it's perverse, but I think about it all the time. I'm not certain what this force is, doctor. I've been hoping it's not a demon possession."

Demonic possession was a bit out of Kutnick's specialty. But it seemed that Eddie, having come from a fundamentalist background, was truly fearful that if not actually possessed, he at least was under attack by an oppression of demonic origin. His church taught that once they received the Spirit, Christians could not be possessed. But they could very well be oppressed by demons. To those who did not hold such beliefs, the construction of this demon world was Eddie's embodiment of the forces in his embattled conscience. The demons were the faces on Eddie's evil impulses. Soon, Kutnick changed the subject to the present.

"Did you rape this seventeen-year-old girl?" Kutnick asked Eddie.

"I guess so," he replied. "I didn't remember doing it at first, but now the memory is coming back to me. These thoughts kept coming into my mind and I tried to fight them. I vaguely remember going into that girl's house, and I remember having some sex with her. I don't remember killing that dog, or taking pictures of her, but they say I did."

Eddie produced a letter from Ronda and showed it to Kutnick.

"She talks about the rape in there, but I don't even remember talking with my wife about it," Eddie said. "I must've just lost control."

Eddie told Kutnick that his sexual relationship with Ronda was normal, in stark contrast to what Ronda had told Barroso. The apparent contradiction was likely the result of different expectations. What little Ronda received was plenty for him. But Eddie told the psychiatrist that there had never been anything abnormal about his sexual activity until recently.

In his written report to Judge Dunham, Kutnick made a provisional diagnosis of an obsessive compulsive disorder revolving around sexual practices the defendant professed to find repulsive. The opinion was provisional because Kutnick could not be sure about his subject's motives. If Eddie was accurately describing what had been going on in his life, his thoughts about sex had certainly become an overriding obsession. But Kutnick pointed out that an obsessive compulsion does not obliterate one's ability to understand the moral issues of the behavior, or the ability to weigh the consequences and cease it if necessary.

"There is a good possibility that the defendant is exaggerating the quality of these obsessive thoughts and in fact does not have any particular psychiatric disorder," Kutnick wrote to the judge. He concluded that at the time of the rape, Eddie Wyatt "had no mental disease or defect which rendered him unable to know his conduct was wrong" and that he was currently competent to stand trial.

As far as the obsession with anal sex, Kutnick found no particular origin, except for Eddie's contention that this force he described had, within the past year or so, brought those thoughts on him. From how deep in Eddie's psyche they had to surface was anybody's guess at this point.

"I have a feeling that he remembers much more than he is willing to admit," Kutnick wrote in his report.

*　　*　　*

Ronda found a job early in March as a clerk in a Lakewood gun shop. She could not yet afford to rent a home of her own, and Paul and Erna made it plain that she and the children were welcomed to stay for as long as necessary in the Newland Street homestead. As much as the assistance was needed and gratefully accepted, it was difficult for Ronda to be starting over back in the home where, as a little girl, she had so often dreamed happy things about her future.

Ronda knew that she could not recover from her depression until she dealt with a host of grueling questions that kept recurring in her mind. One evening she wrote some of them down in her journal, hoping that by seeing them in black and white, it would help her focus on the possible answers. Strangely, while she understood that she was not to blame, she still suffered from gnawing doubts about herself, as if there really had been something wrong with her and not with Eddie. Intellectually, she knew none of this was true. Yet she felt shackled by the sensation that if she had just been a little prettier, or a little more outgoing, she might have prevented this. They were questions Ronda believed no one else could understand unless and until they underwent such treacherous disloyalty themselves and felt an almost total draining of self-esteem:

Why me, God? Why this way? Couldn't you have done it another way?

Why wouldn't Eddie get help? Where did I fail? What could I have done to have prevented this? Is this really happening? Where do I go from here?

Why did Eddie force himself on Allison? Why wouldn't he love me? What is rape? Does it feel something like what I have felt?

Is it really an act of violence and not of passion? If it is, then what was Eddie so angry about? What don't I know about Eddie and what happened?

How could the man I thought was so quiet and gentle be such a different person when he was not with us?

*How far-reaching was his unfaithfulness? How do I let
go of him? How do you stop loving someone you loved
so much?*

And in the midst of those questions, Ronda's compassion had
her wondering who would take care of her husband when he got
sick, and how he would handle the pain of knowing he had lost
his family through his own actions.

Then Ronda turned the questions inward:

*What's wrong with me? Who am I? Am I attractive—
inside and out? What will other people say, and why
does it matter what they will say? Will I ever marry
again? What if I'm not good enough for someone else?
Is it normal to feel what I am feeling? Why am I so
scared? Can I love again?*

*If I failed in such an important area of my life, how
can I succeed in other areas?*

Ronda learned from her brother Randy, who had phoned Botary, that Eddie was asking about a plea bargain. It was through
that call that Ronda learned her husband was being considered
as a suspect in several more rapes in Kingsville, and three sexual
assaults in Norfolk and Virginia Beach. Ronda did not want to
go back to Kingsville to testify, but she knew if there was a trial,
she would have to go. She did not know how she could face Eddie
in that courtroom when each day brought to light other things
he had done behind her back.

While preparing for her divorce, she felt the stinging awareness that for years she had sat on the sidelines and seen other
marriages break up, and she had not even begun to perceive the
depths of their emotional pain. How easy it had been to offer glib
advice and observations on what the other couples should have
done to stay together, even when it was no longer possible. How
easy it was to thoughtlessly condemn others to a life without
love. A week or so later, Erna brought in the mail and handed
Ronda another envelope from Eddie. It contained Eddie's reaction to her divorce filing.

Dear Ronda

Received your letter today and I wanted to write you this last letter to tell you goodbye. It's very hard to do but somehow I knew it would end this way. I just didn't want to give up the slightest hope. I hope like you said, honeybun, that you will never keep me from Paul and Sissy because you know I can never have any more children. You have my only two.

I'm glad you said you had no bitterness in your heart. I hope you mean it, because you know what bitterness and unforgiveness could do to your life. I'm glad we're not parting in hate and bitterness as some, but in understanding and sorrow. I can't deny the hurt inside me, honeybun, because I do feel I still love you. I have never felt so alone in all my life.

So often I've sat here and thought of our first years together and how happy we were. I know these last couple were hard as I was no longer being able to cope with things. How I wish I could undo so much. I always thought I knew so much, but I've really known so little. I'm so sorry, honey, if that means anything at all. I would surely give my life to undo the hurt in your heart. Maybe I no longer deserve you. Maybe I never have. I have learned so much from our seven years together. I could never say I lost because my life was made richer through our years together. I'll never forget you, honeybun.

Then Eddie enclosed a poem for Paul and Diana, which he asked Ronda to give to them when she felt they were ready for it. The poem went on for two pages, in which Eddie sought to reassure his children that the wrong he had done was not a rejection of them, and that he loved them. His father left him when he was the same age, he reminded them:

Paul and Diana, two children of mine,
*   I write this poem for you two*

To remember in time.
Though you don't understand now why I had to go away,
*   In the years ahead, God will show you one day.*
*   Though blinded and twisted as my mind became,*
*   My love for you two always remained the same.*
I want you always to know this day, I tried, I tried, I
tried
*   To be the daddy you needed.*
*   How so often with God I pleaded.*
*   I never wanted you to be cheated*
*   From having a daddy to love.*
My heart broke, it bled, I cried a thousand tears
*   To know I will never see you again, in all my earthly*
years.
*   I love you, I love you, I love you.*
*   Please believe me when I say*
*   I never meant to hurt or deprive you in this way.*
Mommy knows I love you. She'll tell you the way
*   I'd rock you two in my arms till asleep you would*
lay.
*   Then gently, so gently, put you to bed*
*   With kisses and prayers to be said.*
What great comfort it gave me, what great joy I had
*   When you were my children and I was your dad.*

Ron Barroso tried one more time to have some of the evidence
thrown out. A week after losing the motion to suppress Allison
Shaw's identification of Eddie, the defense attorney filed a motion
to suppress the search of the Wyatt house, basing it on questions
he had about Detective Treviño's probable cause for seeking the
warrant.

The hearing on this latest motion was held in the Kleberg
County Courthouse on May 5, twelve days before the scheduled
trial. Judge Vernon Harville was back on the Kleberg bench and
would rule on the motion. In addition to the suppression motion,
Barroso asked Harville for a postponement of the trial. He had

a civil case in Corpus Christi in which the trial had earlier been set for May 17.

During the ninety-minute hearing, Treviño was able to establish to Harville's satisfaction that police had more than enough probable cause to go and search the Wyatt house. The detective spoke in a businesslike, professional tone, the way he always approached his work, as he testified about the way his investigation winnowed its way down to Eddie Wyatt's doorstep. Then once he was in the house after taking the suspect home before the arrest, Treviño told the judge about seeing many of the items Allison Shaw told him she had seen while being raped in the attacker's house. Once Allison identified Eddie's mug shot, there was compelling reason to authorize the search warrant.

Harville ended the hearing by upholding the prosecution's position on the search of the house. The judge then denied Barroso's motion for a continuance. Eddie's trial, he ruled, would go on as scheduled. Barroso respected Harville as a very knowledgeable judge who was almost never overturned, so the lawyer figured he had little chance of carving out some breathing room.

The loss of those motions put pressure on Eddie to forego a trial with a guilty plea. He thought about Ronda coming back to testify, and about listening to Allison on the stand with her explicit testimony about his deeds. He thought about the possibility of being charged with some of the other sexual assaults as well, and of his attorney's assessment of the case, which was not good.

It was time to stop, Eddie decided. Barroso came to visit him on Tuesday, May 11, and Eddie told him to try to negotiate the best deal he could get from Botary. Eddie said he wanted to spare everybody the financial and emotional expenses of a trial whose outcome seemed certain already.

Barroso went to see Botary and Bill Mobley, who would have to approve any plea bargain, especially in a case as controversial as the Kingsville rapes. Barroso told them his client would plead guilty to the felony charge of burglary with intent to commit rape that was in the original indictment. The plea would be entered if the state agreed not to prosecute the other two felony counts in the second indictment, and several misdemeanor charges. The recommended sentence would be thirty years in prison. Mobley and Botary agreed to take it to Harville.

At a short hearing that afternoon, Eddie entered his guilty plea, tearfully admitting in testimony that he had broken into Allison Shaw's house, kidnapped the teenager, and raped her. Prosecutor Botary told Judge Harville that the state's interest in accepting the plea was to spare the victim from having to testify again, only in much fuller detail. Harville then sentenced Eddie to the recommended thirty years. He would languish in the Kleberg jail for several months before the overcrowded Texas state prison system found a bed for him.

Captain Gomez and his detectives finally put away all their files on the Kingsville rapes, including the long sheet of butcherblock paper.

There had been no more rapes in Kingsville since the night Eddie Wyatt was arrested.

"A special day, Lord." Ronda wrote in her diary after learning Eddie would plead guilty. To Ronda's surprise, they were remarkably strong and optimistic sentiments. "I cannot exactly put into words what I am learning, but I am learning."

> *Eddie made his choices, and now must reap accordingly. But where Paul, Diana, and I go from here is up to me. I'm no longer a little girl, but a grown woman and a mother with lives in my hands. I must begin to act responsibly. People have always determined for me how my life should go. Now I have to take the reins and make choices for us. My "walls" are crumbling down and that is very frightening. My "walls" have always been my protection. I thought that they were me. Now I'm finding out that they were not me at all.*

One of the first things Ronda did to reassure her children that they were still a family, even without their father, was to have a

new family picture taken to hang on her wall. They went to the
same photography studio where they had all gone when Eddie
and Ronda, and her brothers and their families, gathered for
Thanksgiving only seven months earlier. Ronda used a small print
of the new family portrait to adorn a scrapbook she began to put
together with Paul and Diana that spring, called "We're Special."
She used the scrapbook to bolster the children's spirits, and made
it a group activity to fill in each new page.

When they first moved back to Colorado, Diana seemed to
be angry and resentful, but she soon enough came out of it. Paul
was more introverted than his sister, and it concerned Ronda
that her son was holding too much inside of him. As talkative as
a six-year-old boy can be, Paul hardly ever brought up how he
was feeling about what had happened to the family. But one night
after his bedtime prayers, he broke down and began to cry terribly. He had loved his daddy so much, and his sobs made Ronda
wonder whether she was right to decide that they should not
exchange letters with Eddie. The children could not simply pretend their father had never existed. Ronda decided that night that
she would let the children write to Eddie.

Ronda filed the divorce papers on May 26. This was rock
bottom for her. From this point onward, she wanted to look up.
In her journal, she wrote her personal prayer of capitulation to
the Lord. Its title was "Ashes," and she would share the prayer
with many people in the ensuing years when she felt they needed
the peace of mind that came with acceptance of their situation.

*Ashes. Here, Lord. Ugly ashes, in an ugly bucket. That's
all I have left. I haven't known what to do with them, so
I tossed it about in my mind and decided to bring them
to you. They're not very pretty. I'm sorry, God, so very,
very sorry. I started out meaning so well, wanting so
much for you to be proud. But look at the mess I've made.*

*All I have left are these ashes. It got hot, so hot, and
we couldn't stand the fire. It hurt so very much to watch
as my husband and my home began to totter, crumble,
and fall. I cried, I prayed, I tried to pick them up, to put
them back together. But it was too late. We waited too*

long. What you gave me was destroyed. And I am left with a rusty old bucket filled with the ashes of my life.

I wanted to bury them so no one would know what happened, but I couldn't. So, here they are. I've heard that for them you would give me beauty. If you will grant me your beauty for these dirty ashes, I will give it back to you through my life. And this time, Lord, this time I will be a planting for you, that you might be glorified.

CHAPTER 11

SEPARATE WAYS

I am lonely and ready to love again. It is as if only now we are beginning to emerge from the dark tunnel in which we have been so long encased. In my heart, I still pity Eddie for what he allowed to come into his life. I look at my lovely daughter and wonderful son, and feel saddened for what I know he has missed in their lives. I am so very grateful that for their sakes, you did not let me give up.

—from Ronda's diary

The town looked almost exactly the same as she remembered it when Ronda returned to Kingsville in December 1990 for the first time in nearly nine years. Small details, such as the white-painted trim on the light brown brick facade of the Kleberg County Courthouse, triggered a flood of unpleasant memories. She felt compelled to return to this institutional-looking building to chase away the ghosts that lingered there. As she walked down the north side stairwell to the sheriff's department, she vividly remembered herself guiding her blind pastor down those stairs to meet with Eddie. She relived the moment when her faith in her husband was crushed and Eddie told her that he was a rapist.

She had left part of herself in this scary place, and she had to return to reclaim it.

At her side was Rob Knuth, a tall, easygoing, and loving man with a pleasant smile who was Ronda's second husband. In the years she had been away from Kingsville, Ronda thought she had come to terms with what had happened, that she had forgiven Eddie, and that no bitterness had taken root.

Amid the hectic pace of life as a single parent for three years, she had had little time to face her feelings. Then her marriage to

Rob and the happiness it brought her made it very easy to ignore
the unpleasant emotions of her past. But they were only packed
away in boxes and shoved in a closet. The closet was now so
crammed full, that everything was ready to tumble out the moment someone, or something, opened the door.

Such was the case just a year earlier, when Ronda and Rob
took a trip to Louisiana. Passing through Texas on U.S. 287, they
drove by the exact spot at the side of the road where she had
lost her virginity to Eddie in the VW bug fifteen years before. She
had repressed the terrible memory of that night so deeply that
she had not thought of it since her wedding to Eddie. While
passing the site, Ronda glanced to the side of the highway and
saw the same clump of three dark tree trunks she had stared at
while Eddie had his way with her. They were larger now, but
they still matched the image that had burned itself into her subconscious memory. The scene immediately brought the entire
episode back, and made her wonder whether she should have
taken it as a clue.

Once Ronda made the first tentative moves to share her story
with friends, she was surprised when the old anger, hurt, and
frustration engulfed her again. They had not gone away after all,
which helped to explain why for a long time, she felt uneasy
looking at her own image in the mirror. She still felt rejection,
shame, and humiliation, despite her new satisfaction as a wife
and mother, now with four children. Ronda began to have regular
sessions with a female psychologist who operated a Christian
counseling practice. During those sessions, it soon became obvious that Ronda had to go back to Kingsville. It was a risky thing
to do—Kingsville remained a place of dread. What filled her with
apprehension the most was making the final discoveries, whatever they might be, about her failed marriage.

In the Kleberg Courthouse, Ronda went with Rob to the sec-
ond-floor clerk's office and asked for case file number 3043. She
opened the dog-eared file folder and read the transcripts of the
testimony given by Hector Treviño, Luis Godines, and Allison
Shaw. She saw the selection of Polaroid mug shots from which
Allison had picked Eddie, with the teenager's handwriting on the
back of Eddie's photo. She saw the police photo of Detective

Durham's hand pulling the unraveled recording tape out of the eggnog carton in her trash, and read the transcript of the tape Eddie made while he raped Allison under the family's Christmas tree. Although she was able to obtain a copy of the tape recording itself, she could not bring herself to play it. The transcript was terrible enough.

After years of repressing it, facing up to all that had gone on behind her back was something Ronda feared. It was something she could not do until her counselor told her she had the courage to do it. Courage, Ronda learned, was not the absence of fear but the ability to go on in spite of fear.

About a year after Ronda returned to Colorado, she took Paul to a derby sponsored by the church's Royal Rangers, and she noticed a mother of one of Paul's friends whom she had seen once before in church. About a week before, Ronda saw the woman off by herself, crying quietly. While their sons played with toy cars, the woman came over to a desk on which Ronda was leaning and sat next to her on it. Ronda wondered what words to use to break the ice, and found herself understanding what others meant when they told her that they had wanted to reach out to her but could not find the right words. It would be so easy to ignore the young woman next to her, and walk away with Paul when the derby was over.

But Ronda overcame her reluctance and began to speak with the woman. Quickly, she discovered that the woman's pain of the previous week was rooted in the same type of personal crisis Ronda was undergoing. The woman's name was Karen. She was a divorcee, she had a son, and she was just now starting over, like Ronda. As Karen spoke, tears started streaming down her cheeks again. Karen turned her head to hide them. But Ronda urged her to share them. She knew they were part of releasing the bitterness and the pain. The two women soon became friends, and Ronda felt strengthened by the new relationship and her sense of usefulness.

That night, Ronda was amazed at the peacefulness she felt. There was something therapeutic in reaching out to someone in need. It made her feel alive again. It made her realize that there would come a time when she would go from dawn to dusk without once feeling her own tears start to flow. And that first day would lead to a second, and then to a week. Ronda now knew that one day, although she would never forget what she went through, she would be able to recall it without the stinging pain. After meeting Karen, Ronda wrote in her diary:

> *I have fought so hard not to let anyone see my tears. But when I stopped up my tears, I also stopped up my spirit. I had determined that no one would touch me to the point of weeping. But when I finally stopped caring that they came, stopped trying to be what I was not, then the softening came to my heart again.*

Ronda soon allowed Eddie to write to Paul and Diana. They exchanged letters, drawings, and poems, and it had an immediate impact on Paul. The little boy's questions—especially "Does Daddy still love me?"—did not come as often, although he still harbored conflicting feelings. He felt unwanted by his father, no matter how often Ronda reassured him that Eddie's problems had nothing to do with his children. Diana told her mom that she felt sad and that she hated policemen.

So Ronda was relieved the morning Paul ran to her and excitedly announced, "I didn't have bad dreams!" She understood bad dreams. Even a year after she returned to Colorado, she needed a night-light to be able to sleep. Late one night, she was jarred awake in pitch blackness in her basement bedroom. She groped for the lamp at the bedside and turned its switch, but it failed to come on. Panic filled her, like the frightening night in Kingsville when both she and Eddie awoke to the sensation of evil in the room. Was there someone in the room who had cut off the lights? Could he see her? Did someone pull the breaker switch outside to plunge the entire house into darkness? She cried herself back to sleep, and awoke later with both lamps burning. Evidently, there had been a power outage in the area.

That morning, she thought about that evil presence in her bedroom in Kingsville. It happened two weeks after the rape of

Kyung Ellis. Looking back, Ronda realized it was the same time her husband was fighting a raging battle against his evil impulses, all while keeping it masked behind his seemingly ordinary lifestyle. It dawned on her that the night they both awoke to the oppressive sense of evil might have been the precise moment when Eddie, spiritually spent by years of both fighting it and hiding it, surrendered to it. If she could have sensed his utter hopelessness much earlier, if he had not kept resisting her comfort by assuring her it was something he could handle, would it have made a difference at that point, she wondered?

Ronda turned to her faith more intensely to find strength to go on. Ultimately, she was nourished by her own spiritual strength. When she sought counsel from a pastor who compared her recovery to that of the biblical prodigal son, returning to the community of believers after she had sinned, Ronda was outraged. She had had enough! Enough of people who would judge her, enough of those who looked for what she had done wrong, enough of people who thought she needed forgiveness.

The most useful tool Ronda found to deal with her emotional turmoil turned out to be her journal. With it, she could watch herself change and grow from the confused, self-blaming wife into the woman who was trying hard to understand that what her husband did was not her fault. What kind of person would be reflected in future diary entries, she wondered? One still more self-confident?

Ronda found part-time work at a local Sears store. She longed for a better-paying job, but she did not want to leave the children alone for so much time. She wanted to move out of her parents' house, but she could not afford that. On a visit to her physician, Vernon Ritzman, who had been Ronda's doctor since she was in elementary school, she mentioned her training in medical records and her job in Kingsville. A few days later, his colleague Dr. Phil McCreedy, an obstetrician, mentioned that he had an opening for a clerk. Dr. Ritzman put the two together, and in May 1983 Ronda began to work for McCreedy. Not only did she earn more money, but it brought her a new circle of friends. Ronda could feel herself emerging. There would be an end to the darkness, and she was putting Eddie behind her.

Ronda dated hesitantly and sporadically. She was not comfortable in the single world. On her first postdivorce date, she broke out in hives! But in August 1983, Ronda got a telephone call from a gentleman who introduced himself as Rob Knuth. He was a new-car salesman in Littleton and a fervent Christian man. He had been at a church service in the south Denver suburbs with a friend when he was spotted by one of Ronda's matchmaking aunts, who knew Rob's friend. She gave her friend Ronda's number and asked him to pass it on to Rob.

After exchanging phone calls for two weeks, Rob asked Ronda out on a date. It turned into a wonderful day as Rob thoughtfully included Paul and Diana in the activities. In Ronda's diary was a list of qualities she wanted in a new husband, and near the top was that he love and understand children. Later, after they dropped off Paul and Diana, they went on a drive up Lookout Mountain. Ronda felt relaxed as they walked along the observation patio, watching the lights begin to switch on across the flat landscape of the city below them. It was in this spot two years earlier, during that tense Thanksgiving trip, that there were bewildering barriers between her and Eddie. But Rob Knuth seemed open and caring, balanced and mature.

Although they became strong in their love for each other, there were several reasons that Ronda and Rob did not rush into marriage. First, Ronda no longer felt that her identity lay in being married. Then, Rob needed time to work out a difficult situation. In the religion of his parents, divorce was taboo. They could not accept the fact that their son was pursuing a romance with a divorced woman, and he was torn between his love for Ronda and his love for his parents. He grappled with the divorce issue for some time before finally concluding that Ronda was morally free to remarry, and that he was free to marry her.

Ronda and Rob were married December 28, 1984, in a small ceremony attended by only the minister and his wife, two friends as witnesses, and Paul and Diana. It did not occur to Ronda until much later that the date she had chosen to begin her second marriage was three years to the day from Eddie's arrest.

Ronda continued to work for Dr. McCreedy until August 1986. Two days after she left, she gave birth to her third child, a boy whom she and Rob named Andrus. In September 1988, they had another boy, Benjamin. In between, there was grief over two other pregnancies, one ending in a miscarriage and another in a stillbirth.

Eddie's letters to Paul and Diana tapered off, eventually stopping just before Ronda's remarriage. Eddie found out about the marriage later from his sister.

Eddie Wyatt's face was almost passionless as he described what at one time had been an obsession. It was that song his wife had sung at Ocean View Assembly, a song of faith with a country waltz beat. Eddie was seated on a tall stool, the only furnishing in a bleak five-by-three-foot enclosure, framed on three sides by a black wire cage with a locked gate. In front of him was a thick glass and a small counter on which he could lean his elbows when he lowered his face into his cupped hands. A rusted screen and wire mesh along the bottom of the glass allowed his voice to filter out. The occasional sounds of clanging metal and the shouting of men punctuated the stale atmosphere.

On the other side of the glass was a writer who had gone through Ronda's diary, filtered through decades-old records, and tracked down the people who thought they knew Eddie Wyatt better. Finally, he had come to a prison in Texas to talk with Eddie. During three separate all-day sessions, alone in the visiting room, Eddie told the writer things he had never said before.

"You know, I do remember this song by the Lanny Wolfe Trio," Eddie said near the end of the third visit. "I used to play it over and over and over. Some of the words were, 'If I lose family and home,' and all this, you know? It said, 'Take the dearest things to me if that's how it must be.' The name of the song, I believe, is 'Whatever It Takes.' I thought at times that I listened to it so much, I brainwashed myself with it. And I used to think to myself at times that maybe this is what would happen. God would have to take my family and my home and my car, and maybe when I lost everything I had and God took it all away, I would be brought to that place where God wanted me to be.

"And then it just came to me one day and I thought, 'Man,

that happened.' That song that I listened to over and over so many times for so long, it happened."

Eddie had arrived at his place, the maximum security Ramsey Unit 1 prison farm outside the country crossroads of Rosharon, Texas, located at the dead end of a five-mile asphalt road. His hair was thinner and grayer, and his face had deeper lines. The prominent discolored mark near his left eye that had been such a crucial identifying factor was less apparent. But the low and soft drawl of the prisoner approaching middle age was identical to the voice of the young Eddie Wyatt, preserved by Ronda on a few cassette tapes back home.

"All of a sudden that hit me, man. The kids are gone, Ronda's gone, you know? I mean, thirty years in prison was one thing, but that was just the beginning of what it cost. It cost my career in the service, my family, all of my possessions, everything I've ever had or worked for. I mean, all of a sudden it dawned on me, everything was gone."

During the same week in 1990 that Ronda returned to Kingsville, Eddie sat down in that crude interview room at Ramsey Unit 1 with a visiting writer and spoke for the first time about what he had done to put himself there.

"I'll tell you where the turning point was. In Colorado, in Denver. I was driving down the street and I told Ronda, I told her mother, I told her dad, but they didn't hear what I was saying. I don't think they did. But I told them, I said, 'I'm feeling depressed, those feelings are coming back and I'm just so tired of fighting it.' Up to that point I was fighting it okay. But then something would happen that would bring it back, some stressful situation. We'd run out of money. I got real upset because of that and I told her mother, 'I'm just feeling depressed,' and I remember what she told me. She said, 'Just think of it this way, you could be back in prison,' she said. 'Things could be a lot worse, you know.' "

In the end, Eddie completely capitulated to his evil impulses. He stopped fighting altogether. But it started off in a small way in Colorado. On the way to work at Arvada Steel, he passed a liquor store, and soon he began to stop in to purchase small airline-sized bottles of whiskey. The first few times he did it, he rationalized that he needed it to help him through the day. Just a splash of whiskey in his Coca-Cola at work, he figured, would help him get through the day because he was so unhappy with where his life was headed. He felt out of place, as if there was something in his delinquent past that had not been forgiven, despite his religious conversion and the forgiveness he wanted it to bring.

He had no friends in Denver. There were no Teen Challenge colleagues to bolster him when he felt weak, to provide him with reassurance the way Steve Griffith had done after Eddie prayed in tongues. He was out on his own, and he realized that each time he went out on his own, he failed. It started like a faraway drumbeat inside his head, and gradually it kept pounding and pounding until it felt so natural for Eddie to pick up that tiny little bottle, like it was the next move expected of him. The responsibility he had so studiously avoided his entire life was square on his shoulders. And that voice he kept hearing said, "You're no good. You're going to fail again." Every time the voice came to him, it had been correct.

But behind the mask of a good Christian man with a loving wife and a handsome little boy, it was more difficult than ever to face his fears. Eddie had never trusted anyone in his life. He felt he could not trust Ronda to stick by him if he showed signs of crumbling, that she would not understand the forces pulling on him. He believed Ronda would turn on him, the way everyone else in his life had. So he tried to fight off those premonitions of failure and inadequacy, sought escape in liquor, and hid it all. It was easy to hide his small amount of drinking. Early in the day, or at lunch break, Eddie dumped a little bottle into his soda pop, and by the time he got home, the slight buzz he had acquired would be gone. In the beginning it was easy to squeeze out a smile when he got home after work. Lying was the next natural step.

The early misgivings he had at Teen Challenge, that he did not deserve a wife like Ronda Hunter, came back to haunt him. How could he make love to such a woman, he thought, when he was living a lie? Her personality and her very presence were reminders of the person he should have been. Eddie's decision to join the navy had little to do with the good of his family. In the navy, he could get away more often and drink to his heart's content. The deeper into depression he went, the more he found himself wanting to get away from Ronda. The perfection he thought he could find when he got out of prison was unattainable, and it gave him a sense of utter worthlessness when he realized it.

But when he got to basic training in Orlando, Florida, he found he could not escape. The fellow recruits in his barracks, on learning Eddie was a fundamentalist Christian, voted him religious petty officer. In rebellion, Eddie went out and drank even more. As he drank and caroused with the guys from the barracks, he experienced an intense relief that was almost sexual in nature. Yet later, back at his bunk, he was overcome with remorse. That was a new twist. As a child, Eddie never had any remorse about anything he did.

Eddie knew where drinking would take him; after all, he lived through the destructive effects of alcoholism on his family, then went through his own drinking problem as a teen. Whereas a night on the town produced no psychological trauma for the other recruits, who went on with their business the next day, for Eddie it was yet another proof of failure.

Moving to Millington, Tennessee, in the month before his pregnant wife came down to join him, Eddie quickly found himself among a group of marijuana smokers. Then in California, he went further. In one of the clubs near the base in San Diego, Eddie hooked up with a sailor named Pete, who had just reenlisted and had about $4,000 in bonus money he was itching to spend on liquor or dope. Pete had no car. Eddie did. For only a few bucks in gas money, Eddie shared all of Pete's dope and liquor money. Over the next four days, the two of them went on a binge. In the end, Eddie was sticking a needle in his arm, shooting speed. It scared him, and he was glad to get away from San Diego. He had lost fifteen pounds that he could hardly spare from his slender frame. When he phoned Ronda from that small motel in New Mexico on his drive back, just to hear her voice, he confronted the hideous lie he was living. The longer he hid his activities from his wife and friends, and the longer he failed to seek help for them, the worse they would become. He knew it. The guilt from knowing that he was doing wrong could only be masked by more liquor and drugs, and ultimately by worse sins.

Eddie was apprehensive when he was assigned to the U.S.S. *Kennedy*. He knew he would be doing drugs whenever he could get his hands on them. He looked forward to the drugs. On one hand, it would be a vacation from having to be a good Christian man all the time, something that increasingly became only a pretense. On the other hand, the more depraved his behavior became, the more urgently he needed to hide it. The *Kennedy* wasn't halfway across the Atlantic Ocean before Eddie made his first score, a small chunk of hashish he bought for ten dollars. He had made a few friends with whom he could smoke it, and they were scoring their own dope to share as well. Dope was prevalent, and not just among low-level sailors. It was common for Eddie and his crew mates working on the planes to find marijuana roaches in the cockpits, where pilots had been smoking. When he was arrested by the military police for having the hash pipe at his bunk, he was put in the brig for thirty days by the ship's captain— something he never told Ronda.

Eddie remembered well his return to Norfolk, when Ronda surprised him by showing up early at the Robin Hood Apartments to greet him. He had gone out with some of the fellows after the ship docked, thinking Ronda was still in Denver, and drank the better part of a case of beer. He remembered being stunned when Ronda appeared smiling on the landing, and then brushing by her without even a kiss of greeting after more than six months apart. A strong odor of beer wafted around him, and for years Eddie believed Ronda detected it as he rushed into the bathroom to brush his teeth. But the truth was that Ronda had never smelled stale beer before, and wouldn't have realized it even if she had not been immediately devastated by a sense of sexual rejection.

During his second Mediterranean cruise, Eddie was stoned almost constantly. He and a friend chipped in together and bought a baseball-sized hunk of opiated hashish as a Christmas present to themselves from a twelve-year-old waif near the docks in Alexandria, Egypt. While the *Forrestal* was docked near Athens, Greece, Eddie had the sexual affair that Dave Houser revealed to Ronda several years later. Eddie met a woman tourist from

Chile in a bar near the Piraeus waterfront, and they hit it off well enough to take their foreplay to a motel for the night. They did drugs and had sex several times before giving in to exhaustion.

Because of the double life he was leading, Eddie felt increasingly uncomfortable around Ronda and their churchgoing friends. So when Pastor Alvin Hall offered him the opportunity to help with the Royal Rangers during the Wednesday evening services, he jumped at the chance. It meant he did not have to sit with Ronda and listen to Pastor Hall preach about the righteous life he should be leading. Ronda and their friends, unaware of his true motivation, admired Eddie for volunteering his time to work with the children.

Eddie knew things were getting out of hand in Virginia. He began to have fantasies springing from strange desires for younger women, mistresses, and even unwilling sexual partners. He thought a lot about anal sex. He had been surrounded by it in reform school, and thought himself fortunate to have escaped it. Yet he told Dr. Kutnick that it obsessed him. His fantasies grew stronger even as his sexual drive with Ronda diminished. Eddie came to loathe the time he had to be with her. He dreaded coming home from the late shift at the base, apprehensive that Ronda might still be awake and want to make love.

He recalled the night a week before his arrest when Ronda entered the bedroom in that lavender negligee. When he saw his wife dressed for lovemaking, it turned him off.

"Somehow or other it didn't seem appropriate. When I thought of Ronda, she was a picture spiritually of what I wanted to be, that's how I saw her. It was nice, I do remember thinking that it does look sexy on her, but I always saw her as a very pure, spiritual person. She had never done anything like that before. It was out of character. It was like, here I'm struggling to get to this place spiritually, and it seemed like she was lowering herself to where I was. I didn't want her to do that."

Into the midst of this confused sexuality, Eddie fulfilled one more fantasy. He returned to Galveston the summer before his arrest to see the woman he could not get out of his mind. But when Eddie took Patty Battaglia to a motel across the causeway in Texas City, and finally had sex with his childhood sweetheart, he found it mechanical and disappointing. He could not believe that he had held onto the memory of her for so many years, and blew up his anticipation of intercourse with her, only to find it falling short in a drab motel room. It was nothing like what he had imagined it would be. It was one more failure.

Ronda closed the court file after she finished reading all of the material and looking through the mug shots. She had learned much about the detective work that brought the Kingsville police to her door Christmas week of 1981, and for a change, she found that dredging up those difficult days was more cathartic than tormenting. She glanced at her watch and then turned to Rob. There were other places she still had to visit.

Outside the Kleberg Courthouse, a friend waited to drive them to Mesquite Avenue. Outside her old home, Ronda and Rob remained in the car while their friend went up the walk to the house. Ronda noticed the mesquite tree in the front yard was much taller, but the park across the way looked much the same as it did the last time she and Eddie walked over there with Paul and Diana, the day Allison Shaw was raped. A pleasant, dark-haired woman wearing thick glasses came to the front door, and Ronda watched as a short conversation took place. Her friend soon went inside, and several minutes later, he and the woman appeared at the door motioning for Ronda and Rob to come in.

The woman who was living in Ronda's former residence was a member of First Assembly of God. Ronda smiled at the coincidence, and at the good fortune of finding the woman agreeable enough to indulge the unexpected visitors. Ronda's stomach was in knots while she walked through her old bungalow and recalled the past for Rob.

After some time, the three visitors headed to Wanda Street, where they parked once more in front of a pleasant-looking wood-frame house, painted white with blue trim. A tall, muscular young man was doing some work out in the yard, assisted by a child. This was the house where Pastor James Fields had lived with his wife, Dolores. The Fieldses left Kingsville a few years after Ronda did. But Ronda hoped to see the house that had been her refuge during the scary days after Eddie's arrest, when the anonymous phone calls made Ronda fear for her safety. The young man greeted the visitors. It turned out that the homeowner was the youth minister at First Assembly, and he listened closely to a brief explanation of the nature of the visit. At that, he welcomed everyone inside, where he and his wife gave Ronda warm hugs and invited her to go through the house.

Walking down the short hallway, Ronda came to the front corner bedroom and glanced through the doorway. This was the room where she had stayed during her gruesome ordeal, and now it was colorfully decorated for a little girl. After holding back tears at the courthouse and at her former Mesquite Avenue home, Ronda finally began to cry. No longer tears of anguish, they were tears of release. Bitterness and anger at Eddie that had somehow stayed intact during all this time were being uprooted.

Returning to Colorado, Ronda formulated a plan she hoped would allow good to come out of that episode in her life. With Rob's wholehearted support, she set aside a place in her home for strangers who are going through intense personal crises. The security she had felt while staying in the home of James and Dolores Fields was a priceless gift during her worst moments. If anything, Ronda's experience had opened her eyes to the pain and suffering of others, and this room in her home would be her way of giving back the shelter she had received.

Ronda called the room Resting Place. It was not long before several individuals in need passed through its sheltering confines. And Ronda remembered to use with them the things that had brought comfort to her. She wrote them down in her journal in the form of a poem she titled "Reaching":

I hurt. You've told me that you care.
"What can I do?" you said.
Let me tell you.
Listen. Link action with your words. Hug my neck. Hold
*   me tight.*
Call me. Come and see me. Let me share. Look me in the
*   eye. I need to talk, and cry, and hurt.*
I need to do those things. Let me.

*Don't look at me with shock, and shame, and condem-
nation. I feel those things already.*

*Remember that healing takes time. Don't hurry me to
heal. If you can't see immediate results, don't assume
that I love my grief, or that I'm just feeling sorry for
myself.*

*Affirm me. I need you. I need to believe in "me" again.
Tell me that I have worth. Tell me again and again
and again! Tell me that the sun will shine once more.
Encourage me to hope. Let me be human. When I fall,
don't walk on me. Pick me up, carry me if you must.
Little things mean a lot—a fresh baked cookie, a bottle of bath oil, a squeeze, a card, a call. Anything.
Anything to let me know that you know I exist. Don't
pretend that I can handle it alone. It's okay that you
don't know what to do and say. Neither do I. I have
never walked this way before. Just don't stop trying,
please.*

*Help me to walk again, to be whole one more, and then
I will touch another with that same love. Perhaps
someday you will need me to be there—and I will
come as you came to me.*

"There's no hope for people like you," one of the prison psy-
chologists at the Texas Department of Corrections diagnostic unit
told Eddie after she looked at his paperwork and found he was
a sex offender. Eddie had heard those words before. But the
psychologist meant it quite literally. When Eddie learned he would
be sent to Ramsey Unit 1, he also found out that there was no
treatment program for sex offenders. He was simply going to be
warehoused for whatever portion of his thirty-year term he
wound up serving.

In Texas, as in most other states, prison math is different
from regular math. Geraldo Nuñez served less than nine years of
his fifty-year sentence. Eddie was considered for parole several
times, the first within five years of his arrival, but was turned
down. The warden considered him a model prisoner, but Eddie's

use of a deadly weapon in the rape, and the protests of Kingsville citizens and police each time a hearing was scheduled, resulted in denials of his pleas for release. If there was going to be any rehabilitation, Eddie Wyatt was going to have to do it himself.

Eddie realized his crime was not about sex—Ronda was starving for sexual attention at home—but a crime of violence in which sex was merely the weapon. Forcible rape is almost always the result of some psychological trauma rather than a need for sex. Met by frustration and failure in his life, Eddie retreated into a fantasy world where he had potency and control. His fantasies soon assumed a pattern of aggressive and even forced sex with younger women. Sometimes the mistresses were in bondage. Sometimes he forced them to submit to everything he wanted, especially the anal sex Ronda had refused him. Eddie's rape fantasies ultimately brought him to the real-life enactment of the fantasy. Initially, he rationalized his crime by telling himself it was for the sex. But the lasting impression he took from rape was the satisfaction of total control and domination over his victim, and how it relieved him at last of his feelings of frustration.

After Eddie raped, he recalled it constantly, sometimes in nearly a trancelike state. He did not want to think about it, yet he became obsessed with intense memories of power and rage. But the relief he felt was fleeting; frustration slowly seeped back. In time, Eddie was struck by the reality of what he had done. The more obsessed he became with it, the more dissatisfying it became. That was when he realized that he would do it again.

"I was thinking about how mad I was," Eddie recalled of his thoughts during the actual rapes. "I was so full of anger. After I was locked up I heard about a guy who was doing that same thing and he was killing the women, and I thought, 'Lord, that could have just as well been me.' I was so full of anger, I don't know how I didn't. I know this one thing, if one of them had've resisted and tried to fight me, I don't know what I would have done. You know, in that state, I probably would have hurt them. But none of them did."

Police suspected Eddie in a total of eleven sexual assaults, occurring as early as when he was still living in Norfolk, but he was only charged in one. There were three cases in Virginia that investigators there wanted to pin on him. There were the two assaults in Galveston that occurred when he was consorting with his childhood sweetheart. And finally, there were the six rapes in Kingsville between June and December of 1981.

At the time of his arrest, Eddie admitted only to the last one and denied any involvement with the others. When this writer told him that police believed he had carried out eleven rapes, Eddie arched his eyes in disbelief.

"There's no way," he said.

Well then, how many did he commit?

Eddie paused for a split second, making an instant decision to say something he had never said to anyone before.

"There was three," he said.

Eddie Wyatt went on to describe how a voice inside his head slowly dragged him down from the lofty position of trust in which Ronda held him, to burglary, drug abuse, and rape. The force led him through increasingly vivid masturbatory fantasies involving younger women he would dominate until, at two o'clock in the morning on Wanda Street in Kingsville, he found himself staring into Sue Wilson's bedroom window. He had intended to commit burglary, which he had already resumed as part of his degeneration to juvenile habits. But when he saw the young woman inside the house, Eddie's inner voice asked him how he thought it would feel to live out his rape fantasy.

"When I started burglarizing, I would think about, you know, what I would do if I was ever in a situation like that, where there was a woman there alone. And I was thinking, would I actually rape one? I had thought about it and I had come to the decision that I didn't really know for sure. But I thought, well, if I get in the situation, I'll just make that decision whenever the time comes.

"On this particular day I remember when I looked in there and I saw her, that thought came to me, you know, to break in."

Eddie knew that the tremendous anger he had inside was rooted in deep unresolved conflicts of the past, particularly his desire for anal sex. In his years in prison, he tried to come to some understanding of his criminal acts.

"It had built up to the point where it could just have easily come out in a murder. It could have come out in any kind of violent behavior and it just so happened that rape was the way that it came out. I thought about it, would I shoot them? Would I actually shoot them? And I didn't know. I thought, 'Man, I don't know what I'll do, I'll just have to wait and see.' I just never knew what I was going to do from one minute to the next. I would break in some place, and something would tell me do this or do that. A thought would come to me, it was like I was being led or guided. And any little thing could have set me off."

When his frustration and guilt rushed back in after the momentary relief he gained through raping Sue Wilson, Eddie found himself prowling Kingsville again. By the time of Halloween night 1981, when he raped Kyung Ellis, Eddie's more extreme urges frightened him.

"I told her to take her clothes off, and she was so afraid that I was going to kill her, she kept saying, 'Don't kill me, don't kill me.' And I thought, why is she saying that? Because I had no thought whatsoever of killing, or of even hurting her really, other than just raping her. But when she said that, later I thought, man, she must have seen something that I'm not even seeing, anger or rage. She certainly thought I was going to kill her. And I kept telling her, 'I'm not going to kill you. I'm not going to hurt you.' And then right before I left she said it again. She said, 'You're not going to hurt me, are you?' And I said, 'I told you that I wasn't, and I'm not,' and then I left.

"But what she kept saying kept bugging me. 'Are you going to kill me?' I kept hearing that, you know, 'Now, was you fixing to kill her?' And I was thinking, 'No, I wasn't going to kill her.' 'Yeah, you were going to kill her.' 'No, I wasn't going to kill her,' and then I was thinking maybe I was about to kill her. Did I do something I didn't remember?

"Some parts I didn't want to remember. The look on some of their faces. The scared look, I was seeing myself in her. I mean, I was seeing what she was seeing. And I just saw some warning signs, like it's getting out of hand."

After he killed Allison Shaw's dog, Eddie felt like a different person. He tore up the Polaroid photos he had taken of his victim and threw the pieces into a garbage bin at a convenience store.

He tried to destroy the tape recording that police later recovered in his trash. And he claimed that two days before his arrest, convinced he was on the verge of a nervous breakdown, he injected himself with a large dose of cocaine in an attempt to commit suicide.

"I stabbed the dog two or three times," Eddie recalled. "I don't remember which. But I remember when I did that, something happened. It was like, man, something real evil took over. It was like there was another presence there over me. And it was like I had given myself over to something. I knew that once I had done that, I had gone too far. It was like I no longer had a say in it. I mean, up to that point I could have turned and left, walked away.

"I knew that after that happened, it was very possible that I could have killed her. Even though, up to that point, my thinking was, 'I'll never kill even if it means me being caught, I'm not going to kill anybody.' I mean, that was like, hey, here's the line. I'll go this far but I'm not crossing that line, see. But when I killed that dog it was like, man, that line was erased."

Eddie's admission that he had raped Sue Wilson and Kyung Ellis, in addition to Allison Shaw, was his first public admission of multiple rapes. He stridently denied involvement in the other three unsolved Kingsville cases, the attacks against Kim Sullivan, Cheryl Palmer, and Shelly Polk. But there was one disturbing piece of evidence that reopened the issue: the diamond ring that Ronda and her mother found in Eddie's coat pocket.

When Lakewood police sent the ring to Kingsville shortly after Ronda moved back to Colorado, Captain George Gomez examined it. The setting held a large diamond in the center, surrounded by a circle of smaller diamond chips. It perfectly matched the description of the ring that was stolen from Shelly Polk by the man who raped her. Although Eddie had already been sent off to prison, Kingsville police decided to follow up the lead in an effort to close the Polk case. Gomez took a picture of the ring and mailed the photo to Polk, who had moved back to her Midwestern hometown.

But Shelly Polk never answered the letter from Kingsville. Perhaps the victim wanted to put the event as far behind her as possible and forget that Kingsville even existed. In time, because Shelly never responded, Kingsville police sent the ring back to Lakewood, and it was returned to Ronda.

Asked about the diamond ring, Eddie seemed certain that it did not belong to any rape victim. He recalled stealing it during an unrelated burglary in Kingsville, and he went on to describe some of the specific aspects of that crime. He estimated he committed at least fifteen burglaries while he lived there, in addition to his sexual assaults. That was how he had obtained the sewing machine for his wife, the speakers for his stereo, and a number of other items that he told Ronda he had earned in trade for his painting work.

Yet for Eddie to be in possession of a diamond ring matching one that was stolen from a woman who had been raped in precisely the way he admitted raping three other women seemed to defy coincidence. He had forthrightly confessed to two other rapes, even though he had kept quiet about them for more than nine years. That alone could have been counterproductive to his upcoming parole request. Having done that, Eddie asked this writer, why would he not confess to the others if he had done them, too?

But as more details surfaced during three grueling and emotional day-long interviews, there were other coincidences.

While confessing to the details of raping Sue Wilson, much of what Eddie said conformed to the evidence found in the police investigation. But there were inconsistences. Eddie said he looked in the window and saw his victim preparing to take a bath or shower. And he recalled that while he was in the act of raping her, he heard water running in the bathroom and the thought came to him that he should go in and turn it off.

The problem was that Sue Wilson was not getting ready to bathe. The police record shows that she was asleep in bed at 2:30 A.M. when she was attacked. The only Kingsville rape victim who was attacked while preparing to shower was Shelly Polk, and the water was running during the assault.

These inconsistences led Eddie to wonder, nine years later,

whether it was possible that he had committed more rapes than he could remember. This writer suggested that perhaps Eddie incorrectly confessed to raping a woman in June, who would have been Sue Wilson, when he actually was recalling raping Shelly Polk in September. (Eddie never knew any of their names, except for Allison because she went to court.) But that was not possible either. He remembered committing his first rape within three months of settling into Kingsville in March. The unsolved June 14 rape of Sue Wilson was the only one that fit his recollection of both date and time. Also, Eddie insisted that he had not used colored tape on his first victim. Sue Wilson was the only victim from the unsolved group not to be bound with colored tape.

Eddie admitted to lapses of memory, particularly when he was heavily into drugs. He hesitated while he considered this information.

"I don't know, maybe there is something that went on," he concluded. "I know there's probably things that I don't remember, but I don't see how I wouldn't remember that. I'll just say this, that it's possible I may have committed another rape during that time and just don't remember, you know. I'm not saying that that's not possible, but I'm just saying that I don't remember it."

Because the number of Eddie's victims remains unclear, the truth may never be known. What did become clear during the visits with this writer was that none of these women was Eddie's first rape victim. For the first time, Eddie talked about something that had been buried deep in his conscience for almost a quarter century. He believed that his motivations went clear back to reform school. And in retrospect, Eddie volunteered, it explained a lot.

Eddie could not wipe from his mind the memory of his victims' faces. They reflected uncomfortable emotions, raw and unformed, yet familiar. During his years in prison, he thought of an event back in reform school that he had repressed for much of his adolescence and early adulthood. It was so threatening to his own sense of self and sexuality that he managed to bury it in the recesses of his consciousness, only to dredge it up in the context of his later rapes.

The event dated back to 1967, when Eddie was returned to the maximum security Mountain View after escaping from Gatesville.

Tommy Harper, the white boy who was widely known to be giving his sexual favors to black teens, was walking through one of the buildings. Eddie, sixteen at the time, had been angered at what he perceived as young Tommy's insolent disregard for the racial and sexual boundaries of the reform school. Then Eddie and his clique of Anglo teens watched in rage as the black inmates, · having worn out their amusement with Tommy, tossed him aside like a spent toy. The Anglo inmates focused intense anger on Tommy.

When Eddie saw Tommy that day, he followed him, grabbed him by the arm, and yanked him into a bathroom area.

"Take off your pants," Eddie ordered Tommy, staring angrily into the boy's glazed eyes. They were filled with fear, but Tommy undid his zipper and stripped off his pants.

"Now a white man's going to have you for a change," Eddie growled as he unhitched his pants and pulled out his penis. Tommy offered no resistance, turning around and bending over to make it easier for Eddie to penetrate him from behind. No one else entered the bathroom area while Eddie raped Tommy, and it was over quickly. Then when the boy turned around to pull his pants back up, Eddie looked into his eyes again. The vacant stare was still there. It made Eddie very uncomfortable, but he did not know why.

Merely a week later, as Tommy Harper was walking back to the dorm from Mountain View's vocational area, one of the members of Eddie's clique rushed up to the young boy and slashed him with a homemade knife. The blade caught Tommy in the neck, and he went down on the path, bleeding profusely. The boy died from a massive loss of blood.

Eddie never told this story to his wife, or anyone else. He tried hard to expel the memory of the dead boy from his mind, and even harder to bury the memory of what he had done to him shortly before his murder. Because of the prison code in which the one penetrated is the one humiliated, and the one who does the penetrating retains his manhood, Eddie convinced himself that he was punishing Tommy for having given himself to the blacks.

"I thought, 'Why is he over there?' I didn't realize he was being held against his will. I didn't understand how somebody can dominate you like that because I had never really experienced it. I saw what was happening and I didn't understand. I thought he was doing it willingly and that was why I resented him. I resented the blacks, seeing that day after day after day after day, week after week. That went on for months.

"Looking back, that to me was worse than anything I've ever done. When they threw him aside, it was like I was blaming him, and I said, 'It's your fault, you disgraced all the whites here.' He was totally and completely crushed. There was no resistance, it was like he was just there. He was like a zombie.

"I felt dirty, ashamed, I felt like I had this secret going on inside of me that was so terrible that if anybody ever found out about it, it was like the most terrible thing that could have ever happened to me."

It was not until years later, through adult eyes, that Eddie came to believe Tommy Harper had not been a willing consort of the black inmates at all. The blank look in Tommy's eyes was one of victimization, and when Eddie saw it, it disturbed him deeply. From a harsh anger, Eddie began to see Tommy as a victim of repeated and humiliating rapes, first by others and then by himself. Tommy was a loner and a misfit, an awkward kid who never quite fit into the protective cliques. Eddie realized that that was how he had felt during his youth on the streets of Galveston. "I never felt normal," Eddie recalled of his childhood.

Eddie believes that is what caused his obsession with anal sex, and why he raped his female victims in that fashion. He did not feel any homosexual tendencies, either before or after cornering Tommy Harper. His urge that day was to punish the boy, demean him, and make him submit to his will.

During his years in Ramsey Unit 1, Eddie received no counseling of any kind. Left on his own, he went back to prayer. In April 1985, he attended the organizational meeting of a prison chapter of Full Gospel Business Mens' Fellowship International. He was elected president, and for six years he remained the leading figure in the group. Volunteers from Houston-area churches brought guest speakers into Ramsey on a regular basis, and some of the men who came to know Eddie became fast friends. They did not know why Eddie was in prison, nor did they ask. But for six years, the volunteers helped Eddie and others in the prison chapter to organize among the inmates. Based on that experience, Eddie Wyatt decided that when he was released, he wanted to be a minister, something he wanted to do as early as his Teen Challenge days in Dallas.

Eddie was aware that there were people watching him, waiting for him to fail again after he got out of prison. High on that list was Judy Hayes, who in the intervening years had been promoted to lieutenant on the Kingsville police force. She was convinced that it was a question of when, not whether, Eddie Wyatt would rape again. Also keeping up to date on Eddie was Sergeant Ray Rubio, the Galveston officer who fished Eddie out of the pond after the 1970 burglary for which he was sent to prison the first time. Rubio was the officer who investigated one of the rapes that occurred the week Eddie went to Galveston, and he considered the case still open.

Eddie said he didn't care what the police thought were his odds of getting back into trouble on the outside. "I don't expect people to believe me. I wouldn't be surprised if you don't believe me when I say that I know that I can get out of here. I wanted to tell that prison psychologist who said there was no hope for people like me that she's going to see an exception. She's not going to be able to say that about me. And what I'm saying is I know that I can't just say that, I've got to show it. Who should believe an ex-con who spent half his life in prison, I mean, who should take my word? I know that I'm going to have to prove myself when I get out. I'm not going to be able to leave any room for mistakes. It's not going to be easy. It hasn't been easy."

That clock started ticking in July 1991. After serving nine and a half years of his sentence, Eddie Wyatt was released from prison.

He went to live for a time with his mother and stepfather, who had moved from Galveston to another part of Texas. Shortly, Eddie began to attend a small-town church, and got work doing odd jobs. On several occasions, he shared with the congregation his testimony about his past.

Months went by. Paul and Diana learned through a roundabout way that their father had been released from prison, and they steeled themselves for the moment when he would contact them. Any time the telephone rang, or the mail carrier pulled away from the front of the house, it might bring a strangely familiar sight or sound. It was not a pleasant wait. They did not know Eddie anymore, and the anticipation was laced with dread.

Eventually, after bracing themselves for something they gradually realized wasn't coming, the children began to wonder even more about their natural father. Had he forgotten all about them? Did he not want to hear from them? Was he resigned entirely to a life without them? Diana, always the more forward of the two, wanted an answer. Over Christmas 1991, the tenth anniversary of her father's abrupt removal from the family, Diana told Ronda that she was going to call her grandmother Eva in Texas to wish her Merry Christmas, knowing full well that Eddie was with her. Ronda stood by while both Diana and Paul went to the telephone to call.

After some pleasant talk with her grandmother, Diana heard Eva tell her to hang on because there was someone there who wanted to speak with her. Eddie got on the phone, and spoke with both of his children for about half an hour. It was mostly chitchat, how-have-you-been conversation. When it was over, it seemed anticlimactic. Eddie had convinced himself that the children did not want to hear from him, and that they were better off without him. So he had put off contacting them.

Ronda could see that her children needed to visit Eddie, whether it was to laugh with him, cry with him, get angry at him, or hit him. She had no clues as to which it would be. Ronda had been through a renewed healing over the previous year, but Paul and Diana had not been part of that. She believed that seeing Eddie again would help the children close some broken circles in their memories. Diana was for it. Paul was ambivalent, but his younger sister prevailed on him to go. There was one significant emotional hurdle to overcome. Rob, their stepfather. He was the father they knew. He was the one who was there for the smiles and the tears, who put food on the table, provided for their schooling, hugged them when they needed security, and loved them as he did his two natural sons. Paul and Diana were concerned that it might hurt Rob's feelings if they made this trip.

In July 1992, Rob took Paul and Diana out to dinner, just the three of them, so they could talk about meeting Eddie. The children told Rob that they considered him their father. At that, Rob looked them in the eye and said that he had thought a lot about what they were going through. He concluded that he would support their decision, whatever it was, and that he did not feel threatened.

"You should do what you feel you need to do," he told them.

July 6, 1992

I had a phone call that took me completely by surprise. I'm glad I didn't know ahead of time that it was coming. I stopped by mom and dad's for just a minute on an errand, and no one else was there. When the phone rang, I answered it. In an instant, it was 1982 again. His voice hadn't changed. I would have known it anywhere. It was Eddie. We had not spoken since I said goodbye to him in the Kingsville jail.

For a minute, I was stunned and taken off guard, and so was he. He was calling to finalize arrangements for the children's trip next week, and I think he expected Diana or my mom. It would have been so easy to be superficial, to take the information and hang up. But another part of me still had some questions for him, and some things to say.

I had heard that he was doing well, and was facing up to the things that had fueled his frustrations with life. But I needed to hear it straight from him. He told me he feels that he has a good support base now, and is making strides to putting his life back together. I hope that is so. I have never wanted anything for Eddie but happiness, and the sometimes harsh frankness he showed in his interviews with Kevin makes me think that he is getting things out into the open where they can be faced down in the light.

As for me, I can finally look back and see that through the fire of my years with Eddie, I have become a much more loving person—Rob has brought that out in me. I think that I am much less naive than I used to be, yet I hope that my capacity to trust others has not diminished. I am now more quick to acknowledge my weaknesses, but I am also more aware of my strengths. I am not as afraid to let people see me the way I see myself. I used to try to be the person I thought others wanted me to be, and that imprisoned me. With Rob, I am free to be me, through the good or the bad. Thank you, Lord, for crossing our paths.

I used to think that what was wrong with my first marriage was my fault, because that was the only way I could fix it. It nearly destroyed my sense of self-worth. When I discovered the truth, it made me doubt my ability to perceive the world around me. How could I have been so wrong? Today, I think I am a much better perceiver of people. I don't let things go unsaid, or stuff my feelings down where no one will ever know them. It helps me bring out those things in others, as I had always prayed I could do with Eddie. I now see my place in my marriage, and with my role as a mother. There were times, when I was lower than I had ever thought possible, that I doubted there would come a day when the pain, anger, and frustration would fade completely. But Lord, on this day, when I picked up the phone and heard Eddie's voice, you touched me and I felt solid again.

We talked about Paul and Diana. They have so many questions, I told him, [that] only he can answer. I hope the three of them sit down together and talk, and talk, and talk.

I've thought a lot about their going. Diana, and es-

pecially Paul, are trying to work through some pretty intense emotions right now. I've often wondered if, when they reached their teenage years, they would have to face some issues all over again, the anger, abandonment, embarrassment, and disgust. They need healing. Rob feels, and I agree, that we need to allow them to do whatever they need to, to resolve their past.

When I hung up the phone, I felt good inside, like a load I hadn't realized was there had been lifted. I've always heard that to forgive is to forget. For so many years, I tried to forget, thinking that would bring the forgiveness. But I heard it said recently that to forgive is to remember . . . without the sting.

The sting is gone.

POSTSCRIPT
November, 1992

On September 11, 1992, after fourteen months of freedom, Eddie Wyatt was arrested by police in Alpine, Texas, and held in the Brewster County jail without bond. Thirty-six hours earlier, police had found a video camera, ski mask, and stool in the car Eddie abandoned as he fled after having been identified as a prowler and suspected burglar. During the ensuing search for Eddie, police sifted through his apartment and turned up videotapes linking him to other crimes. These included footage of a naked woman videotaped through her bathroom window without her knowledge, and a tape he had made of himself trespassing in a home in which the occupants were asleep. This latter tape showed Eddie masturbating while touching and kissing a sleeping ten-year-old girl. When Eddie was finally caught, he was charged, on the basis of the taped evidence, with three counts of burglary, including burglary with intent to commit sexual assault; one count of evading arrest; and one of trespassing. The state of Texas has moved to revoke his parole. At this writing, Eddie Wyatt is awaiting trial.

ACKNOWLEDGMENTS

Ronda Knuth never imagined when she first brought her journals over to my house for a sample reading that this entire process would become part of her healing. What she wanted was to produce a work that, through her family's tragedy, would vividly show others going through personal crises that there is always hope. I warned her that once we started to tap into those emotions again, it would be almost like reliving the pain. If it was not, then we would have failed to tell her story. The pain and tears did come. However, baring her most private moments in this fashion turned out to be less difficult than discovering a hidden swamp of anger and bitterness that still had to be drained. Thus, the trip back to Kingsville became integral parts both of this book and of Ronda's ultimate resolution of her troubles, and I am grateful to have been involved in that with her and her family.

The contribution that Eddie Wyatt himself made to this book was also immense. On the day we met, he began to divulge closely held secrets that he had guarded for many years. He told me that he had often wished he could find a way to allow others to learn from his mistakes, so that those who are on a destructive path can see it in time to stop themselves. For that reason, he answered every question I came up with, even though many of his answers would bring him hurt, reproach, and personal embarrassment.

I owe many thanks to George Gomez, Judy Hayes, Hector Treviño, Ron Barroso, and Steve Thomas. To those friends of the

Wyatts, from Norfolk to Dallas and Kingsville, who shared with me their recollections of what they thought was a wonderful young family, I am also grateful. Stuart Krichevsky helped me to shape the raw ideas into a story, and as before, Joyce Seltzer had the unenviable task of making me hew to the straight path.

Researching and writing this book took me away from my own family a great deal of time, even when I was at home working on it. The very essence of the story made the nature of my family's sacrifice all the more obvious. Kathy, who brought Ronda's story to my attention in the first place, paid a price for her bird-dogging by working doubly hard to keep our family going while I disappeared. I could not have done it without her. And for Brendan, Elisabeth, and Brian, who had to give up an irreplaceable resource, I will be doing my best to try to make up for the time lost.

—K.F.